Changing Corporate Governance Practices in China and Japan

Also by Masao Nakamura

CHANGING JAPANESE BUSINESS, ECONOMY, AND SOCIETY:
Globalization of Post-Bubble Japan (editor)

THE JAPANESE BUSINESS AND ECONOMIC SYSTEM:
History and Prospects for the 21st Century (editor)

THE SECOND PAYCHECK:
A Socio-Economic Analysis of Earnings (with Alice Nakamura)

Changing Corporate Governance Practices in China and Japan

Adaptations of Anglo-American Practices

Edited by
Masao Nakamura

Konwakai Japan Research Chair and Professor, Institute of Asian Research and Sauder School of Business, University of British Columbia

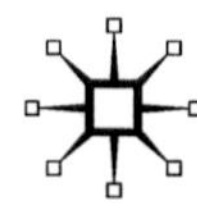

First published 2008 by
PALGRAVE MACMILLAN

Palgrave Macmillan in the UK is an imprint of Macmillan Publishers Limited, registered in England, company number 785998, of Houndmills, Basingstoke, Hampshire RG21 6XS.

Palgrave Macmillan in the US is a division of St Martin's Press LLC, 175 Fifth Avenue, New York, NY 10010.

Palgrave Macmillan is the global academic imprint of the above companies and has companies and representatives throughout the world.

Palgrave® and Macmillan® are registered trademarks in the United States, the United Kingdom, Europe and other countries.

ISBN-13: 978–0–230–22165–9 hardback
ISBN-10: 0–230–22165–3 hardback

This book is printed on paper suitable for recycling and made from fully managed and sustained forest sources. Logging, pulping and manufacturing processes are expected to conform to the environmental regulations of the country of origin.

A catalogue record for this book is available from the British Library.

Library of Congress Cataloging-in-Publication Data
Nakamura, Masao, Ph. D.
Changing corporate governance practices in China and Japan : adaptations of Anglo-American practices / Masao Nakamura.
p. cm.
Includes bibliographical references and index.
ISBN 978–0–230–22165–9 (alk. paper)
1. Corporate governance—China. 2. Corporate governance—Japan. I. Title.
HD2741.N355 2008
338.60951—dc22

2008030441

10 9 8 7 6 5 4 3 2 1
17 16 15 14 13 12 11 10 09 08

Printed and bound in Great Britain by
CPI Antony Rowe, Chippenham and Eastbourne

Contents

Part II Evolving Corporate Governance Practices: Selective Adaptations

List of Tables and Figures

Tables

Figures

Acknowledgments

Earlier versions of the studies reported in most of the chapters in this book were presented in draft form at a research conference titled "Corporate Governance in East Asia." This conference was held at the Shanghai Academy of Social Sciences on July 18, 2005. That conference was sponsored by the Institute of Asian Research of the University of British Columbia and was funded in part by a Social Sciences and Humanities Research Council of Canada (SSHRC) Major Collaborative Research Initiative grant on the Asia Pacific Dispute Resolution Project. The initial research and further development of some of the chapters in this volume were also partially supported by funding from that same SSHRC MCRI grant. We are grateful to this support. In addition, the editor of this volume acknowledges separate research support for completing this volume from SSHRC and from the University of British Columbia Hampton Fund research grants.

Foreword

Pitman B. Potter

This volume is a product of a major research effort by the Institute of Asian Research at the University of British Columbia working with colleagues in Japan, China, Australia and Canada. The project focuses on the role of Selective Adaptation and Institutional Capacity in local application of international regulatory standards. These paradigms emerge from perspectives on the relationship between formal rule regimes and associated normative and institutional contexts.

Legal behavior is strongly influenced by norms of legal and political culture (Etzioni, 2000; Kelsen, 1991) and by the institutional context within which these norms are operationalized (North, 1990). Cultural norms are reflected in rules, including formal laws and regulations and informal procedures and practices. The distinction between rules and the cultural norms they represent becomes especially important when rules particular to one cultural group are used by another, without a corresponding assimilation of underlying norms. Local implementation of non-local rules is also affected by the institutional context. Under current conditions of globalization normative tensions are present as liberal rules of governance generally associated with Europe and North America are disseminated to other areas characterized by local norms that are often in conflict with norms of liberalism. Business regulation is of special importance, where concerns over compliance with international standards often reflect misplaced expectations about the enforceability of rules without agreement on underlying norms. In the context of globalization, economic and political power have allowed standards of corporate governance associated with liberal democratic capitalism to be imposed on societies outside the European tradition, but have had less effect in displacing local cultural norms.

Understanding local implementation of international standards on corporate governance can be furthered through appreciation of the normative and structural contexts for legal performance. This volume offers a valuable collection of chapters that further understanding of corporate governance in comparative context, in light of normative factors of selective adaptation and the structural dynamics of institutional capacity. In contrast to expectations about convergence that suggest development toward a globally unified system of institutional practices (Mattei, 1997), local implementation may be seen as a product of normative and structural factors. Normative dynamics of *selective adaptation* explain variations in compliance with non-local standards by reference to different levels of normative consensus (Potter, 2004). Structural dynamics of *institutional capacity* depict the ways in which relational factors of institutional purpose, location, orientation and cohesion affect local implementation of non-local rule regimes (Potter, 2007).

The role of institutional dynamics in corporate governance is addressed in Part I of this volume. Colleagues from the Shanghai Academy of Social Sciences (Peng Fei Yang, Xiaorong Gu, and Shuliang Wang) and the University of British Columbia (Andrew Yuen and Anming Zhang) examine varying models of corporate governance used in China. Specialists from Tsinghua University (Wei Chi) and Kansas State University (Yijiang Wang) examine corporate governance from the perspective of China's economic policy programs of reform and opening up. Issues of corporate governance in Japan are examined by Masao Nakamura (Institute of Asian Research) and Japan's mergers and acquisitions practices are addressed by Yasuhiro Arikawa and Hideaki Miyajima of Waseda University. Taken together these chapters offer a comprehensive comparative look at corporate governance in the two largest economies in Asia.

The role of local norms is addressed in Part II. Jiangyu Wang (Chinese University of Hong Kong) offers a chapter on independent directors that explores the complex relationship between legal rules and local practices. The treatment of corporate governance norms in China by S. H. Goo and Anne Carver of the University of Hong Kong offers insights about local perceptions and practices. Professor Nakamura's chapter on corporate governance in Japan addresses the role of selective adaptation in local application on non-local rule regimes. By addressing the normative dynamic of local implementation, this section complements the institutional orientation of the chapters in the preceding section.

The work was supported by the Asia Pacific Dispute Resolution (APDR) project of the Institute of Asian Research, funded by the Major Collaborative Research Initiatives (MCRI) of the Social Sciences and Humanities Research Council of Canada (SSHRC), for which I am deeply grateful. The project has shown the wondrous potential for international scholarly collaboration across institutional and normative boundaries, while revealing the utility of cross-cultural communication in academic and policy research. We hope that this collection of chapters will contribute to broader understanding of corporate governance in China and Japan, as well as building appreciation for the role of norms and institutions in comparative regulatory change.

Dr. Pitman B. Potter
Vancouver, Canada
March 27, 2008

References

Etzioni, Amitai (2000) "Social Norms: Internalization, Persuasion, and History," *Law & Society Review*, 34(1), 157–78.

Kelsen, Hans (1991) *General Theory of Norms* (trans. M. Hartney) (Oxford: Clarendon Press).

Mattei, Ugo (1997) *Comparative Law and Economics* (Ann Arbor: University of Michigan Press).

North, Douglass (1990) *Institutions, Institutional Change and Economic Performance* (Cambridge: Cambridge University Press).

Potter, Pitman B. (2007) "China and the International Legal System: Challenges of Participation," *China Quarterly*, 191, September, 699–715.

Potter, Pitman B. (2004) "Legal Reform in China – Institutions, Culture, and Selective Adaptation," *Law & Social Inquiry*, 28(4), Spring, 465–95.

Notes on the Contributors

Yasuhiro Arikawa is Associate Professor, Waseda University Graduate School of Finance, Accounting and Law, Tokyo.

Anne Carver is a professional consultant, School of Law, Chinese University of Hong Kong, Hong Kong.

Wei Chi is Assistant Professor at the School of Economics and Management, Tsinghua University, Beijing, and Department of Economics, Kansas State University, Manhattan, Kansas.

Say H. Goo is Associate Professor, Faculty of Law, University of Hong Kong, Hong Kong, and Honorary Fellow, Monash University, Australia.

Xiaorong Gu is Director, Law Institute, Shanghai Academy of Social Sciences, Shanghai.

Hideaki Miyajima is Professor, at the School of Commerce, Waseda University, Tokyo.

Masao Nakamura is Konwakai Japan Research Chair and Professor, Institute of Asian Research and Sauder School of Business, University of British Columbia, Vancouver.

Pitman Potter is Director, Institute of Asian Research and Professor, Faculty of Law, University of British Columbia, Vancouver.

Peng Fei Yang is Associate Professor, Law Institute, Shanghai Academy of Social Sciences, Shanghai.

Andrew Yuen is a Ph.D. student, Sauder School of Business, University of British Columbia, Vancouver.

Jiangyu Wang is Associate Professor, School of Law, Chinese University of Hong Kong, Hong Kong.

Shuliang Wang is Researcher, Law Institute, Shanghai Academy of Social Sciences, Shanghai.

Yijiang Wang is Professor, Industrial Relations Center, Carlson School of Management, University of Minnesota, Minneapolis, and Special Term Professor, Department of Economics, Tsinghua University, Beijing.

Anming Zhang is Vancouver International Airport Authority Professor in Air Transportation, Sauder School of Business, University of British Columbia, Vancouver.

1
Introduction

Masao Nakamura

Globalization has had major impacts on business activities in countries throughout the world. China and Japan are no exceptions. Effective global business operations involve people and economic entities and governments at all levels from different nations. Hence it is important that many aspects of global business conform to international standards. This is particularly so for countries such as China and Japan which are heavily involved in international trade and investment.

In China, the increasing complexity of the contemporary business operations required to satisfy both domestic and foreign customers' needs means that more transparent corporate governance mechanisms are needed. This would permit potential problem areas in corporate social responsibilities to be more easily identified. The increasing complexity and size of Chinese economic activities also means that many large state-owned enterprises must privatize their ownership, and must seek external public funds from domestic and foreign investors. But private (individual and institutional) investors demand transparency in reporting on how their invested funds are used by corporations and also demand high returns on their investments. This has been an impetus for a new corporate governance system.

Beginning in the early 1990s, massive amounts of production capacity were moved to China from developed economies. Like their U.S. counterparts, Japanese manufacturers have moved millions of jobs to China since the 1990s. This worsened the recession in Japan which was triggered by the burst of Japan's worst ever financial bubble in 1990. The prolonged recession forced the Japanese government and corporations to undertake massive reforms of many aspects of Japan's institutions and business practices. In response to the public's criticism that Japan's then prevailing bank-based corporate governance practices were among the main reasons for the failure of the Japanese economy during and after the burst of the financial bubble, the Japanese government undertook a major reform of the laws related to corporate governance, capital markets and accounting reporting, among other areas. In response to this reform, Japanese corporations also implemented new corporate governance mechanisms.

In both China and Japan, the main objective of the reforms has been the adoption of corporate governance practices from the Anglo-American countries including the United States, the United Kingdom, Canada and Australia. The main reason that the Chinese and Japanese governments paid special attention to the practices in these Anglo-American countries is that their economies were performing much better than other developed economies in the West. Furthermore, certain European corporate governance mechanisms had already been adopted. Also, the Anglo-American corporate governance mechanisms had become accepted as the *de facto* global standard. For these reasons, both China and Japan, though in different stages of economic development, felt that it was in their interests to implement Anglo-American-style corporate governance practices.

Given the institutional realities, local business practices, cultural differences and the history of corporate governance in these countries, China and Japan could not implement Anglo-American practices in exactly the same forms as in the United States and Canada. One main objective of this volume is to analytically explore cultural, social, institutional, historical, economic and other factors affecting the resulting differences in implementation that have been observed in China and Japan.

In the area of international trade, thanks to the ongoing international efforts of the World Trade Organization (WTO) and, previously, the General Agreement on Tariffs and Trade (GATT), on removing obstacles to international trade and investment transactions, a significant level of standardization has been achieved with respect to tariffs on imported goods, allowable trade restrictions, allowable subsidies to firms, and so on. However, the current liberalization efforts, including the rules for international trade and investment, do not extend to corporate governance activities within national borders.

Many aspects of corporate governance (for example, how firms' production and control activities are organized, how their financial results are reported and how their organizations are structured and managed) are closely related to their home country situations. Corporate governance mechanisms within national borders have implications for how (and the extent to which) foreign goods and services, as well as capital, penetrate national borders. For example, certain equity-based interfirm relationships, which are common in East Asia, can impede flows of foreign goods and services into these countries even though the countries involved have formally accepted the WTO rules for liberalized trade transactions.

In recent years the United States, the European Union, Japan and other countries have been working on standardization of the accounting methods used for reporting both international and domestic business operations. National accounting practices are closely tied in with the respective countries' corporate governance practices. These standards affect calculations by firms and governments regarding international taxation liabilities and the expected returns from prospective investments in foreign business operations as well as foreign portfolio investments. It is generally agreed that the Western liberal norms such as individual rights, transparency and information disclosure have been driving forces for standardization of processes in global business around the world. Yet it is also the case that conforming to the new accounting standards being adopted by countries such as the United States and the European Union would require significant changes in corporate governance practices in China, Japan and other countries in East Asia.

In both China and Japan, massive effort has been poured into adapting to Western standards, including adjustments in domestic rules that govern practices related to international trade and corporate governance. For example, domestic laws and business practices had to be changed to accommodate the accepted international rules of the WTO. In China, adaptation to the Western liberal norm-based WTO rules in their domestic practices, where the traditional non-Western legal and social norms had prevailed, has been complicated. Acceptance of the principles of the WTO international trade rules at the national level is one thing, but reshaping a nation's business practices to make these rules compatible with and supportive of the WTO rules is a different matter. In general we observe that selective adaptation, rather than full implementation, of the WTO rules has taken place in China.

Similar observations can be made with regard to the Anglo-American corporate governance rules, which currently serve as the *de facto* global standard. Even though China and Japan, for example, are in quite different stages of economic development and have quite different institutional and cultural circumstances, these countries still face similar issues when it comes to adapting to Anglo-American practices in a domestic context. Chapters in this book address these issues from various perspectives.

In Part I, "New Corporate Governance Practices: Institutional and Economic Considerations," seven chapters are devoted to various issues that have arisen with efforts in recent years to transplant Anglo-American corporate governance mechanisms to China (Chapters 2–6) and Japan (Chapters 7–8). These efforts have caused frictions with the local business norms that underlie traditional corporate governance practices. These chapters pay special attention to the corporate governance practices associated with *share*holder value maximization versus *stake*holder value maximization principles, transparency and information disclosure, protection of minority shareholders, and the market for corporate control.

Translated into corporate governance practices, Western liberal norms such as protection of individual rights and property, transparency, and free market transactions correspond collectively to advocating shareholder value maximization over stakeholder value maximization, advocating full disclosure of accounting and other relevant information to shareholders, protection of minority shareholders, and facilitating development of the market for corporate control including both friendly and hostile takeovers. In both China and Japan, introducing these Western practices has been difficult. One source of friction are large shareholders. The state itself is the main shareholder in China. Corporate group-based shareholders dominate in Japan. These large shareholders continue to play important roles in corporate governance in the two countries, as discussed in the chapters of this book.

In Chapter 2, Yang describes the progress of development for China's corporate governance mechanisms, beginning with the original adoption of a stakeholder value maximization model of the sort found in Germany and Japan in the 1980s. Yang then goes on to explain the shift in the 1990s toward the Anglo-American style shareholder value maximization model. Stakeholder value-based models of corporate governance emphasize the welfare of firms, including the employees, suppliers, managers, and even the customers, rather than focusing on shareholder interests. In contrast, for shareholder value maximization-based corporate governance systems, managers as the agents of the shareholders of a firm are supposed to make decisions based on the shareholder value maximization principle; subject, of course, to the existing contractual relationships with others, including employees and suppliers. Yang discusses issues that have arisen as a result of the shift in the governance practices in China, and proposes mixed corporate governance systems that blend practices from both types of corporate systems.

In Chapter 3, Gu discusses issues associated with firms' misrepresentation of their accounting and other company information in the context of the changing legal situation in China. Despite the ongoing introduction in China of U.S.-style legal norms emphasizing transparency, information disclosure, and the protection of private (individual and institutional) investors, China's securities regulatory agencies continue to face difficulties in enforcing the information disclosure required for protecting public investors in transactions, such as those involving third-party loan guarantees, the treatment of trade secrets, and the veracity of financial statements.

In Chapter 4, Wang discusses the 2005 revision of China's Company Law which was originally enacted in 1993, and the implications of this revision for protection of minority shareholders' rights in China. The Company Law provides the legal framework within which shareholder-owned corporations operate while also satisfying social and other obligations. The issue of how to protect the rights of the minority shareholders of firms is an important one in China where the state is by far the largest majority shareholder of many listed companies. Wang compares how minority shareholder rights are treated under the original and revised Company Law, and concludes that the revised law has yielded significant improvements in the protection of minority shareholders' rights.

In Chapter 5, Yuen and Zhang comment and expand on the discussion of the corporate governance issues dealt with in Chapters 2–4, making use of economic insights. They focus on the implications of recent changes in the legal setting of China's corporate governance system for various aspects of the economic behavior of Chinese firms. Since the majority of listed firms in China are state-owned enterprises, Yuen and Zhang use the principal-agent framework for their analysis of corporate governance issues, including the tradeoffs between stakeholder and shareholder value maximization. In their analysis, they treat the state as the principal and managers of state-owned enterprises as the agents.

In Chapter 6, Chi and Wang discuss corporate governance issues that have arisen since China embarked on market-oriented economic reforms in 1978. The so-called industrial reform, whereby state-owned enterprises began to achieve more autonomy and government interventions in enterprise affairs were curtailed, is of particular importance. This process of change in the corporate governance of Chinese firms has been accompanied by a separation of ownership and control, resulting in a significant increase in the importance in the role of government bureaucrats as managers of state-owned enterprises. Noting that these bureaucrat managers neither own state-owned firms nor represent the best interests of the people of China, Chi and Wang apply agency theory (much as Yuen and Zhang, in Chapter 5, used principal-agent theory) to analyze corporate governance and economic implications of state-owned firm behavior in China under the new legal and institutional settings. They emphasize that, unlike Russia and former socialist countries in Eastern Europe, China has focused on transforming state enterprise corporate control and on the changing relationship between government and enterprises, as opposed to promoting privatization of state-owned enterprises. One of Chi and Wang's conclusions is that, while many aspects of the reform measures may increase the economic efficiency of state-owned firms, including more efficient production operations, nevertheless, state-owned firms do not seem to have reached the level of efficiency of Western corporations. One reason for this may be the lack of genuinely private large shareholders and shortages of managers with the sorts of specialized expertise associated with efficiency gains in productive activities for Western firms.

Chapters 7 and 8 are concerned with new developments in corporate governance in Japan since the 1990s. Since the end of World War II, Japanese firms have worked hard to develop bank-based corporate governance practices which pay attention to the welfare of various stakeholders of firms, including their permanent employees, managers, suppliers and other related firms which collectively own the majority of their shares as the firms' friendly shareholders. Under these circumstances, there was no need to pay attention to minority individual shareholders or shareholder value maximization in general. This post-World War II system of corporate governance served Japan well during its high growth period but, as growth opportunities began to dry up in the late 1980s, the system seemed unable to stop firms and investors from seeking asset returns without paying adequate attention to economic fundamentals. The entire Japanese economy was caught up in a financial bubble of historic size – larger than any bubble the world had experienced before. The bubble burst in 1990. The subsequent public sector policy failures worsened the post-bubble recession which continued into the early 2000s. The public began questioning why Japan's post-World War II bank-based corporate governance mechanisms failed the Japanese economy. At the same time, the banks themselves began to suffer from massive non-performing loans in the aftermath of the bubble burst. Many banks, large and small, faced the prospect of bankruptcy and the government had to bail many of them out, including most of Japan's largest banks. Under these circumstances, the Japanese government, firms and the public came to believe in the need for massive reforms of Japan's corporate governance practices.

In Chapter 7, Nakamura discusses characteristics of Japan's corporate governance reforms in the 1990s: reforms that led Japan to introduce a U.S.-style corporate governance system. The reforms have been significant in substance and are still ongoing, and have involved significant changes in legal and institutional regulations as well as firm business practices. The reform aim is to introduce the Anglo-American corporate governance system as a replacement for the traditional bank-based one. Laws have been implemented to institutionalize transparency, information disclosure, and the protection of individual shareholders, as well as to create a formal place for independent directors and establish the shareholder value maximization principle. As a result of these reforms, hostile takeovers are now possible, for example. They were not possible under the bank-based system when friendly institutional and corporate shareholders typically owned 70 percent or more of many listed firms. Nakamura notes that, while the market for corporate control has been significantly liberalized, resulting in increased mergers and acquisitions (M&A) activities, it is still quite unlike that found in the United States. For example, the majority of transactions are between friendly or related firms and there are still very few hostile takeovers. Indeed, hostile takeovers have not been well accepted in Japan to date. Nakamura also illustrates other corporate governance issues Japan still faces with respect to accepting new practices adopted from the U.S. system. For example, he points out the ambiguity in the process of transplanting the U.S.-style use of independent directors. While the new Japanese law recommends the use of outside directors, the companies choose how many outside directors to have and how to use them. These choices are tied in with the company choice of a U.S.-style executive committee system or a traditional Japanese one. The latitude of company choice under the new Japanese law can potentially encourage the development of (unpredictable) dysfunctionality in the corporate governance system.

One of the main purposes of Japan's corporate governance reform is to enable certain corporate activities that were not possible under the traditional bank-based system. One such activity is reorganization of corporations using M&A. Corporations, facing removal of many of the traditional institutional and business practice restrictions, are now able to reorganize their structures more freely using M&A and other tools for economic gain, while reallocating economic resources across the firms involved in M&A transactions. The number of mergers and acquisitions between domestic firms increased from fewer than 300 in the early 1990s to more than 2,000 by 2005.

In Chapter 8, Arikawa and Miyajima, using recent data on Japanese M&A activities, explore possible economic reasons why the rate of M&A involving Japanese firms has increased significantly since Japan's recent corporate governance reform. Consistent, in part at least, with the existing empirical evidence for U.S. corporations, Arikawa and Miyakima find, at the industry level, that those industries with higher growth opportunities, as well as industries facing negative prospects such as sales declines, are more likely to engage in M&A activity. At the firm level, bidders are generally growing firms, and targeted firms tend to be more mature. Typically older, less productive firms in declining industries are acquired by more productive, younger, growing firms in growth industries. These findings are consistent with the role that M&A transactions play in reallocating capital and other economic resources across industries, and within firms, for improving economic efficiency. Arikawa and Miyajima conclude that Japanese firms improved their efficiency through merger activity in the 1990s, and that this improvement was enabled by Japan's corporate governance reform.

In Part II, "Evolving Corporate Governance Practices: Selective Adaptations," three chapters are devoted to a discussion of the processes of selective adaptation of Western corporate governance mechanisms in China and Japan. Facing globalization of their economic activities, these two countries began their reform of corporate governance mechanisms in the context of quite different economic circumstances. In both countries, Company Laws were at the center of the reform. China's Company Law was created in 1993 and revised in 2005. Japan's Company Law (Commercial Code) and other related laws went through numerous revisions in the 1990s to 2000s, and a new revised and consolidated Company Law was enacted in 2006. In both countries, the revisions of these laws attempted to incorporate Western (particularly U.S.) legal practices. Important corporate governance issues associated with the application of some of the imported legal practices to the business environments in China and Japan have already been considered in Chapters 2–7 of Part I. The chapters in Part II further consider issues of transplanting foreign corporate governance practices, making use of various historical and selective adaptation process perspectives.

In Chapter 9, Jiangyu Wang discusses the process of China's adoption of Western corporate governance mechanisms. He particularly focuses on China's Company Law and also the role of independent directors in the two-tier board structure of governance. Wang notes that the Chinese Company Law system is a hybrid one, containing institutions borrowed from both the collection of common laws, as practiced mainly in the United States, and the collection of continental civil laws, as practiced especially in Germany. The hybrid nature of the legal systems is reflected in the board structure of China's listed companies, which are mandated to have both a management board with independent directors and a supervisory board. With these two "safety nets," however, Wang concludes that corporate governance for China's listed companies is still very unsatisfactory. Previous studies have shown that the supervisory board and the independent directors, as "strange partners" (that is, an odd working partnership, given their different mandates) in China's listed companies, have not brought significant improvements in terms of the overall corporate governance of Chinese companies. In this evolutionary process for China's hybrid corporate governance practices, Wang also concludes that, compared with the supervisory board, which can be regarded as a complete failure, the independent director system has made certain, albeit limited, contributions to the improvement of the corporate governance of China's listed companies. However, given the inherent defects in the overall corporate governance environment in China, it is not easy to be optimistic about how much more the independent directors can accomplish.

In Chapter 10, Goo and Carver discuss the process of selective adaptation of international norms of corporate governance mechanisms in China, paying particular attention to how Chinese culture has influenced the development of China's Company Law.

China's Company Law and the corporate governance system currently in place owe more to the long-standing and deeply held Chinese values upholding the importance of flexibility, sensitivity to context, and tolerance for degrees of freedom in decision making depending upon the context. This has been described as a system of "low structure, high ambiguity" in which the ambiguity itself becomes part of the context for determining what is fair. Chinese Company Law remains ambiguous and, on many important issues, fails to deal with the "who, what, where and how" of legislative drafting that we expect from common and civil law systems. For the Western investor, therefore, the whole system appears to be legally "deficient" when compared with the detailed drafting techniques of, for example, the Hong Kong Companies Ordinance. The problem is further complicated by the fact that there is no body of case law to supplement the gaps, and there is no doctrine of precedent with which to predict outcomes and to give the investor a sense of deeply held traditions of law, structure and stability. Goo and Carver conclude that, when learning from the West regarding an appropriate measure, care needs to be taken to understand the background and reasoning of the measures adopted in the West and whether these measures are likely to work in China. Simply copying from the West without effective implementation and adaptation of the standards may appease the international investors in the short run, but is unlikely to work in the long run. So far, law and regulations appear to be generally in place for listed companies and state-owned banks, though certain provisions in the Company Law still need further adjustments. More difficult is the task of creating an international culture of good corporate governance practices.

In Chapter 11, Nakamura applies a selective adaptation framework to explain the process of the local acceptance of newly introduced corporate governance practices as Japan has shifted its corporate governance mechanisms from the traditional bank-based system to a U.S.-type system. In this framework, the manner (for example, the degree and speed) of the local acceptance of new practices has depended on interactions between the business norms underlying Japan's traditional corporate governance practices and the Western liberal norms that underlie U.S. and other Western corporate governance practices that are being imported into Japan. Nakamura uses five state variables (state of shareholder value maximization, state of independent directors, state of the competition in the market for corporate control, state of transparency and information disclosure, and state of minority shareholders) to characterize the state of corporate governance in Japan before and after the reform. He considers how Japanese business norms can help newly proposed U.S.-style corporate governance practices gain acceptance locally.

The selective adaptation framework that has been adopted does not suggest the outright rejection, on the basis of legitimacy and complementarity in Japan, of new U.S.-style corporate governance practices affecting the state variables. However, Japan's prevailing business norms are more consistent with stakeholder than shareholder value maximization principles. This implies that new laws advocating shareholder value maximization are likely to engender negative perceptions and reactions from Japanese firms and businesses.

Application of the selective adaptation analysis to Japan's new policy of promoting a more competitive market for corporate control suggests that Japan's business norms are compatible with this policy not only on the basis of its legitimacy, but also its complementarity with Japan's existing business environment, particularly where the market for friendly (though not hostile) M&A activities is concerned. This implication seems consistent with what we have observed so far. Another application of selective adaptation is Japan's new policy of giving firms the choice of having (or not having) independent directors with formal involvement in corporate governance. The analysis suggests that firms with significant interfirm relationships (for example, keiretsu[1] firms) are not likely to make this choice. Nakamura concludes that, in the process of selective adaptation of the Anglo-American corporate governance practices, Japan's implementation of these practices is uneven, resulting in significant dysfunctionalities, and that it is not possible to predict the economic efficiency consequences of these dysfunctionalities.

Note

1. "Keiretsu" is the Japanese term for corporate groups in which member firms have some relationship to one another via their common and long-term business objectives. Equity relationships are often involved. One example is the Toyota keiretsu group, which consists of the Toyota Motor Company at the center, and many supplier firms which sell their products to Toyota. Toyota Motor Company owns small amounts of equity in many of these supplier firms in the group.

Part I

New Corporate Governance Practices: Institutional and Economic Considerations

2
The Two Models of Corporate Governance and the Institutional Reform of Chinese Enterprise[1]

Peng Fei Yang

Introduction

The enterprise reform in China since the 1980s has actually been an exploration of establishing a suitable corporate governance mechanism. The process can be divided into two periods. In the 1980s, it was adapting aspects of the German and Japanese model; and from the 1990s, from the Anglo-American model. However, the Chinese system has inherited some of the disadvantages of these two models, such as the dominance by one major shareholder, the absence of employees in corporate management, and the lack of protection of the interests of creditors and local communities. This has caused the misbehavior of corporations. This chapter concludes by summarizing the lessons learned in China's corporate governance reform, and provides analysis of some of the new trends in the reform, such as the reforms in differentiated treatment of shares, and emphasis on the concept of harmonious society.

Nowadays, many Chinese listed companies have a very negative reputation. An important example is that the Chinese stock market is in a record-low downturn and is still going down. It seems that people have completely lost their trust and confidence in it. For many years, small and medium shareholders could not enjoy even the basic privileges and benefits of the stock market and, moreover, suffered big losses in their investments. Moreover, Chinese companies and enterprises also have a bad reputation in the domestic labor market, and legal action against employers is always in evidence. It is not only generally about low salaries, poor working conditions and lack of respect for employees' dignity, but also quite often about worker layoffs. The reputation of Chinese companies is also very bad in terms of society and the environment – the misspending of natural resources, the destruction of the environment, ignorance of enterprises' responsibility towards society, for example. All of these have resulted not only in broad condemnation by the public, but also in many massive public demonstrations taking place which have affected the stability and harmony of the society.

Since the early 1980s, China has been carrying out reforms of its state-owned enterprises. The reform process has been a hard one, evolving from loosening the control of management power to the separation of management and ownership powers, and then to building a modern enterprise system. It has gone from learning from the German experiences of corporate governance by employees in the 1980s, to learning from the American experiences in developing stock markets and introducing the system of independent directors, and so on, in the 1990s. Why have enterprises retained such bad reputations while Chinese economic development has generally achieved great success? What will be the future for Chinese enterprises in corporate governance reform? This chapter will attempt to provide some analysis by referring to China's efforts in introducing the Western models of corporate governance.

The two major models of the corporate governance mechanism

The corporate governance mechanism is an organizational arrangement for the corporation itself. Through this organizational arrangement, it serves the interests of investors in the company (Mayer, 1997). The contents of the corporate governance mechanism include a series of corporate governance systems, such as a board of directors, a supervisory board, the employees' role, and directors' incentives. In modern societies, and in the form of legislative intervention, different countries establish their corporate governance mechanisms based on different backgrounds.

The necessity of state intervention in corporate governance is a conclusion reached by Berle and Means (1932) in their research. According to them, a corporate governance system derives from the separation of ownership from control in modern stock companies under a market economy. In modern stock companies, investors who possess ownership of the company do not directly operate the company like they used to. Rather, they hire professional managers as their representatives and make them responsible for the company's operation. Under this model of "separation of powers," the interests of investors and managers are likely to be in conflict. Without sufficiently effective supervision, managers can very easily exploit their advantage to the detriment of the investors' interests. Under these circumstances, it is necessary for the state and society to establish a corporate governance mechanism to regulate firms' management in order to protect stakeholders (including shareholders, as well as creditors, employees, suppliers and communities, and so on). This is the goal of the corporate governance mechanism.

Currently, and relatively speaking, there are two corporate governance mechanisms which function well in achieving the goal mentioned above: the German and Japanese model of internal control of the organization and the Anglo-American model of external control based on the market.

The German and Japanese model of internal organizational control

Internal control is an essential feature of the German and Japanese model of corporate governance, and this can be seen from the following:

1. Corporations always have a few major shareholders who together own the majority of the controlling fractions of the firms' shares, and they exercise their power as the controlling shareholders' block when the corporations face critical management decision issues. Very often, the views of the minority shareholders are ignored.
2. Banks are shareholders. Banks hold a large amount of stakes in listed companies, and also function as a watchdog for individual shareholders and execute their voting rights.
3. There is a board of directors and a board of supervisors. The supervisory board in Germany even functions as the real decision making body in the corporation.
4. Employees are involved in corporate management.
5. External markets, especially markets for corporate control rights, have little effect in monitoring a firm's management.

Employees' participation in management is the most important feature of the German model. According to German corporate laws, based on the nature and size of the company, employees have different functions in company management. The supervisory council is not required in private limited companies with fewer than 500 employees. For those companies with fewer than 2,000 employees, two-thirds of the members in the supervisory council are elected by the shareholders, while one-third of the members are elected by the employees. For companies with more than 2,000 employees, half the representatives in the supervisory council are elected by the employees and half by the shareholders. As we can see, in the initial stages, companies are operated at the owners' discretion. As the company develops and expands, the corporate governance mechanism changes accordingly, and the "check and balance" function of the employees grows stronger.[2] Moreover, employees in German companies are highly organized; trade unions and factory committees represent workers (including those who are not members of trade unions) in the supervisory council. Accordingly, workers are incentivized when doing their jobs, the companies are thus under good operation, and employees' interests are well protected. In Japan, participation by employees in corporate management is not emphasized. Yet in Japanese enterprises, life-time employment is a social custom. A company is regarded as a family by its employees, and the employees are deemed as family members by the company. Most employees actively take part in corporate operation and management as if they were owners of the company.

Both the German and Japanese models of corporate governance have been influenced by the historical developments of their respective economies, and the structures of their corporate governance systems have certain similarities. German and Japanese economic development and competitive enterprise in the post-World War II era may be attributed to their corporate governance mechanisms.

The Anglo-American model of external control by markets

The Anglo-American model of corporate governance is characterized by external market control that depends on external forces to monitor corporate management. This can be seen from the following:

1. Corporate shares are dispersedly distributed. Investors have little influence on corporate operation and management.
2. External directors (independent directors) play an important role on the board of directors, and become a key part of corporate monitoring.
3. There is freedom of employment. Employees are connected to the company through employment contracts, and they have little influence on corporate governance.
4. There is a developed securities market. If the company performs poorly, the shareholders' response is to sell their shares. Mergers and acquisitions (M&A) based on market pressures are very common.
5. There is a fairly sound legal system in terms of mandatory information disclosure, control of insider trade, and protection of minority shareholders.

A main feature of the Anglo-Saxon model is the "check and balance" of corporate operators through the external forces of the securities market. These external forces include corporate M&A, appointment of independent directors, and other laws and regulations. The Anglo-American model is also related to its historical tradition. For example, securities markets in these two countries have a long history; the common law tradition can quickly respond to the need to update laws. In 2002, after the Enron scandal, the U.S. Congress passed the Sarbanes-Oxley Act immediately and strengthened the supervision of firms' management, thereby reinforcing the securities market system.

What should be noted is that, although both the Anglo-American model and German/Japanese model are recognized worldwide, they are not perfect models. These models themselves are still developing and evolving. Moreover, over the past 20 years, these two models have been "borrowing" from each other. In the 1980s, impressed by Japan's economic miracle, American enterprises and legislature were very much interested in learning from the Japanese experiences. Following the American economic recovery and growth since the 1990s, the Anglo-American model has become a model for Japan and Germany to learn from, and therefore the so-called combination of the two models has become a worldwide trend.[3]

China's enterprise reform and the two models of corporate governance

China began its enterprise system reform in the early 1980s. Its main focus has been on enterprise governance in a micro sense, aimed at strengthening the competitiveness of enterprises and protecting the interests of investors (especially investors in state assets). From the perspective of enterprises, this is a *de facto* reform of corporate governance mechanisms in China.

The reform can be divided into two phases. Phase I is from the early 1980s through the early 1990s; Phase II is from 1993 to the present day. For simplicity, I shall refer to them, respectively, as the 1980s period and the 1990s period.

The enterprise reform in the 1980s is mainly referred to as reforms within state-owned enterprises (SOEs). This is because during that period China had just started its reform and was beginning to pursue its "open door" policy, private enterprises and foreign enterprises were still in their early stages, and SOEs were in a position of absolute dominance in terms of both GDP contribution and products in the market. Major events in this period were the enactment of the General Principles of Civil Law and the Bankruptcy Law in 1986, and the Law on Industrial Enterprises Owned by the People of China in 1988 (these enterprises subsequently became known as state-owned enterprises). These legislations were aimed at gradually recognizing enterprises as entities in the market in order to create incentives for and encourage the competitiveness of enterprises.

Briefly speaking, the SOE reform in the 1980s included the following aspects:

1. *The relationship between the state and enterprise.* Since the early 1980s, government has continued reforming the enterprise management system. This included loosening control of the enterprise by allowing it to operate as an economic responsible system, changing the enterprise management mechanism, and even aiming at the separation of enterprise from government. Article 2 of the Law on Industrial Enterprises Owned by the People of China was seen as a monument: "An industrial enterprise owned by the people (hereinafter referred to as the enterprise) shall be a socialist commodity production and operation unit which shall, in accordance with law, make its own managerial decisions, take full responsibility for its own profits and losses and practice independent accounting." Thus, the basic feature of a "company" – taking responsibility for its own profit/loss – is given to SOEs as a basis for corporate governance.
2. *The relationship between an enterprise and its operators.* According to the new laws and regulations, compared to the pre-reform era, management in an enterprise is entitled to more power in making operational decisions; for example, the introduction of factory director responsibility, which gives heads of enterprises the right to make final decisions. Also, in establishing a system of economic responsibility, according to the contract, major operators in enterprises are entitled to full power in operational control.
3. *The relationship between an enterprise and its employees.* The Constitution and various enterprise laws emphasize that workers are owners of the state enterprise. Employment for workers is usually for life. Although the employment contract system was introduced in 1986, generally it was not implemented until the 1990s. Particularly, according to the Law on Industrial Enterprises Owned by the People of China, enterprises should be managed in a democratic way, and this takes place in the form of the Staff and Workers' Congress, which has rights in issues ranging from discussing enterprise development plans to electing the factory director. The purpose of the legislation was to provide a

check and balance over the factory director's power by allowing the employees to participate in management of the enterprise.

4. *The relationship between enterprises and society at a large.* Enterprises are gradually becoming market-driven and therefore must compete at market prices, but they have a civil responsibility as well because their assets are granted by the state.

In view of the enterprise reform in the 1980s, regardless of the perspective one is taking – historical, theoretical, or practical – we can clearly see that the Chinese enterprise reforms have been greatly influenced by the German and Japanese model. To a certain extent, China was still in a planned economy which was different from the market economy. Yet in terms of the economic mechanism, the Chinese reform measures were very similar to the German and Japanese model, which relies mainly on internal control. For example, German and Japanese enterprises are mainly controlled by majority shareholders (in China, the government is the representative of the owners, the public), and employees participate in enterprise management. Although an enterprise does not have a board of directors, a supervisory board, or a shareholders' general meeting, there are administrative, party, and trade union organizations which play roles in operation and supervision. In terms of employment, Japan also has a tradition of lifelong employment with one firm, and there is a long-term employment system protected by labor laws and collective contracts in Germany. In China's planned economy, providing lifelong employment was one responsibility of Chinese enterprises.

In fact, in the economic reform in the 1980s, it was reasonable for China to take lessons from the German and Japanese model, and especially the Japanese experience. It is not only because the Japanese model was a good example for the whole world at that time (even Britain and America were learning from it), but also because there were similarities between China and Japan in terms of tradition and culture. For example, China, Germany and Japan are all civil law countries, and both China and Japan are influenced by the Confucian culture and tradition.

However, the enterprise reforms in the 1980s did not meet society's expectations. Although the economy in general was developing continuously, lack of incentive in SOEs remained a serious problem. In fact, it had nothing to do with the models we were learning from. Instead, some basic conditions for a sound corporate governance system, such as autonomy of operation and a relatively well-established market system, were not in place at all.

In 1993, when the socialist market economy was beginning to be developed, China started its second phase of reforms. The new reforms are very different from those in the 1980s in terms of both the background and content, and included issues such as the establishment of the goal of a market economy, and rapid growth of private and foreign enterprises. Major events in this period include the enactments of the Company Law in 1994, the Labor Law in 1995, the Securities Law in 1999, and especially the Rules on Corporate Governance of Listed Companies, promulgated by China Securities Regulatory Commission (CSRC) in 2002.

In brief, the enterprise governance reforms of the 1990s have the following features:

1. Substantial progress has been made in the reform of enterprise ownership. Through a series of political decisions and the enactment of company laws, enterprises have become real participants in the market. To a certain extent, many enterprises have even become "super-participants" in the market. In order to attract more investment, enterprises were sometimes permitted to behave illegally by local governments. For example, some illegal activities, such as destruction of the environment, violation of labor laws, and production of counterfeit products, were all protected by local governments and allowed to take place.
2. The securities market was established. Enterprises have been offered opportunities to raise funds from the securities market, but are also becoming gradually more supervised by the market. Listed companies began implementing a modern system of corporate governance, which was an important step in establishing China's corporate governance system. Since the 1990s, the stock exchanges in Shanghai and Shenzhen have developed to a size of some 1,300 listed companies. However, most of these companies still suffer from the dominance of a single majority shareholder.
3. In terms of the corporate governance framework, three boards have been established in accordance with the Company Law in 1993, replacing the three old boards. The supervisory board has become a legal supervisory body within a company. After years of practice, considering the fact that the supervisory board was not able to function well, in early 2001, by reference to American experiences, the system of independent directors, or external directors, was established. Currently there is both a supervisory council and an independent director system in listed companies.

4. Since the enactment of the Labor Law in 1995, except for government agencies, public services, and monopolistic state-owned enterprises, most companies and enterprises have abandoned the system of lifelong employment. Fixed- and short-term labor contracts have become the norm in the labor market, and enterprises have enormous discretionary power in employment decision making.[4]

In view of the reform practice since the 1990s, corporate governance reform in China has obviously and greatly been influenced by the Anglo-American model. The German system of internal organizational balance in the company, such as democratic management by employees, was replaced by its counterpart system in China. The government is much more focused on establishing an external control system for companies, such as a securities market, independent directors, and so on, and has attempted to check and balance enterprise operators through external forces to realize the value of companies.

Evaluation of China's corporate governance reform

Through the enterprise governance reform in the 1980s and 1990s, and after learning from the German/Japanese model and Anglo-American model respectively, what results have the Chinese corporate governance reforms yielded? After a closer look at these 1,300 listed companies, we cannot be optimistic. Some facts are notable, as follows:

1. Dominance by a single majority shareholder is very common in listed companies. This is caused by the stock issuance system. Stock issuance of every listed company must be approved by the CSRC, and stocks in every listed company are divided into two categories, tradable and non-tradable shares. The percentage of tradable shares in most of the listed companies is very low and that of non-tradable shares comprises more than two-thirds. For this reason, although China has some 1,300 listed companies, these companies are dominated by a single majority shareholder, which is the same as that in Germany and Japan, but not the American model, and therefore there is no such check and balance system established from the securities market. The independent directors system introduced from America is not able to function well due to the restriction of dominance by a single majority shareholder (Ying, 2004). It should be noted that dominance by a single majority shareholder has provided firms' management with a great opportunity to infringe other stakeholders' interests.
2. Balance from democratic management by employees has disappeared. Since the 1990s, treating employees "American-style" has become very

popular. Employees are only a component of an enterprise, and the government should establish a free labor market for enterprises. The establishment of the modern enterprise system is accompanied by layoffs and unemployment of tens of millions of workers from SOEs. In the media, people can always see and hear the propaganda that people should find new jobs in the labor market by themselves rather than rely on the government. Although it is possible, according to some laws and regulations, that presidents of trade unions are members of the board of directors or the supervisory board, the traditional system has remained, where the trade union is heavily restricted by the management, and cannot do much in corporate management. In particular, under the rules of fixed- and short-term contracts under the Labor Law, and the over-supply in the labor market, workers are facing an extremely uncertain and competitive market. Many workers are unable to secure a job, let alone ask for democratic rights in enterprises. Thus the check and balance by labor as an important mechanism for enterprise internal control, which is very popular in Germany and Japan, is not in place in China.

3. The check and balance in other aspects is also not optimistic. According to German and Japanese experiences, creditors and residents of local communities are also stakeholders of the company to some extent. Their interests should also be considered in corporate governance mechanism. But the reality is that they are not able to play such a role in China.

   From a creditor perspective, due to the strict financial control system, most creditors of companies are banks, especially state-owned banks. Theoretically speaking, China has relevant civil and contract laws and regulations, but in terms of corporate debt, banks in China are the most powerless in the world. It is not only because banks cannot play a role in corporate governance, but also because they cannot even secure repayment of their loans. These banks are still considered by companies as state-owned, so their loans can be arranged through the government. Some companies take out borrowing with no intention of repaying the loan; instead, they just wait for a waiver from the government or they convert the debt to shares.[5] At an international meeting on December 1, 2004, Zhou Xiaochuan, the president of the People's Bank of China, the central bank, pointed out that "how to solve the big problems of debts converting to shares which ignored the principle of corporate governance" is still a serious problem that Chinese corporate governance is facing (Xiaochun, n.d.).

> From the perspective of the local community, there is no check or balance either. In recent years, the growth of GDP has become the only thing local government officials are concerned about. They are always preoccupied by attracting investment, while paying little attention to supervising enterprises or protecting the interests of local residents. In quite a few cases, some government officials themselves are investors in enterprises, and so have a vested interest in them. Before 2003, in particular, some local government officials were even managers of some large local enterprises. How, then, can they play a role in supervising the company?[6]

Through some 20 years of economic system reform, such as the development of private and foreign enterprises, and promoting foreign trade, the Chinese economy has achieved great success. But in terms of the corporate governance mechanism, despite what has been learnt from both the German/Japanese and Anglo-American models, the core of the corporate governance system, or, in other words, a monitoring and supervisory system upon corporate operators, has yet to be established. We can even say that what China has taken from these models are all of their disadvantages, such as the dominance by one majority shareholder in Germany and Japan, and the lack of labor protection in the Anglo-American model.

The current situation in Chinese corporate governance has caused the lack of even a basic balance in Chinese enterprise. Without such checks and balances these companies can do whatever they want in the market without any restrictions. The interests not only of related parties but also of their investors, such as minority shareholders, cannot be protected. Due to these reasons, as mentioned at the beginning of this chapter, enterprises have a negative reputation.

The future of China's corporate governance reforms

The cause of the problems mentioned above is very complicated: it is related to corporate governance itself. The corporate governance mechanism is still developing even in those "developed" countries such as the U.S. and Japan; and it is also related to specific historical factors in China. For example, China was in transition from a state-owned economy to a market economy, and conflicts during the transition period have been complex. However, I think there have been two issues in which China made mistakes that could have been avoided. These should be particularly noted as follows:

Firstly, China gave up democratic management by employees completely, which was a very important historical tradition and also a basic feature of a socialist country. It is true that enterprises and employees did not have incentives in the old economic system. It is, however, inappropriate to change to a completely capital-controlled system without protecting labor rights, not to mention democratic management by employees. Even in the most typical capitalist countries such as Germany and Japan, protection of employees' democratic rights in management and other labor rights is strongly emphasized, and yet they are both leading global economies.

Secondly, as we can see from the German/Japanese model and Anglo-American model, the core element of corporate governance is the formation of the supervisory system upon corporate operators. However, during the 20 years of China's enterprise reform, particular attention was paid to strengthening the power of corporate operators. This can be seen from the fact that the heads of factories, who are responsible for operational decision making in these firms, may also become the owners of these factories, whereas, before, the state was the sole owner; ownership and control have been separated; shares are being held by management; and, most recently, management buyouts (MBOs) have been implemented. The power and interests of management are increasingly being strengthened while a supervisory system of corporate management has been weakening. Therefore, China's enterprise reform to a certain extent is working in an opposite direction to the basic rule of corporate governance.

The government is probably now aware of the above-mentioned problems in corporate governance reforms, and is seeking to improve the corporate governance reform measures. The two points discussed below are of particular importance to the future of China's corporate governance reform.

Reform in the differentiated treatment of shares

The differentiated treatment of shares is a historical problem in China's securities market: there are different policy treatments between tradable and non-tradable shares upon the issuance of the stock. Non-tradable shares cannot be traded in the market, but the holders of these non-tradable shares control the company. For a long time, this differentiated treatment has caused many problems in corporate governance, such as the dominance by one majority shareholder. Many majority shareholders control all the assets in the company and therefore infringe upon the interests of the minority shareholders.

Obviously, a reform in the treatment of shares was a necessary procedure and measure learnt from the Anglo-American model of corporate governance. If shares are always treated or settled differently, control by external market forces, as in the Anglo-American model, can never be achieved. However, whether or not the external control of the Anglo-American model can be applied to China is determined by the following issues:

1. If we suppose that the reform in differentiated treatment of shares is successful, it will only mean that dominance by one majority shareholder is removed in the legal sense. But the dominance by a hidden majority shareholder will still be possible. Based on the real situation of China's securities market, it may take years, even decades, to solve the problem.
2. If we suppose that the reform in differentiated treatment of shares is successful, and the goal of dispersedly distributing shares according to the Anglo-American model is successful, there is still the question of establishing an external market force, such as providing a complete legal system of information disclosure, control of insider trading, and protection of minority shareholders, and so on. All of these are challenging tasks.
3. Currently, the difficulty of the reform in differentiated treatment of shares is a critical issue. Since the carrying out of the reform was declared in April 2005, investors have considered the reform as a great expansion of the securities market. As we can see from the current situation, people lack confidence in the securities market. Whether or not the reform can be successful is still questionable.

Corporate governance and building a harmonious society

Since coming to power in 2003, facing SARS and other serious social issues, the new generation of leaders in China have put forth a series of new guidelines and policies towards building a socialist harmonious society. These new guidelines and policies have pointed the way for corporate governance.

Currently, some new ideas which meet the requirement of building the socialist harmonious society have played a role in corporate governance. For example, the Decision on Renovating the Socialist Market Economy System passed by the Chinese Communist Party in its 16th plenum raised the ideas of "respecting labor, respecting knowledge, respecting intellectuals, and respecting creativity," and required the strengthening of the labor protection system in enterprise. It emphasized the harmonious development between individuals and society, and between human beings and nature. This provided a basis for establishing a social responsibility system for enterprise.

Naturally, how to build a sound corporate governance system and improve the reputation of Chinese enterprises based on the concept of harmonious society, technically and practically speaking, has a long way to go. Undoubtedly, China should combine its own traditions and needs with the German/Japanese and Anglo-American models of corporate governance.

Notes

1. The editor thanks Mr. Harry Wang (a Ph.D. student at the University of British Columbia) for providing the initial English translation of this chapter originally written in Chinese.
2. As Brian R. Cheffins (1997) noted, in Germany, many investors and managers are not interested in having employees involved in management, but the law makes it unavoidable, and therefore big enterprises in Germany usually provide employees with a right to participate in democratic management.
3. See "The convergence of corporate governance models in the world and its implication to China," http://www.xyfund.com/112003/10/58704.html.
4. For example, Article 20 of the Labor Law states that long-term contracts are only available to employees who have been working for a company for more than ten years; others can only have fixed- or short-term contracts.
5. As a way to lower the risks of banks in China, and to improve the assets and debts structure of state-owned enterprises, since 1999, China has taken the measure of converting the debt in some important SOEs to shares, the so-called "conversion of debts to shares."
6. In March 2003, Central Committee of Chinese Communist Party has promulgated the "Notice on clearance of concurrent post of party or government officials in enterprises." See http://www.people.com.cn/GB/shizheng/1026/2778556.html.

References

Berle, A. A., and Means, G. C. (1932) *The Modern Corporation and Private Property* (New York: Harcourt, Brace and World, Inc.).

Cheffins, Brian R. (1997) *Company Law: Theory, Structure, and Operation* (Oxford: Clarendon Press).

Mayer, Colin (1997) "Corporate Governance in Market and Transitional Economies," in A. Tan (ed.), *Corporate Governance Mechanism in Reform* (China: Economic Press).

Xiaochun, Zhou (n.d.) "Corporate Governance in China is Still in Exploration." See http://www.china.org.cn/chinese/PI-c/846033.htm.

Ying, Tong (2004) "The First Report on Independent Directors: The Current Situation of Independent Directors," *Shanghai Securities News*, May 27.

3
How to Prevent China's Listed Companies from Making Misstatements[1]

Xiaorong Gu

Introduction

If we take a look at the legal and monitoring systems and cases regarding prevention of listed companies from making misstatements in economies such as those of the U.S., the U.K., Germany, Japan, mainland China, Hong Kong and Taiwan, what we can find in common are the following elements which are closely associated with the making of misstatements:

1. Related parties
   (a) listed companies and their staff (directors of the board, supervisors, financial and accounting staff);
   (b) the stock exchange, the securities brokers' association;
   (c) the stock exchange regulatory authorities (the Stock Exchange Regulatory Committee or the Bureau of Financial Administration);
   (d) judicial organs (law courts, prosecutorial authorities) and investigation authorities for securities crime (the public security department or the securities investigation bureau) and their staff;
   (e) intermediary institutions (accounting firms, investment banks, securities consulting and analysis firms, and law firms) and their staff;
   (f) investors (including institutional and individual investors).
2. The legal system and regulatory system: relevant corporate/company laws (including accounting rules) that dictate the substantial framework

of a company's operations; and procedural law, domestic law, international cooperation agreements, and the laws and regulations of every country, provide rules for all the above-mentioned parties. Despite the presence of such laws, rules and regulations, companies still manage to maneuver round them, taking advantage of some of the (sometimes illegal) loopholes and "playing the game" for immediate gain in the hope that they will never be caught.

3. Technical equipment, which includes electronic exchange systems, transaction surveillance appliances, and so on.

The issue we are mostly concerned with is how all of these elements can work together effectively to prevent the making of misstatements. What we mean by effectively preventing the making of misstatements is a comparison of the costs and benefits in pursuing the aim of prevention. There are two elements: one is the aim of prevention, and the other is the comparison of the costs and benefits. The first aim of prevention is to control the systematic risk – so there would be no huge impact on the normal operation of the stock exchange market even if a substantial case of misstatement took place. The second aim of prevention is to punish the violators. In terms of comparison of the costs and benefits, the use of the market mechanism surely incurs lower costs than the use of governmental regulations. However, in the practice of other countries' stock exchanges in the last century, the outcome is not very good. Moreover, since the 1970s or 1980s, every country has been strengthening its governmental surveillance. This issue will not be discussed in this chapter.

The effectiveness of the Anglo-American model in previous practices

Before the exposure of the Enron scandal in November 2001, many people believed that the Anglo-American model was the best (in the regulation of the securities market). The American model is based on the "efficient market" theory which holds that the public disclosure of information is the core to the securities regulatory system. According to this theory, as long as all the important information pertaining to securities and their issuance is disclosed completely, timely, and accurately, the market itself can receive and process the information and reflect it on the price of the stocks so that investors can make informed decisions. The regulatory authorities hence need only to require and urge the corporation to provide full disclosure of information, but need not evaluate the stock.

In other words, they do not need to replace the role of the market to verify and evaluate the stock issuer for its profitability, operating situation, issuance price and condition.

Some scholars have characterized the Anglo-American model as follows: (1) a unified and collective regulatory system; (2) the function of the stock regulatory authority is to implement the laws, make regulations and rules, and provide grounds for the "free" operation of the stock market. Therefore, the regulatory authorities are totally separate from the market, and do not intervene in any specific transactions. In the case of a problem in the stock market, their authority is usually remedial rather than preventative (that is, they tend not to monitor transactions, assuming that the parties involved are abiding by the rules; only after illegal activities are suspected or uncovered do they apply their powers forcefully to investigate and prosecute); (3) the preventive measures are essential to the work of the U.S. Securities and Exchange Commission (SEC); and (4) the SEC has quasi-legislative and quasi-judicial power to ensure the authoritativeness and effectiveness of its regulation of the stock market. The conclusion is, "theoretically speaking, the Anglo-American model of regulating the securities market has functioned relatively well in dealing with the relationship between legislation and implementation, between the federal authority and state authorities, and between the government and the market."[2]

On the prevention of misstatements, there are several features in the Anglo-American model.

The combination of governmental administration and judicial protection

In this combination, not only does the government play a regulatory role, but the criminal or civil litigation raised by the judicial authorities is also in place as a guarantor of judicial power. With regard to governmental administration, it can be divided into two categories: the administration of the federal government and that of the state government. The administration of the federal government is mostly vested in the U.S. SEC.

The SEC's headquarters and its nine local branches had some 2,300 staff in total in 1988, of whom 519 were working directly on the information disclosure system for enterprises and 712 on the prevention of improper relationships[3] (about half of their workload was related to the prevention of misstatement). In total, there was a staff of 1,231 staffs working on the prevention of misstatement. The number of securities criminal cases exposed by the SEC was recorded as 312 in 1986, and 303 in 1987, among which 72 cases, about 24 percent of the total, were in violation of information disclosure obligation; 40 cases, about 13 percent, were in violation of the issuance rules; 117 cases, approximately 39 percent, were in violation of registration rules. In total, 229 out of the total 303 cases were cases of misstatement in 1987, which is about 76 percent.[4]

In 1996, 28 percent of the cases processed by the SEC were related to the issuance of securities, and in half of these cases, the companies did not submit their statements to the SEC for approval. For the other half, the companies made substantively misleading statements, 17 percent of which were related to false financial information.[5] The SEC has thus put most of its resources to dealing with misstatements.

With regard to judicial protection, this includes both the criminal litigation brought by the federal prosecutor to the court, and the cases in which investors themselves appealed to the court. In 1995, American judicial authorities received 92 items of information from the SEC which resulted in 98 rulings imposing penalties upon listed companies, of which about half were related to securities issuance and misstatements.[6] In the United States, the number of civil litigation cases filed by investors was even greater. The accused can be listed companies and their management, or securities dealers and accounting firms. According to the estimate of some American scholars, during the period from 1991 through 2001, about 80 percent of the cases relating to securities were settled through mediation before the court session began, and the other 18 percent were rejected by the court. Only the remaining 1 percent went through the whole judicial process. Among those cases settled through mediation, if listed companies were charged with making false statements, the compensation amount in these cases would be 30 percent more than that for non-listed companies. If such charges were proved to be true, the compensation amount in these cases would be 90 percent higher than that in other cases. If the big five accounting firms were involved as a defendant, the compensation amount in these cases would be 79 percent more than that in other cases. In past practices, once one of the "Big Five" was accused, and if the case was not rejected by the court, each case would be settled through mediation with very high compensation.[7]

The self-regulating administration of stock exchanges and securities dealers associations

In the United States, there are eight major stock exchanges, such as the New York Stock Exchange (NYSE) and the American Stock Exchange. The National Association of Securities Dealers (NASD), which has some 5,200 member companies, is the only registered national securities dealers association. In 1971, it introduced the National Association of

Securities Dealers Automated Quotations system (NASDAQ), through which dealers can make securities transactions with high efficiency and low cost. The stock exchanges and NASD are the major self-disciplined organizations. They cooperate with each other and function as self-disciplined organizations in the following aspects:

The administration of professional qualifications

The main purpose of professional administration is to prevent unqualified people from entering the profession. People working in the field, including chief financial officers, investment dealers, financial consultants or other dealers, must register with correspondent institutions. They also need to register in their own state.

Individuals must be formally recommended by members in the field to qualify for registration. The applicants must provide their details in a V-4 form for registration, including major experience in the past ten years, educational background since high school, and details of any arrests or involvement in litigation, and so on. The applicant must provide a fingerprint on the application form and be subject to investigation for integrity.

After the registration process is complete, the applicant will undergo a probationary period of at least four months. During this period, they must pass the Series-7 Examination to obtain the basic professional qualification.

The Series-7 Stockbroker Exam is jointly held by the NYSE and NASD. It has 250 multiple choice questions, and should be completed within six hours. The pass mark is 70 percent. The applicants must prove that they have a basic knowledge of the profession in the exam. The failure rate is about 25 percent. Of course, submitting a résumé and passing the exam do not guarantee that an applicant, once qualified and registered, will not engage in illegal securities activities. However, at least those people who do not meet the lowest standard will be prevented from entering the profession. This standard is far higher than the one for entering such fields as banking, insurance, and real estate.

The Code of Professional Conduct

A registered broker should behave according to the rules of the company he or she works with as well as abiding by the rules of the profession. Most securities companies have some prohibitive rules, such as prohibiting the transaction of securities which are not recommended by the company's research department. Securities companies will often provide a list of recommended securities along, with a brief introduction, and introduce their client to their professional agent (stockbroker, investment advisor, for example). The internal rules of the company always prohibit staff from recommending those securities with unfavorable prospects.

Although registered brokers can provide their clients with some investment suggestions, they cannot call themselves investment advisors because, under the Investment Advisors Act of 1940, investment advisors must be formally registered. Brokers simply buy and sell securities on behalf of their clients.

Activities prohibited by the professional rules include: (a) providing unclear suggestions (strongly recommending clients to buy certain securities regardless of whether they are suitable or not; (b) pressurizing clients; (c) using clients' accounts to make transactions without written or oral authorization from the clients.

If a registered agent violates the rules or behaves unethically, he or she faces punishments such as formal and severe reprimands, penalties, suspension, or even termination of their professional qualification and registration.

Self-regulation of stock exchanges

Stock exchanges are the major securities markets. The self-regulation of stock exchanges can generally be seen from the following four aspects:

1. *Supervision of securities transactions.* This is the primary aspect of self-regulation, and is mostly concerned with the formulation and implementation of transaction rules, including transaction methods, operational procedures, prohibited conducts in the transaction, the format, effectiveness, and termination of the contract, the clearance of the transaction, the opening and closing of the stock exchange, dealing with unusual situations and the detection, avoidance, and handling of violations. Due to their supervisory role, the stock exchanges are always the "front-line regulatory institutions." Stock exchanges are always equipped with advanced monitoring facilities, which can automatically detect unusual transaction situations.
2. *Supervision of listed companies.* This includes the formation and supervision of the listing standard, the corporate governance structure, and the information disclosure rules. Unqualified companies' requests to be listed will be rejected.
3. *Supervision of members of the stock exchange.* The members of stock exchanges should abide by the rules of the stock exchange on the administration of the seats and representation. They should refrain from transferring or renting their seats to others. They should abide

by the rules concerning self-operating transaction risk control and obligations in buying and selling, submitting financial and operational reports to the stock exchange, and being subject to the inspection of the stock exchange. The stock exchange can take measures against those members who violate the rules or the agreement with members.
4. *The dispute resolution mechanism*. Each stock exchange has its dispute resolution organizations. When the stock exchange is performing its self-regulatory function, disputes and conflicts often take place between the members and the stock exchange, or between the members themselves, or between the members and the clients. Such disputes or conflicts can be presented to the dispute resolution organizations in the stock exchange according to the dispute resolution mechanism and the consensus between the parties.

Besides the stock exchange, the NASDAQ can also perform some of the functions mentioned above.

The stock exchanges and the NASDAQ are only different in terms of the listing standard, transaction fees, and information disclosure requirements; they both have the same rules on self-regulation in transactions.

The obligation of the agencies

This mainly refers to the obligations of accounting and auditing firms, distributors of securities, and law firms in ensuring the accuracy of financial information. Article 7 of the Securities Act of 1933 states that a financial statement audited by an independent accountant must be included in the securities issuance registration statement, which is submitted by the company to the SEC. This is a significant requirement in ensuring the accuracy of financial information. Stricter requirements on accounting and auditing are imposed by the Accounting Reform Act of 2002 (including the supplementary rules of the SEC).

A significant obligation is imposed by the SEC on securities distributors. They have responsibility for the accuracy of the information disclosed by the company and will bear the civil, administrative, and criminal responsibility if the information is inaccurate.

Avenues open to investors for complaint

Complaints

If a client is not satisfied with the services of his agent (or broker), he could complain to the department manager of his agent company. The manager can usually handle the minor troubles well, such as insensitivity on the part of the broker, lack of necessary knowledge, failure to pay dividends in time, operational mistakes, or unwillingness to wait for better opportunities. However, when the client's complaints are likely to affect the interests of the securities company, the manager will always stand by the broker. In that case, the investor (client) has two further ways to claim compensation. One is to complain to the stock exchange, provided that the securities listed in the stock exchange are involved. The other way is, when it involves legal securities outside the stock exchange, to complain to the NASD directly. Such complaints should be as detailed as possible, indicating the time, date, and price of the transaction and including witness statements and copies of related documents.

Request for arbitration or litigation

If the amount is lower than US$10,000, it can be settled through a summary arbitration procedure. The arbitration is final and the parties cannot go to the courts for any resolution through litigation afterwards. Of course, if the client is not bound by the arbitration agreement, he can choose to file a suit to the court directly against the securities company or other clients. If the conflict does not involve a large sum of money, the client usually avoids litigation because of the time, money and energy that this would involve. Even if the client wins, the compensation won can sometimes be lower than the client's litigation and legal fees. For that reason, under certain circumstances, even if the cases are accepted by the court, the conflicting parties will still probably reach an out-of-court agreement.

The U.S. situation

In the United States, the securities regulatory system is well established and continuously being refined in the wake of practical experience. The supplementary rules set by the SEC are more detailed and practical. Furthermore, the cases adjudicated by every level of court can be referred to when dealing with new situations. In addition, the technical equipment for communication, transactions, and clearing are highly advanced, and the real-time monitoring tools are also extremely effective.

In summary, each element mentioned above has contributed to a network for preventing securities misstatements. As long as every element can function well, the prevention of misstatement should be effective. Thus, although the stock market was adversely struck in 1987, it was able recover very quickly. Any violations or illegal conduct are able to be punished criminally, civilly, or administratively.

How to prevent large companies from making misstatements

In 2002, the world was scandalized by the false accounting by Enron and WorldCom. The effectiveness of the American model was widely doubted. In early 2002, the Chairman of the SEC said in his speech that "our disclosure and financial reporting system ... had long needed improvement. Its inadequacies are more visible after Enron's failure, and the need for change cannot be ignored any longer. This is not a problem that arose overnight ... There are many aspects to this problem."[8] Renowned American economist Paul Krugman noted that "the Enron debacle is not just the story of a company that failed; it is the story of a system that failed. And the system didn't fail through carelessness or laziness; it was corrupted."[9]

Since there are many countries in the world, including China, using the American model, it will be useful to discuss the lessons learnt from its systematic malfunction.

Corporate governance

The reasons why large companies make misstatements

An analysis of misstatement cases of big companies shows that there are three main circumstances in which misstatements occur. Firstly, in some companies which have had a good operational record in the past but are facing significant deficits or even bankruptcy, the management may make misstatements to cover up the company's failings. Some Japanese and Chinese companies always behave in this way. Secondly, in companies which introduced an incentive mechanism, under which the management's income is related to the profits of the company during a certain period, the management may make misstatements in order to receive a higher income (such as a financial bonus) even though actual profits do not reach the set qualifying target. It is reported that this was used by some large American companies such as Enron. Thirdly, companies may make misstatements in order to become listed. China's Hongguang Industry Co. is one example.

The countermeasures and mechanisms aimed at preventing misstatement differ according to these three circumstances.

The general prevention of misstatement by the corporate governance structure

The corporate governance structure always refers to the shareholders' general meeting, the board of supervisors, the board of directors, management, and their interrelationship. The goal for corporate governance is to ensure that the interests of the investors (the contributors of the company's capital) are protected. Corporate governance has different effects on different types of misstatement.

Under the first circumstance, the company is facing a large deficit or even bankruptcy. If making misstatements minimizes the shareholders' loss, or even gives the (false) appearance that the shareholders are in profit, it is impossible to hope that the corporate governance system will function automatically to correct the misstatements. In this case, the board of directors will decide to make misstatement, the manager will implement, the board of supervisors will take no action, and no one calls for a shareholders' meeting, or raises the issue even if a shareholders' meeting is held. This is because at this point, from an economic perspective, the shareholders, the management, and creditors will all benefit from the company's misstatements. Thus, in this sense, prevention of misstatement must rely on the external forces such as laws.

Under the following two circumstances, the corporate governance system will perform its function in preventing misstatement.

A system with constraints on stock options must be established in the corporate governance structure. The stock option system was established in mid twentieth century, and was used as an incentive for company executives to make more profit for the shareholders. The mechanism can be divided into three phases. In Phase I, based on the market price or an even lower price of the company's stock, the board of directors will sign an agreement with the executives of the company, indicating that the executives can purchase a certain amount of the company's shares with an exercise price[10] provided that the executives can achieve a certain goal in a certain period. This period can be two to four years. In Phase II, which is around the expiry date of the agreement, the board of directors and the executives, will decide, based on whether or not the goal was achieved, if the option can be taken; in other words, whether or not the executives can buy the agreed amounts of the company shares at the exercise price. In Phase III, the company executives can sell their shares legally at the market price. The key point of the stock option system is whether or not it is profitable for executives to purchase the stock. If the market price is higher than the exercise price, then the executives can make a profit through the stock option. In order to make the market price higher than the exercise price, the executives must work hard to improve the company's performance. Only thus will the stock price in Phase III be higher than the exercise price, enabling the executives to make a profit from the stock option. In the whole process of granting the stock option, the risks for executives are low and the costs are fixed, but the potential profits are huge; therefore the disproportion of risk to potential profit is an incentive to make misstatements. The income of the company may be falsified in the balance sheets of the period from Phase II to Phase III in order to raise the value of the company and therefore increase their profits. Some executives do not trade their stocks for cash, but become majority shareholders of the company through the granting of stock options; in this way they gain control of the company.

As we can see, the lack of restrictive measures in granting stock options is a major reason for company executives to make financial misstatements. Moreover, the new economy, as represented by the knowledge economy (involving knowledge-intensive activities and transactions of information), is making it easier for company executives to make financial misstatements. Enterprises in the new economy have a high portion of intangible assets, and the value of intangible assets is much less stable than that of tangible assets. The value of intangible assets cannot be easily accessed by the investors. Thus executives can use the advantages available to them through access to information job position to exaggerate the value of intangible assets, and make misstatements of the profits in Phases II and III, in order to gain extra profit through the stock option.

In Phases I and II of the stock option system, the corporate governance structure can perform effectively. In these periods, the interests of the board of directors, the board of supervisors, the board of shareholders and company executives are divergent, thus a system of checks and balances exists. The three boards are able to function effectively; for example, the board of directors and the supervisory board can check the company's financial accounts any time, or request for specific auditing. Shareholders can present a motion to prohibit executives from exercising their stock options.

In Phase III, however, the situation is different. During this period, the executives have either sold their stock options or used them to become majority shareholders, and therefore reform the board of directors and the supervisory board, and the votes of minority shareholders thus do not count much. Thus, for the stock options system, the corporate governance structure must set up a "firewall" to prevent company executives from making misstatements.

For those companies that have been making misstatements ever since they were first listed, theoretically speaking, the corporate governance system could have played a role. But in reality it is not effective, and some of these companies are even in league with officials from local government and securities companies in their deception. In China, it was common before the implementation of the Securities Law. The China Securities Regulatory Commission (CSRC) has now strengthened its review powers, as have the securities companies, law firms, and accounting firms. The corporate governance structure can play a role in the following aspects. Firstly, by changing companies' share structure – currently a single majority shareholder dominates the management and voting process of a listed company – they should make the share structure more reasonable, and the stake of the largest shareholder in the company should not exceed 50 percent. The combined stakes of the second and third largest shareholders should be more than the largest shareholder, in order to form a system of checks and balances.

Secondly, the function of independent directors should be effective; according to the rules of the CSRC, the number of independent directors should be no less than one-third of the total number of directors on the board. Independent directors should not only meet with the requirements in terms of their number, but also be knowledgeable and informative about the operation and financial situation of the company. Only in this way can they play their role effectively.

Thirdly, the supervisory board should play its role effectively. Some members of the supervisory board are full time, so they are able to ascertain the operational and financial situation of the company and get feedback from the employees, and thus provide as much information as possible to the board of directors in order to maximize supervision. With the combination of all three measures as mentioned above, the function of corporate governance in preventing misstatements will be well developed.

In order to achieve the basic goal of corporate governance (to protect investors' interests), the key point of corporate governance is to allow investors to supervise the operation of the company effectively. Moreover, when problems arise in the company's operation, the supervisors and investors should be able to respond timely. Therefore, corporate governance depends on the transparency of the company. In order to ensure that companies disclose their operational and financial information to investors timely, truthfully, and completely, the domestic laws of many countries have mandatory requirements for listed companies on the authenticity of their disclosed information. Misstatement of financial information is therefore illegal. Refraining from such illegal conduct should be a significant function of corporate governance.

The function of the shareholders

Shares in a listed company are dispersed, and it is a major problem that shareholders depend mainly on the company's financial reports for learning about the company's operations. As the shares are highly dispersed, the shareholders are unable to participate in the administration of the company, and can only exercise their power in the annual shareholders' meeting in approving some proposals prepared by the management. The separation of ownership and management in the company has provided the grounds for abuse of power by internal people including management. The stock option system provides management with a great incentive to manipulate profits. The investors' money has often been used by management to take risks in order to make profits so that the management can be granted with stock options worth billions of dollars. When management fails in a venture, they will manipulate the balance sheet to hide it because the disclosure of a decrease in profits will cause the stock price to fall, which affects the shares that they hold. To avoid such a situation, management will try their best to keep the stock price of their company high, and the most effective way is to show "profits" on the balance sheet.

The function of the board of directors

Most of the time the board of directors of a listed company cannot be really independent of the company management; instead, it is often dominated by them. In the American system, there are independent directors who account for a great percentage of the board. In order to be on the board, independent directors must be nominated either by majority shareholders or by the management (when the shares are highly dispersed). For example, of the 15 independent directors of Enron before the scandal, ten had a business relationship with the company. This made Enron a "club" with strong interpersonal relationships. When the CEO takes control, other directors, including independent directors, cannot challenge the authority of the management, and the board has to perform as directed by the management. Here, the supervisory role of independent directors is minimal.

The function of the supervisory board

Common law countries emphasize the establishment of independent directors, while civil law countries emphasize the establishment of a supervisory board. In China, however, in the corporate governance structure, there are both independent directors and a supervisory board – a dual supervisory system (though of course, the role of independent directors is not only that of supervision). For the members of the supervisory board, some of them are company employees, such as representatives of the workers; others are external supervisors. These external supervisors are full-time members, and are designated by the State Assets Administration Commission (a person may act as a supervisor in three or four companies). They have professional knowledge, and know the situation well, and therefore can play their role effectively.

Intermediary agencies which provide a service for the market

Intermediary agencies which provide a service for the market should have an independent role. These agencies include accounting and auditing firms, law firms, stock and financial analysts, investment banks, consulting firms, and credit rating agencies. In recent Wall Street scandals, the supervisory role of intermediary agencies with regard to listed companies was quite problematic. Arthur Andersen (AA), KPMG, Ernst & Young, and the other two of the "Big Five" accounting firms were accused of violations of law, with AA being found guilty. In fact, these agencies not only helped listed companies in making misstatements, but because of their then high reputation, the investors tended to trust the findings of auditing carried out by them.

The conflict of interest in the role of intermediary agencies is an important issue. As mentioned above, AA were not only the external auditors for Enron, but also provided consulting services to the company, and these two roles were in conflict. Moreover, an investment bank provides services for both companies and the investors. For instance, it provides services for a company in selling stocks, issuing bonds, and implementing M&As, whereas it also provides investors with investment services, including investment consulting services. This makes it very likely that their own interests are in conflict with the interests of the investors they serve. Investment banks' collusion with securities analysts will not only hurt investors' interests, but also create a crisis of confidence for the public regarding the financial system. The Wall Street misstatement scandal in 2001 began with an investor who had suffered huge losses as a result of investing in internet companies, who took out a lawsuit against Merrill Lynch, who had provided him with investment consulting services. The Attorney General of New York later conducted a wide investigation into every large investment bank, and found out that more and more securities analysts were involved in the sales of stocks, and had made huge profits according to their sales. This is the reason why the securities analysts always raised the ratings of enterprises; they always recommended that the investors buy the stock they were selling. Even after a big fall-off in the American stock market, securities analysts suggested "selling out" in only 5 percent of cases.[11] Honest securities analysts cannot survive in this field. If a securities analyst deems a company to be unworthy of investment at present, then that company will usually not provide information to that analyst in the future. This exists not only in the United States, but also in China. The issue is less serious in China only because the role of securities analysts is not as crucial as that in America.

Government supervision and the judicial system

With the development of the securities market, the transaction amounts have become larger and larger and the context of each transaction has become more and more complicated. The staff and resources of the regulatory authorities are limited. To use the SEC as an example, it needs to review the documents and information of 17,000 listed companies every year; to supervise investment funds which have increased fourfold in the last decade; to discover and expose countless potential cases of internal transactions, and to be responsible for investigating any mistakes in the market. The SEC does not have enough staff to deal with all these issues. A chief accountant working for the SEC admitted that in 2000, only one out of every 15 annual reports would be reviewed by the SEC. And the number of senior financial experts with the skills necessary to uncover flaws such as those in Enron's balance sheets is decreasing. Because of the low salary, lack of funding, and the high mobility of staff, the supervisory agencies have to deal with many disadvantages and their functions have thus been greatly affected.[12] China has a similar situation. The CSRC is responsible for supervising not only the securities market, but also the futures market. Although for now the securities issuance system has been changed from one of "examine and approve" to one of "examine and check," there is still a lot of work to do. It is still debatable whether or not it is appropriate for the CSRC to be in charge of both the approval and the supervisory functions. (The supervisory function of the People's Bank of China has already been transferred to the Banking Supervisory Commission.) We must say that, for those countries which have a collective administration of the stock market, such as the U.S. and China, preventing misstatement relies mainly on government supervision. Thus, the need to strengthen supervision is emphasized each year in the National Conference on Financial Works.

In terms of the judicial system, the United States has a system for investors (shareholders) to sue the company and management to protect their own interests, such as group litigation, and there are some successful cases in claiming for compensation. To some extent this has lessened the occurrences of misstatement in the securities market, but the fact that misstatement still occurs regularly shows that this is not the ultimate solution. Take China as an example. Although the judicial interpretations by the Supreme People's Court enacted in January 15, 2001 and February 1, 2003 have opened the door for investors to claim for civil compensation, there is still a long way to go . In civil law countries, there have been hardly any successful cases brought for civil compensation regarding securities. This shows that the securities civil compensation system for preventing misstatement is not very effective. Nevertheless, criminal punishments in many countries are more common than civil compensation and may be more effective.

Legal responsibility

Following the Enron scandal and other notable cases, in July 2002 the U.S. Congress amended some of the relevant laws, which now impose more legal responsibility on the board of directors, the senior management, the accounting firms and other relevant people.

At the end of 2001, Japan also revised the relevant laws, but the revisions were aimed at alleviating the legal responsibility of corporate directors, supervisors, and managers. For example, in the past, they were held responsible for affixing liability; but after the amendment, they are held responsible for general liability.[13] These two changes have warranted attention in China.

China has a traditional saying of "Heavier punishment in an unordered society." In the transitional process from a planning economy to a market economy, there has naturally been a "mainstream voice" in China (that is, the predominant powers, such as government and Communist Party officials, and so on) to impose punishment upon those companies and people who have made misstatements. But the amendments of Japanese laws must draw Chinese attention because they seem to run counter to the Chinese mainstream voice. Chinese law is neither incomplete nor loose, but there are still many violations occurring. Why is this so? Some have suggested that the main reason lies in the lack of abidance by law and the lack of implementation of law.

It has been argued that the major problem China faces is to create the necessary preconditions through ownership reform for establishing a modern enterprise system which is able to prevent the current prevalent problem of financial misstatement in Chinese enterprises; whereas the problem that Western developed countries are facing is to improve the corporate governance structure and reform the accounting system to solve the problem of misstatement. As a matter of fact, these two issues are not in conflict. The modern enterprise system that China is trying to build must be based on corporate law (including securities law). On the one hand, we should carry out ownership reform and establish a modern enterprise system; on the other hand, we should improve the corporate governance structure and reform the accounting system. We should take both of these two measures in order to solve the problem of misstatement. Also, in terms of the punishment for economic crimes, especially those for financial misstatement, it is more important to find out and deal with these matters timely, rather than setting up a retrospective but more severe punishment, and the laws must be implemented strictly. In sum, a modern enterprise system must be built based on a clear and definite ownership system, a sound external legal environment should be created for the companies, and the companies should have a well-ordered environment in which to compete. The board of directors, the supervisory board, the shareholders, and the management should be able to interact well, so as to ensure the healthy conduct of the company.

Practical measures

In China, some people hold with the idea of establishing a system like that of the United States, which includes group litigation and case law. But at this point in time it seems impossible for such a system to be realized in China. However, the following measures could be taken to deal with the relevant issues. Firstly, lawyers represent minority shareholders in individual or group litigation, according to the Civil Procedure Law and the two judicial interpretations by the Supreme Court; if China sticks to this system, then it will become effective in preventing misstatements. Secondly, China should create a system, in which financial experts, through careful analysis of the financial reports of listed companies, can uncover misstatements (such as that of the Lan Tian Corp). The system must be created to encourage more financial experts to take this role, and to allow them to rewarded commensurately. Thirdly, financial analysts and lawyers should be able to review and check financial reports and relevant information thoroughly and widely in order to uncover any problems. If a problem is found, the lawyers must not be able to do what some lawyers in Western countries have done: they must not be able to make a deal with the company and help the company to cover it up and then be rewarded for it. Rather, the lawyers should submit their evidence to the CSRC or any of the other government agencies concerned, and be rewarded by the government for doing so, or at the very least be rewarded with a good reputation among investors for work in the exposure of misstatements. Fourthly, China should strengthen its system of administrative punishment. According to the statistics, from 1993 through October 2001, the CSRC and the stock exchanges in

Shanghai and Shenzhen have punished 17 listed companies 218 times for violations in information disclosure. Of these violations, only 29 (13.3 percent) were penalized with warnings by the CSRC; the punishments carried out by the two securities exchanges were mainly in the form of internal criticism (61.9 percent), and public condemnation (22.9 percent), which amounts to a total of 84.8 percent.[14]

Thus there is still a lot of room for strengthening administrative punishment.[15] Fifthly, China should make use of the police and judicial organizations to reinforce the criminal punishment for securities misstatements. It will be more effective if China could combine all these measures.

Issues to be studied regarding the corporate legal system in China

Significant loan guarantees for a third party

If a person's conduct is in violation of a certain article in administrative rules, but there is no specific prescription regarding the corresponding responsibility in the law, what kind of responsibility should that person take? Is he only subject to administrative responsibility, or should he also take civil or criminal responsibility? This is a controversial issue.

As an example, one listed company in China did not disclose information about a significant loan guarantee for a third party (henceforth referred to as a "significant guarantee") in its annual report, which is in violation of Article 46(2) of the "Rules concerning contents and formats of information disclosed by listed companies No. 2. – the content and format of annual reports". Of course, the CSRC could apply an administrative punishment to this company. But what if some investors file a lawsuit claiming for the loss in purchasing the company's stocks as a result of the company's significant guarantees? How should the court deal with the case? Will it support the investors' appeals?

The defendant (listed company) held that disclosure of a significant guarantee in the annual report is a requirement of CSRC rules, but it is not required under Company Law and the Securities Law. Article 61 of the Securities Law, in particular, has a clear prescription on information disclosure in annual reports, but a requirement regarding disclosure of significant guarantees is not specifically mentioned. For this reason, the company can accept administrative punishment by the CSRC (a light penalty), but it is not subject to any civil responsibilities (which would carry a harsher penalty) according to Article 63 of the Securities Law.

In response to the defendant's explanation, the plaintiff held that Article 61(3) of the Securities Law has clearly prescribed that the contents of annual reports should include "Other matters as prescribed by the securities regulatory agencies of the State Council." Naturally the significant guarantee should be included here. The defendant did not disclose the contents which should be open to the public; at least it can be categorized as "significant neglect" as defined by the Article. Therefore Article 63 should be followed.

I think that we should analyze the problem from the nature of the significant guarantee.

Firstly, "Other matters as prescribed by the securities regulatory agencies of the State Council" is a part of the content which must be put on the annual report. Since it is required by the CSRC, the listed company must be required to include it in their report. But the omission of any of the information on the annual report does not necessarily mean that the company should take civil responsibility for that. For example, omitting the registration date of the company in the annual report should not result in any legal liability, but for other significant omissions the company should take legal responsibility.

Secondly, a significant guarantee comes under "significant matters" as prescribed in Article 62(2) of the Securities Law, "the following matters should be regarded as significant matters ... When the company is signing an important contract, and that contract may have some significant impacts on the company's assets and liabilities." A significant guarantee is *de facto* a guarantee of loan repayment, and although it does not really have any significant impact on the company's assets, liabilities, rights, and interests, it does have some possible significant impacts. A significant guarantee should therefore be considered as one of the company's important contracts. In sum, a significant guarantee can be categorized as a significant neglect as defined by Article 63. Of course, whether the court is supportive of the plaintiff's requests depends on whether or not the plaintiff's loss is a consequence of the omission of any significant guarantee in the annual report. Only if the causality is confirmed (that is, that the non-disclosure resulted in the plaintiff's financial loss) will the plaintiff's requests be supported.

Whether or not the missing statement of significant guarantee in the annual report should be subject to Articles 160 and 161 of the Criminal Law regarding the "disguising of significant facts" depends on whether the omission is intentional or not. If a company intentionally does not mention the significant guarantee, then naturally this can be categorized under the disguising of significant facts. Secondly, are "significant events" and "significant facts" different in a legal sense? "Significant facts" refers to the situation which already happened. A "significant guarantee" is a fact (signing the guarantee agreement is a fact), but in terms of the results, it is only a "possibility," because the guarantee might be removed if the debtor repays the money himself. Therefore, only when guarantee agreements are due to expire soon, and there is clear evidence that the company intended to hold back the possible affixing liabilities, can it be construed as the disguising of significant facts. In sum, generally speaking, the missing statement of significant guarantee should not be included in the disguising of significant facts as described in Articles 160 and 161 of the Criminal Law, except in the circumstances mentioned above.

The disclosure of "soft information"

The term "soft information" refers mainly to (1) information regarding the development of the issuer's operation; and (2) information about the prospect of the issuer's development in the current year.

There is still some controversy regarding the disclosure of soft information, both theoretically and practically. Supporters hold that if investors invest in securities, then they are confident in the future of the company, but not necessarily the past or current situation. If a company only discloses its historical information, and makes no mention of its future plans, investors cannot make the right investment decision. Therefore, listed companies should disclose soft information. On the other hand, an alternative view is that soft information is only a listed company's estimate on its future, which is very subjective and always different from the actual results. Thus it may only confuse investors.

From a legislative perspective, many countries are changing their attitude towards soft information disclosure from one of rejection to one of encouragement. As for its disadvantages, they have taken some corresponding measures. For example, the United States has introduced the "safe harbor" statement, which requires that the estimates made on the company by the issuer should be honest and reasonable. If it proves that the real situation is different from the estimated one, the issuer will only be responsible when it can be proved that he or she is in violation of the principle of honesty.

In recent years, China has incorporated the experience and practice of the Western countries that have a well-developed securities market. China also requires listed companies to release soft information. For example, Article 26 of the "Administrative rules on the issuance of new stocks by listed companies" prescribes that "the listed company should make its estimate carefully, and be audited by a certified securities accountant.

An analysis and explanation must be provided in case there is any uncertainty which may influence the estimate." But in fact, since some of the listed companies in China do not exert strong self-discipline, they have used the uncertainties of soft information to make false estimates, such as those in the Hongguang case. In that particular case, it was proved that all of the estimates made by this company were false, and the investors simply became victims. For this reason, China should take some supplementary measures regarding soft information in order to help prevent the misconduct of listed companies.

The relationship between information disclosure and commercial secrets

"Commercial secrets" may be defined as technical and operational information which can be of economic benefit to those who are party to it, but which is not available to the public. Listed companies have commercial secrets, but they also have the obligation to disclose information. If any information is required by law to be disclosed, it therefore cannot be regarded as a commercial secret.

In order to leave some room for listed companies to protect their commercial secrets, foreign countries have some privacy laws which allow a company to apply to the authority to keep some information secret within a certain period if the disclosure of information may be harmful to it. The listing rules of the stock exchanges in China have also given some room for listed companies to protect their commercial secrets, and they prescribe the exceptions in information disclosure: if a listed company has enough reason to prove that the disclosure of certain information will be harmful to the interests of the company, and such information does not have a great impact on its stock price, with the permission of the stock exchange, the information need not be disclosed. However, whilst other countries prescribe periodical application and review, China does not, and listed companies are able to use this as an excuse to avoid liability for making misstatements.

I believe that the exception of information disclosure should be strictly limited, and that companies should be obligated to report to the regulatory authority. A definition of "commercial secret," a shorter time limit, and periodical review should be included in the rules.

The definition of a "misstatement"

The effectiveness and timing of information disclosure

In terms of its effectiveness, the information to be disclosed should be accurate and important, but how to define "important" is still in question. The rules in China do not have a clear definition of "significant matters", nor of "significant contracts." Therefore, some listed companies have not disclosed information regarding some important contracts they have signed, whereas others have declared the signing of some relatively unimportant contracts in an attempt to exaggerate their operational achievements.

In terms of timing, the covering period of the temporary report is limited, but the annual report refers only to one point in time. Some listed companies have behaved illegally during the period *between* the two points in time, but the information they have disclosed *at* each of these two points in time has been correct. This makes it hard for their activities to be defined as a misstatement.

The liability of intermediary agencies and their staff

Intermediary agencies and their staff who provide services for listed companies in information disclosure should be held responsible for misstatements by those companies, but in reality there are complex technicalities involved which make it difficult for lawyers, accountants or evaluators to assign legal responsibility.

Because of all of these issues mentioned above, it must be hoped that "misstatement" in China is clearly defined, based on sufficient discussion, by the laws and rules.

Coordinating laws and regulations

At present, the rules on information disclosure are very basic. The "contents and format rules" and the "editing rules" have some detail, but since the rules are promulgated by different levels of institution, the effectiveness of their implementation is different. Therefore, they should be coordinated, and the corresponding accounting rules should also be modified in accordance with the information disclosure rules, so as to improve regulation.

Notes

1. The editor thanks Mr. Harry Wang (a Ph.D. student at the University of British Columbia) for providing the initial English translation of this chapter originally written in Chinese.
2. See Yang Zhihua, *Study on Securities Legal System* (China Law Press, 1995), p. 43.
3. "Improper relationships" here means various types of illegal relationships between/among securities issuers (usually companies), underwriters and investors (buyers) during securities transactions. The securities being transacted could either be newly offered for the first time to the public, or

securities that have already been circulating in the market. The most common sort of improper relationships are those that cause "insider trading," which occurs, for example, when the spouse of a company's executive sells/buys the shares of that company for profit based on information provided by the executive that is not available publicly.

4. See Gu Xiaorong (ed.), *Crimes and Violations of Securities Regulations* (China Prosecution Press, 1998), p. 361. Cited from *The Real Situation of American SEC* (Japanese version) (Japan Economic Press, 1991), p. 30.
5. See Shan Changzong (ed.), *Analysis on Research and Cases of Chinese and Foreign Regulations on Securities and Futures* (People's Court Press, 1997), p. 188.
6. See Fu Chunhong, *The Supervision and Administration of U.S. Federal Government for Stock Markets* (Southwest University of Finance and Economics Press, 1997), p. 94.
7. See Zhang Haibo, *The Claims for Compensation in China's Stock Market* (Guangdong Economic Press, 2002), p. 31.
8. Cited from Wang Qingli, "The Malfunction of Wall Street," *China Securities Daily*, July 30, 2002.
9. Ibid.
10. The "exercise price" is the price pre-agreed between a company executive and the board of directors at which, if the executive decides to exercise his/her stock option, the stock will be bought. In this option arrangement, the executive can choose to buy a pre-specified number of his/her company shares at the exercise price per share if the company's performance (measured, for example, by its stock price) at a particular agreed-upon time (for example, at the end of the current fiscal year) exceeds the pre-specified target level (standard). Usually the exercise price is set much lower than the expected market price, so this type of stock option provides a financial incentive to the executive.
11. See He Fan, "The Reconstruction of Confidence," *China Securities Daily*, August 7, 2002. During a stock price collapse/sell-off, it often makes sense for investors to sell the shares they hold. But few securities analysts would recommend this course of action to their clients, because doing so would likely be against company policy, or at least would not be in the personal interests of the securities analysts.
12. Qingli, "The Malfunction of Wall Street."
13. In Japan's previous Company Law, company directors held unlimited responsibility for any liability their company might have caused to the third party ("affixing liability"), but, in Japan's revised Company Law implemented over the last few years, company directors are responsible for company liability to the third party to the extent that they were negligent ("general liability"). Furthermore, in the latter case (that is, under the revised Company Law), company shareholders can vote to limit the upper bounds for such liabilities. The legal profession generally agrees that Japanese company directors' liability has been lessened under the revised Company Law.
14. See Mao Zhirong, "Study on the Effects of Punishments on Information Disclosure Violation,", *Shanghai Securities Daily*, May 20, 2002.
15. According to the statistics reported by the *Shenzhen Business Daily*, from 1994 through April 2004, the CSRC has resorted to punishment 93 times in 52 cases.

4

Issues in the Protection of Minority Shareholders' Rights and Interests under China's Company Law[1]

Shuliang Wang

On December 29, 1993, the Standing Committee of the National People's Congress (NPCSC) of China adopted the Company Law of the People's Republic of China (PRC), which was the first of its kind since the establishment of the PRC. Because of the historical background of the era when economic reform was begun, the contents and description of the Company Law were rather simplistic, and some of its articles simply didn't make sense. Following the development of the market economy in China, the Company Law obviously could no longer meet the practical requirements of the economy. Although amendments were made by the NPCSC on December 25, 1999, and August 28, 2004, respectively, appeals for a complete revisal of the Company Law grew stronger and stronger. After a draft of the revised version was reviewed a number of times, the 10th NPCSC adopted the revised Company Law at its 18th General Session on October 27, 2005. (The revised Company Law is hereinafter referred to as the "New Company Law," and the original version before this revisal is hereinafter referred to as the "Former Company Law.")

Among the appeals for the revision of the Company Law, a notable aspect was the addition of new rules protecting the rights and interests of minority shareholders in a company. This reflected both the fact that infringements on minority shareholders' rights and interests were occurring, and that the Former Company Law did not contain the necessary measures for prevention and remedy of such infringements. The New Company Law consists of a number of supplements and amendments to compensate for the defects and shortcomings of the Former Company Law.

This chapter will attempt to provide some comments and explanation of the issues in Chinese law on protecting minority shareholders' rights and interests from the perspectives of the forms of infringement of minority shareholders' rights, and the protection against this under the Former Company law and the New Company Law.

Possibilities for and forms of infringement of minority shareholders' rights and interests

In contrast to other countries, the Company Law of China has introduced a special dual-board system in terms of a company's organizational structure. According to China's Company Law, a "shareholders' general meeting" should be established within the company and serve as the organ of authority of the company. A board of directors should be established to serve as the decision making authority (but if the shareholders of a company are comparatively few in number and the company is comparatively small in scale, such a company may have an executive director rather than a board of directors) and a manager should be appointed to serve as the operational authority for the shareholders' general meeting. A board of supervisors should be established as the company's supervisory authority (but, as above in the case of a board of directors, a small-scale company with few shareholders may have one or two supervisors rather than a board of supervisors).

Under the Company Law, the shareholders' general meeting is the highest authority of the company, and the voting rights of shareholders are based on the percentage of shares they hold in the company. This is the so-called principle of "capital majority rule." No doubt, under the Former Company Law system in China, without other regulations to balance and supplement it, such a principle has unavoidable defects in protecting minority shareholders' rights and interests. According to the principle of majority rule, majority shareholders can make proposals and have them implemented regarding the management and operation of the company, while the minority shareholders are not able to do so. Even if some minority shareholders may be elected as directors of the board, since the organization, function and voting of the board of directors are decided by the shareholders' general meeting, the board of directors cannot control majority shareholders at all, and this makes it possible for majority shareholders, based on their own interests, to infringe the minority shareholders' rights and interests by controlling the company.

In China's economic practices, forms of infringement of minority shareholders' rights and interests by majority shareholders are mainly as discussed below.

Transferring profits and assets of the company to majority shareholders' related companies

Some majority shareholders control the listed company in question while at the same time controlling some other companies. In order to obtain extra profits and interests, they always, by using their dominant power in the company, transfer and, ultimately, possess the assets or profits of the company through certain deals with some other companies they own. For example, majority shareholders of Company A make the company purchase materials from their related companies at a high price, and at the same time sell the products of Company A to their related companies at a low price; or, transfer assets from Company A at a low price to their related companies, thus infringing the interests of Company A's minority shareholders.

Making the company take potential risks by being a guarantor of majority shareholders' related companies for financing purposes

Usually, the operation of a company needs financial support in the form of loans. The successful operation and development of the company therefore depends on its successful financing activities. However, guarantees are always needed in financing activities, and in those that involve large amounts of funding, the financial situation of the debtor usually cannot provide a satisfactory guarantee to creditors. In such cases, for example, it is necessary to seek a third party to be its guarantor. Thus, some majority shareholders of Company A, through its dominant power in the company, make the company the guarantor of the related companies. These companies then receive operational and development funding while Company A shoulders the liability as a guarantor. If majority shareholders' related companies cannot repay the debts to financial institutions, Company A, as the guarantor, has to repay it on behalf of the related companies. This makes Company A take potential risks and may thus infringe the rights and interests of minority shareholders.

Issuing new shares to increase registered capital to avoid distributing dividends to minority shareholders

According to the Company Law of the PRC, if a company, after its establishment, plans to increase its registered capital, the shareholders have the preferred rights to purchase the increased capital according to their shareholding percentage. However, some minority shareholders are not very enthusiastic about this, for a number of reasons. For example, since majority shareholders control the company, minority shareholders worry that dividends to be distributed at the end of the year will be used for reinvestment rather than dividend distribution, and purchasing their portion of the newly issued shares (the new shares registered to minority shareholders) is often beyond their capacity. Under these circumstances, minority shareholders can do nothing but give up their preferred rights to purchase the increased capital, and thus it is the majority shareholders who purchase the capital and increase the percentage of shares they hold, whilst minority shareholders' percentage of shares in the company are diluted.

Protection of minority shareholders' rights and interests under China's Former Company Law

Generally speaking, China's Former Company Law lacks a series of systemic and specialized rules, let alone making provision for the protection of minority shareholders' rights and interests. It is only prescribed in Article 11 of the Former Company Law that "if any decisions made by the Shareholders' General Meeting or the board of directors are in violation of any provisions of laws or administrative regulations, thus causing any losses to the shareholders, the shareholders may initiate legal proceedings in the People's Court to stop such illegal activities and infringements." Nevertheless, the Article itself has some defects:

1. The Article is only applicable to the decisions made by the shareholders' general meeting and board of directors which are "in violation of ... laws or administrative regulations." It is not applicable to the violation of the articles of association of the company.
2. The Article makes no mention of what qualifies shareholders to be eligible to initiate legal proceedings in the court, or of the effective period of initiating the legal proceedings, which, in practice, may result in the abuse of such rights by some shareholders.
3. The Article only prescribes that the shareholders are entitled to request the court to "stop" such illegal activities and infringements, but does not say whether or not shareholders are entitled to claim compensation. Articles 214–17 of the Former Company Law prescribe imposed legal responsibilities on directors, supervisors, and managers for their violation of legal obligations, but does not include the legal

responsibilities which should be imposed on dominant shareholders who could, by using their advantage as majority shareholders, force the shareholders' general meeting to pass illegal decisions or resolutions.

4. The right of shareholders' derivative suits was not prescribed in the Article or other Articles in the Former Company Law. Therefore, in legal practice, such rights of minority shareholders cannot be secured.

Improvements in the protection of minority shareholders' rights and interests under the New Company Law of the PRC

As mentioned above, the principle of majority rule is a basic principle in China's Company Law. However, under the Former Company Law system, due to the lack of an effective mechanism to limit majority shareholders' rights and to protect minority shareholders' rights and interests, the minority shareholders' rights and interests were always infringed by majority shareholders. Therefore, it is a key feature in the revision of the Former Company Law to strengthen the protection of minority shareholders' rights and interests in order to balance the rights and interests between the majority and minority shareholders.

Upon the promulgation of the New Company Law, defects in the protection of minority shareholders' rights and interests in the Former Company Law have been remedied in many aspects, including those discussed below.

Minority shareholders' rights to access information on company affairs are secured

The protection of shareholders' rights to participate in company affairs and have access to information is significantly improved in the New Company Law, compared to the Former.

Firstly, the requirements to convene a shareholders' general meeting are relaxed. According to Article 43 section 2 of the Former Company Law, an interim shareholders' meeting can be convened upon request by shareholders representing one-quarter of the voting rights, or one-third of directors or supervisors. The New Company Law has loosened the requirements for convening a shareholders' meeting. It is prescribed in the New Company Law that, if the shareholders representing more than one-tenth of the voting rights, more than one-third of the directors, the board of supervisors, or the supervisors of any company that has not established a board of supervisors propose the convening of an interim shareholders' meeting, such an interim meeting shall be convened. Here the requirement for convening an interim shareholders' meeting has been changed from one-quarter of the voting rights to one-tenth, which has significantly loosened the previous requirements. This enables minority shareholders to propose an interim shareholders' meeting when their rights and interests are infringed, and negotiate with other shareholders, especially majority shareholders, to solve potential disputes, which, to a certain extent, protects minority shareholders' interests.

Secondly, minority shareholders' rights to access information are improved and protected. It is added in the New Company Law that shareholders of a limited liability Company can access the company's accounts. Article 34 of the New Company Law prescribes that the shareholders of a company shall have the right to look into and make copies of the articles of association of the company, the minutes of meetings of the board of directors, resolutions passed at meetings of the board of directors and the board of supervisors, and financial and accounting reports.

If a company refuses to grant any of its shareholders access to its accounts, the shareholder may submit a petition to the People's Court requiring the company to provide such access. Although this Article applies to all shareholders, since the company is controlled by majority shareholders who have no need to request access to such information whereas minority shareholders' rights to access to information was not legally protected for a long time, this Article in the New Company Law undoubtedly provides effective legal support to grant and protect minority shareholders' rights to access information.

An accumulative voting system is introduced

Under the Former Company Law of PRC, in terms of the election of directors and supervisors in companies based on shares, a direct voting system was used, under which each share had one voting right. An accumulative voting system has been introduced in the New Company Law, which is a remedy to minority shareholders' voting rights. It is prescribed in Article 106 of the New Company Law that, when any directors or supervisors are elected at a shareholders' general meeting, an accumulative voting system may be implemented in accordance with the provisions of the articles of association of the company or a resolution passed at a shareholders' general meeting.

The accumulative voting system means that, when any directors or supervisors are elected at a shareholders' general meeting, each share shall have the same number of votes as that of the directors or supervisors to be elected, and the shareholders may pool their votes when such votes are cast. The purpose of the accumulative voting system is to avoid majority shareholders' control over the election by using their advantage of voting rights, and to compensate for the defects of the voting system of "one share, one vote." According to this voting system, not only does each share equal one vote, but each vote is multiplied by the number of directors to be elected: thus the total number of votes each shareholder has is the number of shares he holds in the company multiplied by the total number of directors and supervisors to be elected in the meeting. When voting, a shareholder can pool his votes to cast for one or several candidates. Through this system, minority shareholders can have representatives of their interests elected to the board of directors to avoid the monopoly by majority shareholders in the election. For example, five directors are going to be elected in Company A, the total number of shares of the company is 1,000, there are ten shareholders in the company, a majority shareholder holds 510 shares which counts for 51 percent of the shares, the other nine shareholders hold 490 shares in total which amounts to 49 percent of the total number of shares. According to the direct voting system, each share has one vote, and accordingly, the majority shareholder who holds 51 percent of the shares can have all the five candidates he recommended elected to the board, while the other shareholders do not have a say at all. In the accumulative voting system, however, the total votes are 1,000 [shares] × 5 [directors to be elected] = 5,000 votes, with the majority shareholder holding 2,550 votes, and the other nine shareholders 2,450 votes. According to the accumulative voting system, shareholders can pool their votes and cast for one or several candidates, and directors are elected according to the total votes they receive. Theoretically speaking, the minority shareholders can at least elect two directors to the board, and the majority shareholders who hold more than half of the shares can only elect up to three. As we can see, the control by the majority shareholder through its voting advantage can thus be balanced by the accumulative voting system. It can strengthen the voice of minority shareholders in corporate governance, and help to improve the system of corporate governance.

A system of dissenters' right of appraisal is established

As discussed above, according to the principle of capital majority rule, when significant events take place in a company, since majority shareholders can always control the shareholders' general meeting and have their proposals passed despite any objections from minority shareholders, particularly when minority shareholders' interests are being infringed, this cannot be remedied under the Former Company Law, which is a significant disadvantage in protecting minority shareholders' legal interests.

Foreign company laws were referred to during the drafting of the New Company Law, which introduces the system of dissenters' right of appraisal. According to Article 75 of the New Company Law, if any of the following events occurs, those shareholders that have cast a vote against the relevant resolution made by the shareholders' meeting may request that the company purchase their equity at a reasonable price: (1) if the company has not distributed any profit to the shareholders for five consecutive years when the company has been making profit consecutively for these five years and the company satisfies the conditions of profit distribution as prescribed in this law; (2) if the company is to merge or split or to transfer its major assets; or (3) if, upon expiration of the term of operation as prescribed in the articles of association of the company or upon occurrence of any of the other events in which the company shall be dissolved as provided in the articles of association, the shareholders' meeting has passed a resolution to make amendments to the articles of association so that the company may continue to exist. Article 75 of the New Company Law also prescribes that, if such shareholders and the company fail to reach an equity purchase agreement within 60 days after the resolution is passed at the shareholders' meeting, such shareholders may initiate legal proceedings in the People's Court within 90 days after the resolution is passed at the shareholders' meeting.

The establishment of the system of dissenters' right of appraisal is beneficial to achieving a balance between the interests of majority and minority shareholders, and to protecting minority shareholders' rights and interests.

A system of shareholders' derivative suits is added to the New Company Law

When the rights and interests of the company are infringed by the majority shareholders or directors, shareholders can initiate legal proceedings in court in their own name for the benefit of the company, known as a shareholders' derivative suit. Theoretically, only the company is entitled to initiate such legal proceedings, therefore, such a suit is *de facto* a proceeding on behalf of, and for the benefit of, the company.

When the interests of the company are directly infringed by majority shareholders through abuse of the principle of majority rule, theoretically speaking, the company should use its right to file a suit. However, since the company is controlled by the majority shareholders, such rights cannot be implemented, leading to the infringement of minority shareholders' rights and interests. Although Article 111 of the Former Company Law had relevant prescriptions, they were incomplete: they lacked effective remedial measures for minority shareholders. In order to protect the rights and interests of the company from being infringed, and also indirectly to protect the rights and interests of all the shareholders, especially minority shareholders, it has been necessary to add shareholders' derivative suits to the New Company Law.

Therefore, Article 152 of the New Company Law has established the system of shareholders' derivative suits as follows. If a director or senior officer violates any provisions of laws or administrative regulations or the articles of association of the company in the performance of his official duties, thus causing any losses to the company, the shareholders may petition in writing to the board of supervisors or the supervisors of a limited liability company that has not established a board of supervisors to initiate legal proceedings against such director or senior officer in the People's Court; if a supervisor violates any provisions of laws or administrative regulations or the articles of association of the company in the performance of his official duties, thus causing any losses to the company, the shareholders may petition in writing to the board of directors or the executive director of a limited liability company that has not established a board of directors to initiate legal proceedings against such supervisor in the people's court. If the board of supervisors or the supervisors of a limited liability company that has not established a board of supervisors, or the board of directors or the executive director refuses to initiate any legal proceedings upon receipt of the written petition, or fails to initiate any legal proceedings within 30 days of receipt of such petition, or the situation is so urgent that the company will suffer irreparable losses if legal proceedings are not initiated immediately, the shareholders shall have the right directly to initiate legal proceedings in the People's Court in their own name for the benefit of the company. Besides, it is also prescribed in the New Company Law that, if any person encroaches upon the lawful rights and interests of the company, thus causing any losses to the company, the shareholders may also initiate legal proceedings in the People's Court in accordance with the provisions mentioned above.

The establishment of the system of shareholders' derivative suits enables other shareholders to initiate legal proceedings in the court for the benefit of the company and themselves if any director, senior officer, or majority shareholders encroach upon the lawful rights and interests of the company and the company refuses to take action.

A system of abstinence from voting by shareholders has been established

The system of abstaining from voting by shareholders means that, when a shareholder is a related party of a proposal to be voted on at the shareholders' general meeting, such a shareholder or his proxy cannot participate in the voting. Abstinence from voting was not prescribed in the Former Company Law, and as a result, regardless of whether the shareholders are majority or minority, they were all entitled to voting rights under the principle of "one share, one vote." In order to respond to the cases where majority shareholders always used their dominant power in the shareholders' general meeting to pass a proposal that was beneficial to themselves but which encroached upon the interests of minority shareholders, restrictive rules pertaining to this have been added to the New Company Law, which has thus created a form of abstinence from voting.

It is prescribed in Article 16 of the New Company Law that, if a company is to provide security for any of its shareholders or its *de facto* controller, a resolution thereon shall be passed at a shareholders' meeting or a shareholders' general meeting, and such a shareholder or any shareholder under the control of the *de facto* controller shall not take part in the vote on such resolution. Such a resolution shall be passed by a majority of the voting rights held by the other shareholders who attend the meeting. This rule to a certain extent establishes a system of abstinence from voting, which, through limitations to the voting rights of shareholders as a related party, strengthens the voting rights of minority shareholders and achieves the balance of interests between the majority and minority shareholders, and prevents the minority shareholders' legal rights and interests from being infringed by the majority shareholders through the abuse of their advantage in the company.

Generally speaking, compared to the Former Company Law, the New Company Law has made a distinct improvement on the aspect of protecting minority shareholders' rights and interests. The contents added to the current version include prevention in advance, intervention in the course of infringement, and remedy afterwards. It has referred to some experiences and practices of company laws in foreign countries. It is undoubtedly a positive impetus to improve Chinese Company Law legislation and also the overall investment environment in China, and to establish a fair and sound market economy.

Note

1. The editor thanks Mr. Harry Wang (a Ph.D. student at the University of British Columbia) for providing the initial English translation of this chapter originally written in Chinese.

5
An Economic Perspective on Recent Corporate Governance Developments in China with Comments on Chapters by Yang, Gu and Wang

Andrew Yuen and Anming Zhang

Introduction and overview of the chapters by Yang, Gu and Wang

The almost three decades of economic reform have resulted in some fundamental and structural changes in China. The basic theme of the Chinese economic reform is to shift away from a central planning economy to a largely market-based economy. In the central planning economy, the central government collected information from its subsidiary units, which included local governments and state-owned enterprises (SOEs), made central plans (for example, the medium-run "Five-Year Plans") and then required the subsidiaries to implement the plans through a "chain of command" administrative structure. Thus, the relationships among the central government and its subsidiaries were administrative. On the other hand, in the market economy, economic decisions are decentralized and so the subsidiaries enjoy more autonomy in making their decisions, while the relationships among the economic agents are governed by the market. During the transition, while the previous administrative relationships are dismantled, a new framework needs to be constructed.

The Chinese economic reform since 1979 can be divided into three stages (Guo, 2003).[1] In the first stage, between 1979 and 1987, the introduction of the "household production responsibility system" in China's rural areas successfully stimulated the productivity in its agricultural sector. The reform of SOEs began in 1984: in the initial phase, decision rights were decentralized to lower levels of governments and SOE managers through the "profit retention mechanism" and the "production responsibility system." The second stage of the economic reform was characterized by the implementation of the "management responsibility contract system" (MRCS) in 1987. Under this system, the government transferred management authority to enterprises and allowed them to retain some of their profits.

However, the first two stages of the reform were still implemented within the framework of traditional state socialism without making any significant changes to the existing ownership structure (Guo, 2003), in which case the state was still ultimately responsible for the loss of SOEs. Various studies show that these reforms improved the productivity of SOEs. For example, Groves et al. (1994) provide empirical evidence that the MRCS improved productivity of SOEs and increased the workers' compensation. On the other hand, they also find that the government subsidies to the SOEs were not reduced, nor were the profits of SOEs increased. This reflects a general problem of SOEs' rising productivity but falling profitability (see Table 5.1), and implies that the state, as the owner, could not gain from the improved productivity in SOEs. This conflicting result about Chinese SOEs' productivity and profitability may be understood if we take a closer look at SOEs' operation. Qian (1996) suggests that SOE managers used their effective control over the assets of SOEs to benefit themselves at the expense of the state in many cases. For instance, SOE managers borrowed money from state-owned banks, but some of the loans were not channeled into production; rather, they were channeled into their compensation. In the extreme form, the managers stole money and assets from enterprises. Indeed, the so-called "state asset stripping" problem increased at an alarming rate during that period. In a study conducted by Kernen (1997), for example, some SOE managers admitted that they had created a number of collective or private enterprises for their relatives using SOEs' assets. These kinds of misconduct behavior undoubtedly hurt the state's interest. Being also

Table 5.1 Profitability of state-owned enterprises

Year	*1986*	*1987*	*1988*	*1989*	*1990*	*1991*	*1992*
Return on fixed assets (%)	10.23	10.25	10.14	7.31	3.34	2.97	3.41

Source: compiled by the authors using figures from the National Bureau of Statistics of China (various years).

the owner of the banks, the state was the ultimate bearer of bad debts which were due to the inappropriate use of the bank loans.[2]

As a result, further reforms were required to address the issues that arise in dealing with the relationship between the owner of SOEs (the state) and SOE managers. Thus, the third stage of the Chinese economic reform began in 1993. The critical step in this stage was to establish a "modern enterprise system" (MES) under which shareholders would assume the role of residual claimant on an enterprise's assets.[3] The corporation system established under MES involves different stakeholders (including the state, SOE managers and employees, domestic and foreign investors, and local communities) who are economic agents having an interest, financial or otherwise, in a corporation (see Figure 5.1). How to manage the relationships among them is an important issue in the reform. Thus, the corporate governance system – with a set of processes, customs, policies, laws and institutions affecting the way a corporation is directed, administered or controlled – needs to be established which aims at dealing with these relationships.

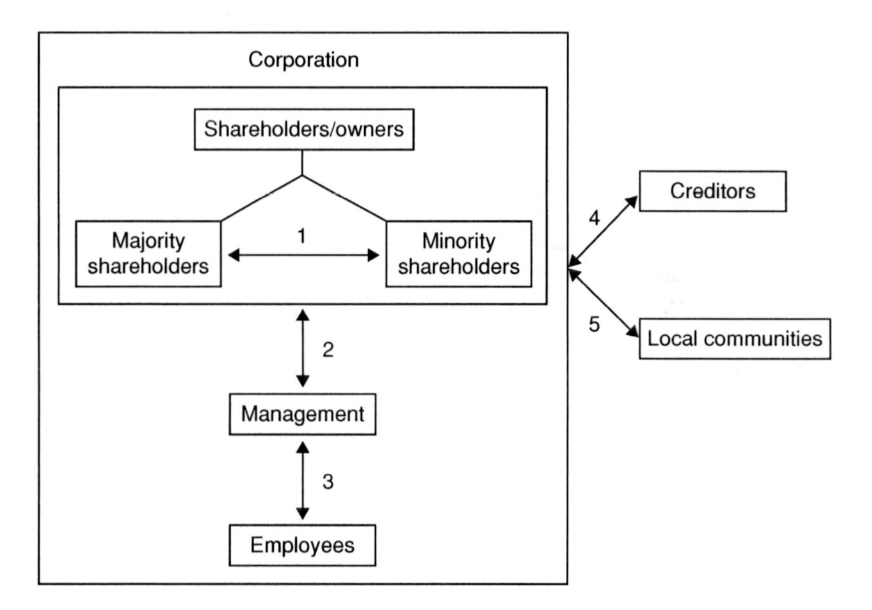

Figure 5.1 Major stakeholders of a corporation

The three previous chapters of this volume, by Yang (Chapter 2), Gu (Chapter 3) and Wang (Chapter 4) are all concerned with the corporate governance issues of MES. Specifically, Yang discusses two major corporate governance systems in developed market economies, namely, the Anglo-American model and the German-Japanese model. He points out that in essence, the Anglo-American model centers on how to deal with the relationships between majority and minority shareholders and between shareholders and management – Links 1 and 2 in Figure 5.1 – while considering that other relationships are governed mainly by the market mechanism (including various market-based contracts). The German-Japanese model, on the other hand, focuses on how to deal with the relationships between shareholders/management and employees/local communities/creditors – Links 3, 4 and 5 in Figure 5.1. This model is less concerned with the relationship between shareholders and management, owing to the existence of relatively stable and large shareholders in their corporations.[4] Yang suggests that China learned from the German-Japanese model when reforming its state enterprises in the 1980s (the first and second stages of the Chinese economic reform), whilst the system that has developed since the 1990s (the third stage of the reform) followed the Anglo-American model.[5] In particular, he contends that there appears to be lack of attention paid by companies to the interests of employees and local communities in the recent reform.

Information disclosure of listed companies in China's stock market is an issue examined by Gu (Chapter 3). In the Anglo-American system, as indicated by Yang (Chapter 2), the force from capital markets provides a vital external discipline for good corporate governance and practices. For example, takeover threats can be an effective measure to mitigate the agency costs of managerial discretions (Shleifer and Vishny, 1986) and further, investors can simply sell their shares in response to poor management performance. The relationship between shareholders and management – Link 2 in Figure 5.1 – may properly be dealt with as a result. For the external discipline to work effectively, however, quality of information disclosure – that is, accuracy and completeness of information and timely disclosure – plays a critical role. In Chapter 3, Gu indicates that in China, misstatements by listed companies have been a prevalent phenomenon and a disturbing issue among regulatory bodies and investors. He discusses three major types of misstatement, and then reviews the Anglo-American system in preventing listed companies from making a misstatement and evaluates its effectiveness in China's context.

In recent years, many investors have complained about poor protection of minority shareholders in Chinese stock markets. The issue of a proper relationship between majority and minority shareholders – Link 1 in Figure 5.1 – is addressed by Wang (Chapter 4). He describes three major types of infringement on minority shareholders' rights and interests by majority shareholders in China, and discusses how the protection of minority shareholders' interests is addressed in the amendment of the recent Company Law.

All three chapters have approached the Chinese corporate governance issues, and offered remedies to them, resorting to the means of laws and corporate legal systems. To complement this legal perspective, the present chapter focuses on an economic evaluation of these problems. Our "economic perspective" may also be helpful in providing a general paradigm to understand these issues. Using a principal-agent framework, we examine the relationship between the owners (the state) and SOE managers in the next section, since the vast majority of China's listed companies are state-owned enterprises. The shareholder-management relationship in the Chinese corporate governance system is examined in the third section. From an economic perspective, the fourth section discusses Chinese corporate governance, centering on the issues examined in the three previous chapters, including information disclosure and the protection of minority shareholders' interests. Finally, the fifth section contains concluding remarks.

Relationship between the state and SOE managers

Revitalizing SOEs is the central theme throughout the 20-year industrial reform in China. As mentioned above, the modern enterprise system was introduced into Chinese SOEs in the third stage of the economic reform, under which ownership was assigned to the shareholders of enterprises. More specifically, the treatment of SOE ownership varied, depending mainly on the size of SOEs and their relative importance to the economy. Under the slogan "grasping the large and letting go the small" (or "*zhua da fang xiao*" in Chinese), the ownership control over small- and medium-sized SOEs was loosened (Cao et al., 1999). Most of them were privatized and their shares were sold to their management, employees and local governments. Investments from Hong Kong, Macau, Taiwan and foreign countries were also encouraged to participate in those enterprises. Table 5.2 shows that the number of SOEs has declined continuously since 1995, and particularly so since 1998. Surveys also suggest that by the end of 1996, up to 70 percent of small SOEs had been privatized in "test run" provinces (Cao et al., 1999). On the other hand, the Chinese government is still holding controlling shares of large SOEs. Four types of industries, namely, national security, natural monopoly, important public goods and services, and key high-technology enterprises, are still required to be under state control.

Table 5.2 The number of state-owned and state-holding enterprises in China (in thousands)

Year	*1995*	*1996*	*1997*	*1998*	*1999*	*2000*	*2001*	*2002*	*2003*	*2004*	*2005*	*2006*
	118.0	127.6	110.0	64.7	61.3	53.4	46.8	41.1	34.3	35.6	27.5	25.0

Source: compiled by the authors using figures from the National Bureau of Statistics of China (various years).

It is generally accepted that the reform of small and medium SOEs is relatively successful. Empirical evidence regarding the performance of large SOEs under the third-stage MES is mixed, however. Although numerous studies (for example, Groves et al., 1994; Jefferson et al., 1996; Li, 1997) have been conducted on the performance of Chinese SOEs, most of them use data from before 1993. Thus they could not reflect the performance of the enterprises in the third stage of the economic reform, which is the main concern of the three chapters under review. Several recent empirical studies examine the performance of SOEs in the third stage. After controlling for the effects of capital structures, taxes, and welfare burdens, Zhang et al. (2002) find that SOEs still lagged behind other Chinese firms in both profit level and its growth. Zhang et al. (2001, 2002) also find that SOEs exhibited lower productivity than firms of other ownership types, namely, collective-owned enterprises, private-owned enterprises, foreign-owned enterprises, and Hong Kong-, Macau-, and Taiwan-owned enterprises. Furthermore, Zhang et al. (2003) find that the state sector has significantly lower efficiencies in both research and development (R&D), and productive activities than does the non-state sector. These empirical results are consistent with most of the theoretical literature that considers state ownership to be a negative factor contributing to Chinese SOEs' performance (for example, Zhang, 1997; Zhou and Wang, 2000).

The major step of SOE reform since the second stage of the economic reform is the separation of business management from state ownership. As a result, it is necessary to have a proper arrangement for the relationship between the owner and management. In economics terminology, this means we should deal with the principal-agent problem. In this regard, the corporate governance system aims at aligning the agent's interests with those of the principal. The principal-agent issue in public enterprises has been widely discussed in the economics literature. Shleifer and Vishny

(1994), for example, argue that, under state dominance, the control rights rest with bureaucrats who have only an indirect interest in profit, which leads to inefficiencies. On the other hand, most of the studies have focused on the economic efficiency in Chinese SOEs by employing a principal-agent framework. For example, Zhang (1997) examines the principal-agent problems in Chinese SOEs. That paper argues that if shifting both decision rights and residual claim from the government to SOE managers, the accounting profitability is improved through the direct incentive effect to the managers, and indirectly hardening budget constraints and selecting management by capitalists. Xu et al. (2005) empirically find that the profitability of SOEs is negatively correlated with the agency costs in SOEs, where the "better" corporate governance system implies lower agency costs in SOEs.

It is noted that in a general principal-agent analysis, how to define economic agents to be principal and agent in the analysis may lead to different analytical implications. To study the Chinese SOE reform, Cauley and Sandler (1992) assume that the principal is SOE managers, while the agent is workers in the enterprises. In other studies, such as Zhang (1997), and Zhou and Wang (2000), the principal is the state, while the agent is SOE managers. Qiang (2003) further argues that there exists a long and multiple series of principal-agent problems among the central government, line ministries, local governments and SOE managers. In principle, we may consider that the ultimate "owner" of SOEs, the general public, is the ultimate principal. Moreover, for large countries like China, there are different levels of governments, as local governments and line ministries are usually responsible for operating and monitoring SOEs. These "governments" perform the roles of both principal and agent in those structures. It is questionable whether the central government can write an optimal contract with the local governments and line ministries to align their interests with the general public. This kind of multi-level principal-agent problem is worthwhile to explore further, as it has been observed in practice that public-owned enterprises are usually quite efficient in economies with a simple government structure, such as those of Singapore and Hong Kong.

As the optimal principal-agent contract is absent, the agents, different levels of governments and SOE managers often have less incentive to improve the performance of SOEs for the sake of the general public. Instead, as mentioned in the introduction, they may derive their own benefits from the power given by the central government or, in principle, the general public. In China, it is common for local governments directly and their officials to be personally involved in local businesses. For example, Shenzhen Airport International Express Supervision Center Co. Ltd., which provides customs supervision and express cargo handling services at Shenzhen Airport, is 50 percent owned by a subsidiary of Shenzhen Government (Fung et al., 2005). Obviously, there is a conflict of interests for the government in performing its roles as market regulator, SOE operator and owner in other local businesses. There are also numerous other opportunities for the officials to obtain benefits at the expense of SOEs. For example, they can sell their products or services to SOEs at a high price and buy materials from SOEs at a low price. Moreover, some assets of SOEs were transferred to the companies owned by the local officials (Qian, 1996).

As substantial political and administrative reform is not expected to occur in China in the near future, the above-mentioned multi-level principal-agent problems are not likely to be properly handled in a short period through a better political and administrative system. An alternative strategy to deal with the problems is to privatize the SOEs. With privatization, the ownership of enterprises is clearly defined, with investors as the principal and managers as the agent, thereby simplifying the principal-agent relationships significantly. As a result, an efficient contract between them may be easier to attain, mitigating the agency cost.

Relationship between shareholders and management

For a typical listed company in mainland China before 2004, there were five major types of shares outstanding: state shares, legal person shares ("*fa ren gu*"),[6] employee shares, and common A- and B-shares, where common A- and B-shares are denominated in Chinese (renminbi, RMB) and foreign currencies respectively, and are tradable shares listed in Chinese stock exchanges, whereas the others are not. The composition of different types of shares between 1992 and 2004 is shown in Table 5.3. As can be seen from the table, while the overall size of the markets had grown rapidly during the period, the portion of tradable shares did not change significantly and remained at about 35 percent. The state was the dominant shareholder in most listed companies. Tenev et al. (2002), based on a survey of the Shanghai Stock Exchange, estimate that in 1999, the state was directly or indirectly in control of listed companies in more than 95 percent of the cases.

The existence of non-tradable shares results in different prices for shares of a company and creates different status among shareholders. Yang (Chapter 2) considers this a barrier to industry consolidation, such

Table 5.3 Tradable and non-tradable shares of Chinese listed companies, 1992–2004 (in 100 million shares)

	1992	*1993*	*1994*	*1995*	*1996*	*1997*	*1998*	*1999*	*2000*	*2001*	*2002*	*2003*	*2004*
A-shares	10.9	61.3	143.8	179.9	267.3	442.7	608.0	812.9	1,079.6	1,318.1	1,509.5	1,714.7	1,992.5
B-shares	10.3	24.7	41.5	56.5	78.7	117.3	134.0	141.9	151.6	163.1	167.2	175.4	197.0
H-shares	0.0	21.8	40.8	65.0	83.9	111.5	120.0	124.5	124.5	331.9	360.1	377.6	387.6
Tradable shares sub-total	21.2	107.9	226.0	301.5	429.9	671.4	861.9	1,079.4	1,355.7	1,813.2	2,036.8	2,267.6	2,577.2
State shares	28.5	190.2	296.5	328.7	432.0	612.3	865.5	1,115.5	1,473.9	2,410.6	2,774.8	3,046.5	3,344.2
Legal person shares	18.3	80.1	154.2	209.0	331.4	596.5	716.2	822.2	904.2	954.2	1,022.3	1,068.9	1,172.7
Employee shares	0.9	9.3	6.7	3.1	14.6	39.6	51.7	37.0	24.3	23.8	14.7	11.0	8.9
Non-tradable shares sub-total	47.7	279.7	457.4	540.7	778.1	1,248.4	1,633.4	1,974.7	2,402.4	3,388.6	3,811.8	4,126.4	4,525.8
Total	68.9	387.5	683.4	842.2	1,207.9	1,919.8	2,495.3	3,054.1	3,758.1	5,201.8	5,848.6	6,394.0	7,103.0
Ratio of tradable to total shares (%)	30.8	27.8	33.1	35.8	35.6	35.0	34.5	35.3	36.1	34.9	34.8	35.5	36.3

Note: "H-shares" refers to Chinese companies that are listed in the Hong Kong Stock Exchange.
Source: compiled by the authors using figures from the China Securities Regulatory Commission (various years).

as efficiency-enhancing merger and acquisition, taking place, and argues that a reform in differentiated treatment of shares is necessary. To address the issue, the China Securities Regulatory Commission (CSRC) and the State-owned Assets Supervision and Administration Commission (SASAC) jointly issued a proposal to promote experiments on split-share structure reform in 2005.[7] The reform aimed at making state shares and legal person shares tradable in the market, and had been controversial for a long time. Investors worried that the sudden increase in the number of tradable shares would exert a downward pressure on the stock market. In order to gain support from investors, the proposal by the CSRC and the SASAC also required that the resolution of a listed company about the split structure reform should be approved by at least two-thirds of all participating shareholders holding tradable shares at the shareholders' meeting.

The new shares, named G-shares, include the previous tradable A- and B-shares, and non-tradable state and legal person shares. By July 2006, a total of 1,092 – or more than 80 percent of Chinese firms listed domestically – had completed or were in the process of split-share reform, and more than 35 firms announced plans to float shares previously barred from trading in the stock markets.[8] Furthermore, non-tradable shares with a total market value of RMB 500 billion were expected to be traded in the first two months of 2008.[9]

Although state and legal person shares are now going to be legally tradable, it does not mean that the Chinese government will give up its dominant position in listed companies in the immediate future. In 2005, the SASAC released the "Guidelines on the Reform on Non-tradable Shares of State-controlled Companies" specifying the requirements on the proportion of state shares in state-controlled companies. Any sale of state shares requires the approval of the SASAC, and the state should maintain a controlling stake in companies that are in sectors vital to the national economy or security.[10] In particular, these enterprises are required to include a restriction in their reform proposals that state shareholding cannot be below a particular level.

Theoretically, the dominant position of major shareholders increases their incentive to monitor the management and alleviate the agency cost. As the benefits of monitoring are shared by all shareholders while the costs are borne completely by the monitoring party, large shareholders internalize the costs and benefits of monitoring to a greater extent than small diverse investors and therefore undertake more monitoring efforts (Shleifer and Vishny, 1986). Grossman and Hart (1980) also argue that a substantial shareholding can give the large shareholder an incentive to collect information and monitor the management, thereby avoiding the traditional freerider problem. Indeed, Morck et al. (1988), Wruck (1989), and McConnell and Servaes (1990) find evidence of the positive effects of ownership concentration on firms' performance, whereas Anderson et al. (2000) find that dispersed private ownership leads to worse performance than state ownership in Mongolia.

However, the argument that concentrated shareholding improves firms' performance may not apply to listed companies in China, given the fact that the dominant shareholder of Chinese listed companies is the state.[11] As mentioned, the general public is the "owner" of SOEs. The property rights belong to everyone – yet to no one in particular. The phenomenon is also called "absent owner" ("*suo you zhe que wei*"). As a consequence, the "owner" (that is, the principal) is unable to write an explicit contract with the government (that is, the agent) to align the interests of both parties. The incentives for the government to exert a full effort to monitor SOEs and improve their efficiency are unclear. On the other hand, other (dispersed) investors also have less incentive to monitor and participate in the operation of listed companies, owing to the fact that their effort will not be compensated accordingly.

There are a number of studies empirically examining the performance of Chinese listed companies. Sun and Tong (2003) find that there is an improvement in SOEs' earning ability, real sales and worker productivity, but not in profit returns and leverage after listing. Wang (2005), on the other hand, finds a sharp decline in post-issue operating performance of initial public offering (IPO) firms. The impact of ownership in Chinese listed companies is also widely studied in the literature. It is found that the performance of Chinese listed companies is negatively correlated or uncorrelated with the proportion of state ownership (Xu and Wang, 1999; Chen, 2001; Tian, 2001; Sun and Tong, 2003; Wang, 2005).

Consider Chinese airport industry as an example. Six Chinese airport companies (managing seven airports) are now listed on stock exchanges in Hong Kong, Shanghai and Shenzhen. Table 5.4 shows that the state still maintains the dominant shareholding of all airport companies even after the share-split structure reform. (The state ownership was greater prior to the reform, ranging from 60 percent to 75 percent for the listed airports.) Fung et al. (2008) compute the productivity growth of listed and non-listed airports in China between 1995 and 2004. They show that although there was, on average, a slight increase in productivity growth after IPOs, this growth appeared to be slower than that of non-listed airports. Using their data, Zhang and Yuen (2008) further investigate whether privatization through public listing improves airport performance, and find a positive and statistically significant relationship between Chinese airport productivity and public listing. Yet the result may only be due to the fact that the government chose more productive airports to be listed. Furthermore, they find that the correlation between productivity growth and listing is statistically insignificant.

Table 5.4 Chinese listed airport companies

	Listed exchange	*Listed year*	*State and legal person shares in 2006 (%)*
Beijing Capital International Airport	Hong Kong	2000	53.8
Guangzhou Baiyun International Airport	Shanghai	2003	52.4
Hainan Meilan International Airport	Hong Kong	2002	52.0
Shanghai International Airport Ltd.	Shanghai	1998	57.6
Shenzhen Baoan International Airport	Shenzhen	1998	54.7
Xiamen Gaoqi International Airport	Shanghai	1996	68.0

Source: compiled by the authors using figures obtained from publicly available company annual reports of the cited companies for fiscal year 2006.

Corporate governance issues in China

In general, it is expected that there will be an improvement in productivity and profitability for listed companies. Since the listed companies need to fulfill stricter corporate governance requirements and are subject to external market disciplines, listing could improve their corporate performance, leading to improvements in efficiency and profitability. However, the above discussion depicts an unclear picture of the efficiency improvement. In this section, some major corporate governance issues faced by Chinese listed companies are discussed, which may explain why the expected improvement of the companies after listing is not being realized. The discussion will center on the issues examined in the three previous chapters by Yang (Chapter 2), Gu (Chapter 3) and Wang (Chapter 4).

Information disclosure

In order to improve the operation of listed companies and facilitate capital flows, governments and related regulatory bodies in different countries have established their own systems to control the quality of information disclosure. Under these systems, listed companies are required to comply with information disclosure requirements in accordance with a set of accounting standards and listing rules, with the aim to strengthen the effectiveness of the external market discipline. In China, the information that listed companies must disclose to the public includes prospectus, offering circular, periodic report, and some special reports for major events, which is unknown to investors but may considerably affect the companies' share price.[12]

In China, misstatement is a disturbing issue among both the regulatory bodies and investors. Gu (Chapter 3) discusses three major reasons for the management to make a misstatement: (1) to cover up its current poor performance; (2) to increase share prices so that managers can cash their stock options; and (3) to get the company publicly listed. Gu divides the Chinese regulatory system on information disclosure into two parts: the administrative system and the judicial system. For the administrative system, the laws and regulations on information disclosure are implemented by the CSRC and the stock exchanges in Shanghai and Shenzhen. Currently, warnings are the major form of penalty for misstatement from the administrative departments (Gu). Another form of penalty is administrative fines, yet they are rarely used. A few examples include the case of the DaMing Group and Yinguangxia Enterprise mentioned in Chen (2003). Furthermore, in 2006, the CSRC imposed an administrative fine in the amount of RMB 600,000 on Guangdong Kelon Electrical Holdings Co. Ltd. for its violation of information disclosure requirements. However, it is still not common for the administrative departments to impose administrative fines.

Gu also points out that the limited resource of the CSRC has also adversely affected its role in preventing misstatement. In China, the CSRC is responsible for supervising not only the stock market, but also the futures market. In addition to resource constraints, the potential ineffectiveness of the CSRC in preventing misstatement may result from conflicts among its statutory roles. Specifically, the CSRC is responsible for examining the documents and related financial reports of firms that apply for IPOs. After the firms are listed, any misstatements found in those documents may put the CSRC into an embarrassing position. Yet, at the same time, the CSRC also plays the role of discovering misstatements. To avoid this conflict, the Chinese government may consider that the approval and supervisory functions are handled by two independent administrative departments, as has been done in the Chinese banking system. Since 2003, the supervisory function of the People's Bank of China has been transferred to the China Banking Regulatory Commission.

For the judicial system, its role in preventing misstatement, and protecting shareholders in general, may be questionable. Chen (2003) argues that the Chinese judicial system is still treated as part of the government's administrative system. Therefore, there is no effective judicial independence in China, and politics and adjudication are often mixed together. Chen suggests that, although related laws and regulations exist, Chinese courts are reluctant to accept private securities litigation, because granting damage compensations in private litigation would amount to the loss of state assets (to the extent that the state owns a majority of the shares outstanding). However, the attitude of the court regarding this issue has been changing. On January 9, 2003, the Supreme People's Court announced a judicial interpretation on civil compensation concerning breaches of the stock market standards on financial reporting. According to the interpretation, investors can sue not only the companies for compensation in violation of information disclosure requirements, but also the information providers such as the directors of the companies.[13]

Although some progress has been made, there is still a long way to go for the judicial system to strengthening its role in protecting investors. On one hand, as mentioned above, the independence of the judicial system has not yet been in place in China, and there is no clear sign that this will be changed in the near future. It is still doubtful whether the government will change its mind if more damage compensations in private litigation are granted – hence, the greater loss of state assets. On the other hand, the ability of judges in handling those cases is also questionable. In China, many judges do not have solid legal training, especially in less developed provinces (Chen, 2003). Furthermore, handling those cases requires some basic knowledge of securities markets, which the judges in China generally do not have.

Gu (Chapter 3) suggests that intermediary service providers, which include accounting and auditing firms, law firms, stock and financial analysts, investment banks, consulting firms and credit rating agencies, could have played a much stronger role in preventing misstatement. Yet to perform the role effectively, the independence of the intermediary agencies is crucial. In the newly amended Company Law (in 2005), in order to strengthen the independence of auditors, companies are now required to provide true and complete meeting minutes, accounting books, financial reports to their auditors and other accounting materials; any refusal, cover-up, or concealment is prohibited. Yet whether the amendment could improve the situation in China is still doubtful. In some recent misstatement cases, the accused auditing firms had almost full information access. The most well-known of these is the Yinguangxia case. Zhongtianqin, the auditing firm for Yinguangxia, and previously the largest and most renowned Chinese accounting firm, was found to be helping the company to fabricate its profit reports.[14] In the case, the CSRC withdrew Zhongtianqin's permit to audit listed companies,[15] and the China Institute of the Certified Public Accountants (CPA) revoked CPA licenses of the two auditors of the auditing firm. In another example, Deloitte was inspected by the CSRC and sued by investors for its role in the Kelon case in 2006.[16] The situation may be even worse in the cases of small auditors, as they have less to lose from the revocation of their licenses, thus less incentive to act independently in comparison to larger auditors (De Angelo, 1981).

Internal control system

In addition to the external market force, the internal control system is another critical component in the corporate governance system. According to section 4 of the Company Law, the statutory power hierarchy of a company includes the shareholders' general meeting, the board of directors and the supervisory board. The shareholders' general meeting is at the top of the power hierarchy. It is responsible for electing members of the board of directors and the supervisory board, examining and approving reports from the two boards, and making other important decisions for the company. As the shareholders' general meeting is only required to convene once a year or under special circumstances, the board of directors is usually responsible for most of the business decisions.

To improve the corporate governance system in China, the independent director system has been introduced since 2001. The CSRC now requires all the domestically listed companies to hire at least two independent board directors. Similar requirements were also added into the Company Law in its recent amendment. Yet both Yang (Chapter 2) and Gu (Chapter 3) argue that so far the independent director system has not worked as effectively as expected. In many cases, independent directors in a listed company cannot be really independent of management. Instead it is often dominated by management. On the other hand, the supervisory boards in most Chinese listed companies are also ineffective in supervising the performance of the board of directors and management. For instance, the supervisory boards played almost no role in many disclosed cases of misconduct of the board of directors and management in China. Dahya et al. (2000) suggest five causes for the ineffectiveness of the supervisory board in China, namely, a lack of legal power and responsibilities, a lack of independence, technical incompetence, information shortage, and a lack of incentives.

Protection of minority shareholders' interests

The above discussions (better information disclosure and stronger internal control systems) are also relevant to the protection of minority shareholders' interests in Chinese stock markets, a popular complaint by investors and scholars in recent years. We will further discuss some other issues on minority shareholders protection in the following. Wang (Chapter 4) suggests that there are three major types of infringement on minority shareholders' rights and interests by majority shareholders in China: (1) major shareholders transfer profits or assets of the listed company to their own companies by using their dominant power in the company; (2) the company takes an extra risk by being the guarantor of majority shareholders' related companies; and (3) the company issues new shares to dilute minority shareholders' ownership, as well as their power in the decision process of the company.[17]

The protection of minority shareholders' interests is addressed in the amendment of the Company Law in 2005 in the following areas (Wang). First, the requirements to convene the shareholders' general meeting are relaxed.[18] If minority shareholders want to propose an interim shareholders' meeting, they can assemble at the shareholders' meeting and vote against a decision unfavorable to them. Its effectiveness may be doubtful in China however, as most companies are dominated by majority shareholders. Under the "one share, one vote" system, the majority shareholders can still pass a resolution in favor of their previous decisions in the shareholders' meeting. And in practice, dispersed shareholders in China are seldom able to participate in the shareholders' meetings. Hence the system of abstaining from voting by shareholders – in which, when a shareholder is a related party of a proposal to be voted on at the shareholders' general meeting, such a shareholder or his proxy cannot participate in the voting – has also been established. Furthermore, the accumulative voting system is introduced under the amendment.[19] The purpose of the system is to avoid majority shareholders' control over the election by abusing their advantage of voting rights.

In addition to strengthening minority shareholders' voting power, several other amendments are included in the new Company Law: A system of dissenters' right of appraisal is established under the amendment; shareholders that have cast a vote against the relevant resolution made by the shareholders' general meeting may request the company to purchase their equity at a reasonable price under some specific conditions. On the other hand, minority shareholders' rights to information access are improved. Under the amendment, shareholders of limited liability companies can access the accounting books of the companies. Finally, the system of shareholders' derivative suits is introduced, under which shareholders can initiate legal proceedings to the court in their own name for the benefit of the company, when the rights and interests of the company are infringed by the majority shareholders or directors.

Generally speaking, the amendment of the Company Law has made gradual progress in protecting minority shareholders' rights and interests in China. Yet legislation is only the first step. Attitudes of different levels of governments and courts are crucial. Without a well-established legal system in China, judgments in the courts are largely affected by the officials. As mentioned above, Chen (2003) argues that the Chinese judicial system is still treated as part of the government's administrative system and hence there is no effective judicial independence. Hence, we should look at more fundamental forces affecting the protection of minority shareholders' interests.

Protecting minority shareholders' interests should, in our view, also rely on market forces. One of the fundamental incentives for the Chinese government and listed companies to provide better protection to shareholders and improve corporate governance is that it can facilitate the flow of capital.[20] In particular, if investors lose confidence about the corporate governance in listed companies, they are not willing to participate in the stock market, thereby decreasing market liquidity. As a result, the companies would be unable to raise funds in the stock market (or would do so at a higher cost than necessary). After a series of scandals, the protection of minority shareholders' interests has become a critical issue for domestic and international investors in making their China investment decisions. The stock prices of Chinese enterprises could well be undermined by its notorious reputation in this aspect of the corporate governance. On the other hand, as most state shares become legally tradable and selling state shares could be a source of funding to its social welfare programs, the market value of state shares also becomes more important to the government. Taken together, both Chinese companies and the government are expected to be more eager to improve the shareholders' protection and other aspects of corporate governance in the near future.

Institutional investors

In discussing the misstatement issue and the protection of minority shareholders' interests, both Gu (Chapter 3) and Wang (Chapter 4) do not pay much attention to the role of institutional investors in those aspects. In general, institutional investors are usually capable of monitoring the performance of managers in an effective way. First, institutional investors have more expertise in finance, accounting and law, and better resources to discover misstatement than other investors. Second, they have better information access, since managers are usually more willing to share information with them than with others. On some occasions, institutional investors are also willing to share that information with other shareholders. Finally, institutional investors' and other shareholders' interests are largely aligned: both want to maximize a firm's profit and its stock price. Therefore, minority shareholders could benefit from the effort made by institutional investors in monitoring and participating in the operation of the company.

In effect, Xu and Wang (1999), Qi et al. (2000), and Chen (2001) find that in general, corporate performance of Chinese listed companies is positively correlated with concentrated ownership by institutional shareholders other than state agencies, and is negatively associated with dispersed ownership. This finding suggests that the type of majority shareholders is important. As we discussed above, state ownership may be subject to substantial political costs and agency costs in monitoring a company. Yet the dominance of private institutional investors may improve the corporate governance of listed companies. In China, there are two kinds of institutional shareholders: those who hold legal person shares and those who hold common A-shares. Xu and Wang (1999), Chen (2001), and Sun and Tong (2003) find that firms' performance is positively correlated with the percentage of legal person shares. It is expected that their impact will become more significant as most legal person shares have just become tradable in the market.

Nevertheless, the role of institutional investors holding common A-shares is limited at present. The shareholding of these institutional investors in Chinese listed companies is too low to provide them with an incentive to monitor corporate performance. The situation is changing, however, after a series of liberalization measures in the Chinese stock market. In 2001, the Chinese government lifted the stock investment ban on its social security fund and chose six domestic mutual fund companies to manage the social security funds, some of which have been invested in domestic stock markets since 2003. In December 2002, China implemented the Qualified Foreign Institutional Investors (QFII) scheme to attract foreign institutional investors to put their money into its domestic stock markets. At the end of 2007, 52 foreign institutional investors were granted QFII status by the CSRC; the number of QFII increased by 73.3 percent compared with that in October 2005. Thus, domestic and foreign institutional investors are going to be important participants in the Chinese stock market. With more participation on the part of institutional investors in the Chinese stock market and the reduction of state ownership in many listed firms, it is expected that there will be a better corporate governance system, including stronger protection for minority shareholders in the near future.

Concluding remarks

Since the 1980s, the Chinese economy has been transforming from a planned economy to a market economy. During this transitional period, the old system of relationships among economic agents has been dismantled. Under the new so-called modern enterprise system, properly dealing with the relationships among various stakeholders of a corporation becomes perhaps the most important issue. In particular, with further development of the Chinese stock market, a new corporate governance system for listed companies is developing in China, which includes both internal and external controls. It is noted that information disclosure may play a dominant role in external control, whereas for internal control, a dual-board system, namely, the board of directors and the supervisory board, and the independent director system have been introduced in China. The recent legislation, especially the amendment of the Company Law, provides a better legal basis for the corporate governance system, including protection of minority shareholders' interests. However, more fundamental changes, such as properly handling the role of the administrative system and the judicial system in the Chinese corporate governance system, remain to be accomplished.

The present chapter focuses mainly on the relationships between majority and minority shareholders and between shareholders and management. In principle, the corporate governance system also needs to address and monitor the relationships of the shareholders/management with the employees and other stakeholders outside a corporation, such as local communities and creditors – that is, Links 3, 4 and 5 in Figure 5.1. The development of the Chinese corporate governance system in these areas is still in progress. Since the enactment of the Labor Law in 1995, most companies and enterprises have abandoned the system of lifetime employment. Fixed-term and short-term labor contracts have become the norm in the Chinese labor market. Enterprises (shareholders and/or management) now have almost complete discretion in making employment decisions. It can also be seen clearly from Table 5.3 that the proportion of employee shares has declined continuously and has now become negligible in a listed company. Thus the "check and balance" from democratic management by employees has disappeared (Yang, Chapter 2). Although the issue was recently addressed and remedied to some extent in the amendment of the Company Law, considerable work remains.[21] Thus, a proper arrangement for the relationship between a company and its employees – Link 3 in Figure 5.1 – is also required to be dealt with in the future development of the Chinese corporate governance system.

Furthermore, although there is no consensus about the exact value of bad debt in Chinese state-owned banks, the issue is certainly a disturbing one in the Chinese banking system. The improper relationship between enterprises and Chinese banks – Link 4 in Figure 5.1 – is undoubtedly a contributing factor to the bad debt issue. On the other hand, in recent years, the growth of GDP has become the only thing that many local government officials were concerned about. They were also focusing their efforts on attracting investment, but not on supervising enterprises or protecting the interests of local residents (Yang, Chapter 2). Thus, the relationship between a corporation and local communities – Link 5 in Figure 5.1 – is still not handled properly in the current Chinese corporate governance system.

As a result, how to manage the three relationships – Links 3, 4 and 5 – is an important issue in the future development of Chinese corporate governance. Yang argues that the current campaign of "building a socialist harmonious society" has paved the way for Chinese corporate governance, especially in dealing with the relationship between shareholders/management and other stakeholders. However, it is still unclear how the concept can be put into the proper context of corporate governance and be implemented. These issues need to be examined in the future development of the Chinese corporate governance system.

Notes

1. For a case study on a particular industry, see Zhang and Chen (2003). In the paper, the authors examine how the three-stage reform is reflected in the airline industry.
2. While SOEs accounted for 34 percent of gross domestic product (GDP), they absorbed three-quarters of domestic credit, which was mainly from the state-owned banks (Su, 2005).
3. "The Decision on Issues Concerning the Establishment of a Socialist Market Economic Structure" issued in the Third Plenum 14th Central Communist Party of China held in November 1993.
4. The effect of the ownership concentration on monitoring corporate performance will be discussed later in the chapter.

5. More discussions about the two models and their recent developments can be found in Buck and Tull (2000), O'Sullivan (2003), and Lane (2003).
6. "Legal person" here means companies and other types of organization that are legally allowed to perform economic and other functions. An incorporated business, for example, is a legal person. If it owns shares in another company, it is known as a legal person shareholder; the shares they own are said to be owned by a legal person.
7. *China Daily*, May 31, 2005.
8. *China Daily*, July 4, 2006.
9. *China Daily*, February 23, 2008.
10. *China Daily*, June 18, 2005.
11. Board members in these companies consist mainly of representatives or officials from the SASAC, local governments, and other state enterprises (Su, 2005). On average, 90 percent of the board members are government officials and delegates of other state enterprises. All top managers must be approved by the Organization Department of the local or central governments. Thus the government maintains ultimate rights for changing managerial positions.
12. "Implementation Guidelines on Information Disclosure for Companies Seeking Public Offering of Stock" issued by the CSRC.
13. According to *Mingpao* (April 27, 2006), some investors sued directors of Kelon for the company's falsified disclosure.
14. *China Daily*, 2 May 2002.
15. *China Daily*, overseas edition, September 8, 2001.
16. Mingpao, April 27, 2006.
17. Although shareholders have, according to the Company Law, pre-emptive rights, which allow current shareholders to maintain their fractional ownership of a company by buying a proportional number of shares of any future issue of common stock, minority shareholders usually cannot exercise the rights due to limited capital.
18. Under the amendment, if the shareholders representing more than one-tenth of the voting rights (one-quarter before the amendment), more than one-third of the directors, the supervisory board members, or the supervisors of any company that has not established the supervisory board, propose the convening of an interim shareholders' meeting, such an interim meeting shall be convened.
19. It is prescribed in Article 106 of the Company Law that, when any directors or supervisors are elected at the shareholders' general meeting, an accumulative voting system may be implemented in accordance with the provisions of the articles of association of the company or a resolution passed at the shareholders' general meeting.
20. By using a large database of various institutional and economic variables for a cross-section of countries, La Porta et al. (1997, 1998) show that stronger legal protection for minority shareholders is associated with deeper and more liquid capital markets.
21. It requires, for instance, that one-third of the supervisory board members should be elected by the company's employees. Before the amendment, the supervisory board should consist of shareholders' and employees' representatives. Yet there was no specific requirement about the minimum portion of employees' representatives on the board.

References

Anderson, J. H., Lee, Y., and Murrell, P., 2000, "Competition and Privatization amidst Weak Institutions: Evidence from Mongolia," *Economic Inquiry*, 38(4), 527–49.

Buck, T., and Tull, M., 2000, "Anglo-American Contributions to Japanese and German Corporate Governance after World War Two," *Business History*, 42(2), 119–40.

Cao, Y., Qian, Y., and Weingast, B. R., 1999, "From Federalism, Chinese Style, to Privatization, Chinese Style," *Economics of Transition*, 7(1), 103–31.

Cauley, J., and Sandler, T., 1992, "Agency Theory and the Chinese Enterprise under Reform," *China Economic Review*, 3, 39–56.

Chen, J., 2001, "Ownership Structure as Corporate Governance Mechanism: Evidence from Chinese Listed Companies," *Economics of Planning*, 34, 53–71.

Chen, Z., 2003, "Capital Markets and Legal Development: The China Case," *China Economic Review*, 14, 451–72.

China Securities Regulatory Commission, various years (1993–2005), *Statistical Reports*, Beijing.

Dahya, J., Karbhari, Y., and Xiao, J., 2000, "The Supervisory Board in Chinese Listed Companies: Problems, Causes, Consequences and Remedies," *Asia Pacific Business Review*, 9(2), 118–37.

De Angelo, L., 1981, "Auditor Size and Audit Quality," *Journal of Accounting and Economics*, 3(3), 183–99.

Fung, M., Zhang, A., Leung, L., and Law, J., 2005, "The Air Cargo Industry in China: Implications of Globalization and WTO Accession," *Transportation Journal*, 44(4), 44–62.

Fung, M., Wan, K., Hui, Y. V., and Law, J., 2008, "Productivity Changes of Chinese Airports 1995–2004," *Transportation Research Part E*, 44(3), 521–42.

Grossman, S., and Hart, O., 1980, "Takeover Bids, the Free Rider Problem, and the Theory of the Corporation," *Bell Journal of Economics*, 11, 42–64.

Groves, T., Hong, Y., McMillan, J., and Naughton, B., 1994, "Autonomy and Incentives in Chinese State Enterprises," *Quarterly Journal of Economics*, 109(1), 183–209.

Guo, S., 2003, "The Ownership Reform in China: What Direction and How Far?" *Journal of Contemporary China*, 12(36), 553–73.

Jefferson, G. H., Rawski, T. G., and Zheng, Y., 1996, "Chinese Industrial Productivity: Trends, Measurement Issues, and Recent Developments," *Journal of Comparative Economics*, 23(2), 146–80.

Kernen, A., 1997, "State Enterprises in Shenyang: Actors and Victims in the Transition," *China Perspectives*, 26–32.

La Porta, R., Lopez-de-Silanes, F., Shleifer, A., and Vishny, R., 1997, "Legal Determinants of External Finance," *Journal of Finance*, 52, 1131–50.

La Porta, R., Lopez-de-Silanes, F., Shleifer, A., and Vishny, R., 1998, "Law and Finance," *Journal of Political Economy*, 106, 1113–55.

Lane, C., 2003, "Changes in Corporate Governance of German Corporations: Convergence to the Anglo-American Model?" *Competition and Change*, 7(2–3), 79–100.

Li, W., 1997, "The Impact of Economic Reform on the Performance of Chinese State Enterprises, 1980–1989," *Journal of Political Economy*, 105(5), 1080–106.

McConnell, J., and Servaes, H., 1990, "Additional Evidence on Equity Ownership and Corporate Value," *Journal of Financial Economics*, 27, 595–612.

Morck, R., Shleifer, A., and Vishny, R., 1988, "Management Ownership and Market Valuation: An Empirical Analysis," *Journal of Financial Economics*, 20, 293–315.

National Bureau of Statistics of China, various years (1987–2004), *China Statistical Yearbook*, Beijing.

O'Sullivan, M., 2003, "The Political Economy of Comparative Corporate Governance," *Review of International Political Economy*, 10(1), 23–72.

Qi, D., Wu, W., and Zhang, H., 2000, "Shareholding Structure and Corporate Performance of Partially Privatized Firms: Evidence from Listed Chinese Companies," *Pacific-Basin Finance Journal*, 8, 587–610.

Qian, Y., 1996, "Enterprise Reform in China: Agency Problems and Political Control," *Economics of Transition*, 4(2), 427–47.

Qiang, Q., 2003, "Corporate Governance and State-owned Shares in China Listed Companies," *Journal of Asian Economies*, 14, 771–83.

Shleifer, A., and Vishny, R., 1986, "Large Shareholders and Corporate Control," *Journal of Political Economy*, 94, 461–88.

Shleifer, A., and Vishny, R., 1994, "Politicians and Firms," *Quarterly Journal of Economics*, 109(4), 995–1025.

Su, D., 2005, "Corporate Finance and State Enterprise Reform in China," *China Economic Review*, 16, 118–48.

Sun, Q., and Tong, W. H. S., 2003, "China Shares Issue Privatization: The Extent of its Success," *Journal of Financial Economics*, 70, 183–222.

Tenev, S., Zhang, C., and Breford, L., 2002, *Corporate Governance and Enterprise Reform in China: Building the Institutions of Modern Markets* (World Bank and International Finance Corporation).

Tian, L., 2001, "Government Shareholding and the Value of Chinese Modern Firms," *William Davidson Working Paper*, 395.

Wang, C., 2005, "Ownership of Operating Performance of Chinese IPOs," *Journal of Banking and Finance*, 29, 1835–56.

Wruck, K., 1989, "Equity Ownership Concentration and Firm Value," *Journal of Financial Economics*, 23, 3–28.

Xu, X., and Wang, Y., 1999, "Ownership Structure and Corporate Governance in Chinese Stock Companies," *China Economic Review*, 10, 75–98.

Xu, L., Zhu, T., and Lin, Y., 2005, "Politician Control, Agency Problems and Ownership Reform: Evidence from China," *Economics of Transition*, 13(1), 1–24.

Zhang, A., and Chen, H., 2003, "Evolution of China's Air Transport Development and Policy towards International Liberalization," *Transportation Journal*, 42, 31–49.

Zhang, A., and Yuen, A., 2008, "Airport Policy and Performance in Mainland China and Hong Kong," in C. Winston and G. de Rus (eds.), *Aviation Infrastructure Performance: A Study in Comparative Political Economy* (Washington, D.C.: The Brookings Institution).

Zhang, A., Zhang, Y., and Zhao, R., 2001, "Impact of Ownership and Competition on the Productivity of Chinese Enterprises," *Journal of Comparative Economics*, 29, 327–46.

Zhang, A., Zhang, Y., and Zhao, R., 2002, "Profitability and Productivity of Chinese Industrial Firms: Measurement and Ownership Implications," *China Economic Review*, 13, 65–88.
Zhang, A., Zhang, Y., and Zhao, R., 2003, "A Study of R&D Efficiency and Productivity of Chinese Firms," *Journal of Comparative Economics*, 31, 444–64.
Zhang, W., 1997, "Decision Rights, Residual Claim and Performance: A Theory of how the Chinese State Enterprise Reform Works," *China Economic Review*, 8(1), 67–82.
Zhou, M., and Wang, X., 2000, "Agency Cost and the Crisis of China's SOE," *China Economic Review*, 11, 297–317.

6
The "Grabbing Hand" and Corporate Governance in China[1]

Wei Chi and Yijiang Wang

Introduction

China initiated its market-oriented economic reform in 1978. The success of the reform is evident: in the three decades since its implementation, China's economy grew at an average of 9 percent per year. A vital part of the economic reform is known as the industrial reform, which gradually gave state enterprises autonomy and reduced government intervention in enterprises. The reform touched on many aspects of corporate governance in state enterprises.

This chapter has three sections. The first section describes the transition of the state enterprises' corporate governance mechanism during the reform. The laws and regulations that led to the changes are also presented. The second section applies economic theories to address ownership, decision making, and control issues in Chinese state enterprises. The final section offers some concluding remarks.

Evolution of Chinese state enterprises' corporate governance

Pre-reform period (before 1978)

In the pre-reform period, under the centrally planned system, state enterprises were essentially the extension of government bureaus. Enterprise corporate governance was tied to government divisions. The central government structure was established by the Organizational Law of the Central People's Government of the People's Republic of China, which was passed by the Chinese People's Political Consultative Conference in 1949. According to the law, the State Council comprised a sub-committee in charge of economic and financial affairs. This sub-committee supervised the Heavy Metal Ministry, the Textile Manufacturing Ministry, the Food Industry Ministry, and the Fuel and Chemistry Industry Ministry. All other manufacturing industries that did not belong to the above four industries were put under the "Light Industry Ministry." Each ministry controlled the state enterprises operating in its industry. Managers in state enterprises were appointed by the supervising government agency.

Managers were given administrative titles commensurate with their qualifications. Their wages and non-wage benefits were linked to their administrative titles. They had the same compensation as a government official at the equivalent administrative level. Pay differences among managers of the same level were minor. Good performers were rewarded in the form of promotion to a higher administrative position. Managers often had the goal of eventually being promoted into the government bureau; if promoted, they would receive a better wage and non-wage compensation.

Since there was no input market (from which firms buy their raw materials, labor services, and so on) or output market (in which firms sell their products), the government's control over state enterprises ranged from obtaining input materials, assigning workers and engineers, setting labor compensation, and designating a production target, to distributing outputs. State enterprise managers simply carried out state-designated output targets. As state enterprises had to turn in all their profits to the government, the managers' autonomy was therefore very limited.

Post-reform period

1979–83

In 1979, the State Council issued a memorandum, "Several Regulations on Increasing State Enterprise Operating and Management Autonomy," followed shortly by another memorandum, "Regulations on Increasing State Enterprise Retained Profits." The former granted some decision making powers to enterprise managers to make purchases and sell products, provided that managers fulfilled the production target first. The latter permitted state enterprises to keep part of their profits. However, based on the Regulations, firms could only use retained profits to develop products, reward employees, and increase employee benefits. Thus, managers' discretion over the use of retained profits was highly restricted.

1983–86

In the 1983–86 period, the main focus of the reform was on enterprise tax systems. In April 1983, the State Council delegated to the Ministry of Finance the authority to allow state enterprises to make the transition from the previous system of turning over all their profits to one of paying tax. Shortly afterwards, the Ministry of Finance issued the "Interim Regulations on State Enterprise Income Tax." Based on this new policy, state enterprises would no longer turn in all the profits to the state but would only pay the required amount of tax instead. As a consequence, enterprises gained some control over their retained profits.

Since 1984, the government had started to implement the "chief executive responsibility" policy in state enterprises. The core of the policy was that the chief executive is considered as the legal representative of a state-owned enterprise, taking full responsibility for the enterprise. Prior to this policy, a group of party representatives held collective responsibility for the firm.

In October 1984, the 3rd Plenary Session of the 12th Central Committee of the Communist Party of China (CPC) passed the "CPC Central Committee's Decision on the Economic Reform." For the first time, Chinese government declared that in state enterprises, government and enterprises as well as ownership and control rights would be separated. State enterprises would become independent producers and suppliers, make decisions regarding production, and be held responsible for performance. The Decision marked a historic breakthrough: state enterprises would no longer be treated as an extension of government.

1987–92

Subsequent to the Decision, many state enterprises, especially large ones, started to experiment with separating ownership and control rights. Managers were deemed as lessees or contractors of state assets. The managers' task was to best utilize state assets to generate profits and increase capital. These experiments became common practice after the State Council issued the "Interim Regulations on Delegating or Renting State Assets to Enterprises" in 1988.

Later in 1988, the 1st Plenary Session of the 7th National People's Congress passed the People's Republic of China's State-Owned Enterprise Law. The law consolidated previous regulations concerning state enterprises, such as the "chief executive responsibility" policy and the separation of ownership and control rights.

According to the law, the chief executive of a state enterprise would be appointed or recruited by the supervising government agency or elected by the enterprise employee assembly. Government would consider employee representatives' recommendations when deciding on the chief executive. The chief executive elected by the employee representative assembly would have to be approved by the supervising agency.

Furthermore, according to the law, after meeting its output target set by the government, an enterprise would have the right to refuse to increase production above target if requested by any government bureau. If an enterprise, based on its own interests, decided to produce in excess of target, it would have the right to sell the excess product in the market. More importantly, enterprises were given the right to request an adjustment of the output target.

The firm had the right to decide from whom it purchased input materials, and the price of its products (other than those under the government's direct control, such as tobacco). It had the right to sign contracts with foreign companies and to decide how to use retained profits, following the guidelines set by central government. It also had the right to decide its internal employment structure, to hire and fire workers, and to determine employee salaries and benefits. Finally, the firm could refuse any government agency's request for monetary or non-monetary contributions.[2]

The law also defined the scope of the government's control over state enterprises. The government would set the output target and guarantee the supply of input materials that enterprises needed to meet the production target. It would have the authority to review and approve important business decisions, such as fixed asset investment or product development. It could appoint, dismiss, and reward managers. However the government could not interfere with state enterprises' daily operation and production decisions or assign redundant personnel to the enterprise. Its functions also included setting industrial guidelines and maintaining fair competition.

1992–97

The period 1992–97 was often known as the "modern corporation reform" period. The benchmark of the reform was the enactment of the Company Law in 1994. The objective of the law was to transform state enterprises into modern public corporations. Under the law, two types of companies might be established: if a former state enterprise had investors other than the state, it might be transformed into a limited liability company (LLC); if the state was the sole owner, the enterprise would remain as a solely state-owned enterprise.

To form an LLC, there must be 2–50 shareholders who need to invest the required minimum funds. After an LLC is founded, a shareholders' assembly would be formed. The assembly would be the top decision making organ of the LLC, with decision rights regarding business strategy, the election, appointment and change of directors and supervisors, and the salaries and benefits of the directors and supervisors. The directors would form the management body of an LLC, the board of directors. The board could call for shareholders' meetings, report to shareholders, execute shareholders' decisions, draft budget plans, or plans for profit sharing, capital increase and decrease and mergers and acquisitions. It would also be responsible for appointing or dismissing managers and determining managers' remuneration. The large LLCs could also have a board of supervisors consisting of at least three members; with a certain proportion of supervisors being employee representatives. Supervisors would be responsible for examining the company's finance, monitoring the board of directors, and calling for special shareholders' meetings.

In enterprises solely owned by the state, no shareholders' assembly would be formed. Government agencies in charge of state enterprises would delegate some of the shareholders' rights to the board of directors. However, the government agency would retain the right to decide on mergers and acquisitions, capital increase or decrease, and important investments. The government agency would appoint the directors, and the board would contain a certain number of employee representatives elected democratically by all employees. The board would be responsible for appointing and dismissing managers. Provided that the government's approval had been obtained, the directors might also serve as managers.

In China, there are two stock markets. The Shenzhen Stock Exchange was founded in 1987 and The Shanghai Stock Exchange in 1990. The substantial growth of the stock market took place in the 1990s. The 1994 Company Law also specified requirements and procedures for listing in a stock exchange.

1998 to the present

After 1998, the modern corporation reform has deepened. Government has started to allow state enterprises to lay off workers and file for bankruptcy, which were two bottom lines that had not been challenged by previous reforms. The State Council also decided to separate the government's social functions from its functions of monitoring state enterprises.

In 2003, the State Council founded a relatively independent agency solely responsible for supervising state enterprises, known as the State-owned Asset Supervision and Administration Commission ("the Commission"). The founding of provincial state assets commissions is also under way, and they would be responsible for supervising provincial state enterprises. The Commission's functions include appointing, monitoring, and rewarding directors, and also dismissing the directors for poor performance, provided the appropriate legal procedures are followed.

Since the end of the 1990s, there had been a rise in management buyout offers in state enterprises. Managers, in profit-making enterprises, wanted to buy ownership interests from the state, so that they could acquire a greater share of the enterprises' profits. The Commission, in consideration of the fact that managers have inside information, has been concerned that state assets may be undervalued in the buyout offers, which would lead to a major loss of state assets.

In 2003, the Commission issued a memorandum, "Interim Regulations on Transferring of State Ownership," which became effective on February 1, 2004. This regulation tightened the rules governing transfer of state ownership to non-state entities. On April 14, 2005, the Commission issued another memorandum, "Interim Regulations on Management Buyouts of State Ownership," which banned management buyouts in large state enterprises. In medium and small firms, management buyout may proceed in compliance with the Commission's guidelines, and the buyout offer is subject to the approval of provincial government and state asset commissions.

Agency theory, large shareholders, and the "grabbing hand"

Our review in the previous section demonstrates that the three-decade industrial reform in China has been a process of the government gradually loosening its control of state enterprises, and enterprises gaining independence in conducting their business. The Company Law of 1994 has afforded enterprises full autonomy in daily business operations, caused state shares to withdraw from many firms, and limited the state's sole ownership to a few selected industries such as natural resources, tobacco, oil production and refinery, and telecommunications.

The goal of industrial reform is to transform the corporate governance structure of state enterprises into that of modern corporations in Western market economies. In this section, we synthesize the theories relevant to the principal-agent relationship and property rights, and then apply them to address efficiency gains and losses associated with Chinese state corporations.[3]

Modern corporations in Western market economies

The survival and prosperity of modern corporations characterized by separation of ownership and control rights have posed a theoretical challenge to organizational scholars. According to Berle and Means

(1932), "The separation of ownership from control produces a condition where the interests of owner and of ultimate managers may, and often do, diverge, and where many of the checks which formerly operated to limit the use of power disappear … ."

Thus, according to Berle and Means, management and owners do not naturally have the same interests. Separation of ownership and control and broadly spread ownership among a large number of shareholders afford managers greater freedom to use the owner's resources to pursue their own interests without being effectively monitored. This type of organizational form potentially suffers loss of efficiency and may not survive in the long run. This speculation, however, contradicts the observation that modern corporations not only have survived, but have also flourished. Much effort has been spent in finding convincing explanations for this contradiction, and organizational theorists have attempted to rethink the nature of the firm.

The definition of the firm

In his seminal work on "the Nature of the Firm," Coase (1937) rationalized the existence of the firm as the outcome of high transaction costs associated with using the market to effect contracts and exchanges. He argued that if the cost of using the market were greater than the cost of using direct authority then the activities would be included within the firm. Alchian and Demsetz (1972) put less emphasis on the notion that activities within the firm are governed by authority but more on the voluntary nature of the exchanges among various input holders[4] in the firm. Viewing firms as organizations of joint input production,[5] they stressed the difficulty of determining each input's marginal productivity and the greater potential for input holders to shirk under this type of organizational form, and therefore emphasized the necessity of having a "common monitor" overseeing all input holders, who was then self-monitored by holding the residual claim rights.[6] Jensen and Meckling (1976) agreed with Alchian and Demsetz on the importance of voluntary exchanges in a firm, but believed that the Alchian-Demsetz characterization of the firm was too narrow. They instead considered firms simply as "legal fictions, which serve as a nexus for a set of contracting relationships among individuals."

Despite the differences, the aforementioned theorists share the view that firms are not simply individuals who only maximize profits, a view that prevails in the neoclassical economic thinking. Firms are "the outcome of a complex equilibrium process" in which individuals with conflicting interests interact on an equal and voluntary basis defined by the contractual relationship (Jensen and Meckling, 1976).

Efficiency gains from the separation of ownership and control rights

The form of modern corporations is determined in a process that balances all sorts of efficiency gains and losses associated with the separation of decision making control and ownership. Efficiency gains suggested by previous theorists are summarized as follows:

Reducing on-the-job consumption and shirking. Demsetz (1983) began the analysis with a simple case assuming that ownership and management are bestowed on one person (owner-manager), and thus there are no incentive issues. He proposed that the owner-manager maximized utility, which is a function of both pecuniary payoff (profits), and non-pecuniary on-the-job consumption, such as executive amenities and perks (use of a company car; use of the company jet, use of executive dining facilities, and so on), and personal taste or distaste for workers of a certain color or gender. The owner-manager pays for his on-the-job consumption by accepting a lower take-home wage. When marginal utility from the increase of on-the-job consumption and take-home wage is equal, the combination of both would be optimal. As a result of separating control from ownership, the owner-manager becomes a "specialized owner" and can no longer derive utility from on-the-job amenities. He would prefer higher pecuniary returns to on-the-job amenities. Demsetz concluded that "in general, the specialized ownership, in and of itself, creates pressure for less on-the-job consumption."

Specialized risk-bearing and decision control. Another benefit of separation of ownership and decision making control, pointed out by Fama and Jensen (1983a), is increased efficiency due to task specialization of risk bearing and decision making functions. A specialized owner is willing to bear greater risks because he can lower risks by diversifying his portfolio. As a matter of fact, portfolio theory suggests that the optimal portfolio for investors is to hold diversified securities of many firms. Furthermore, with the separation of ownership and decision making control, selecting decision makers need not rely on the decision maker's wealth and willingness to bear risks, but is instead based on his decision making skills. Consequently, decision making efficiency will increase.

Specialized knowledge of management. Managers or decision makers are required to have specialized knowledge as well as the skills and ability relevant to making decisions. The requirements are especially high in large, complex corporations which consist of a large number of individuals and the contractual relationships among them. With the separation of ownership and management, managers are able to concentrate on acquiring and accumulating the specialized knowledge, experience, and skills needed for decision making and the control of the corporation, so that their decision making qualities increase, which is important to the survival of the organization (Fama and Jensen, 1983a).

However, the efficiency gains derived from the separation of ownership and decision making control do not come without costs.

Costs of separation of ownership and control

In modern corporations, shareholders purchase stock, become owners and residual claimants, and bear the risk of stock performance by holding diversified portfolios. Professional managers are contracted to manage the firm, develop strategies and make decisions. Thus, shareholders and managers form a principal-agent relationship: shareholders are the owners/principals who hire managers (the agents) to manage the corporation on their behalf. Both parties are assumed to be utility maximizers, but they do not always share the same interests, and the agent does not always act in the best interests of the principal. The costs associated with the principal-agent relationship, known as "agency cost," include monitoring and bonding costs as well as the "residual loss" due to the divergence of the agent's interest from that of the principal (Jensen and Meckling, 1976; Williamson, 1964).

The survival of the separation of ownership and decision making control relies critically on whether the agency cost can be effectively regulated and reduced. Theorists have noted both internal and external forces for controlling the agency problems, with the emphasis being placed on the role of the market in monitoring management behavior. The methods for controlling agency cost are summarized below.

The stock market. The stock market has coexisted with modern corporations ever since the separation of ownership and decision making control. Stock prices are an indication of management performance and exert pressure on managers to direct their efforts toward the interests of shareholders. To control management behavior effectively, the stock market has to be well functioning in the sense that stock ownership must be transferable; and, more importantly, can be transferred at a relatively low cost (Fama and Jensen, 1983a).

The managerial labor market. Fama (1980) acknowledged the importance of a well-functioning capital market (stock market) in signaling and controlling management performance, but he also pointed out that the external managerial labor market plays an important role in sorting and rewarding managers according to their performance. A manager's pay in the current period would reflect his marginal productivity of previous periods. Thus, due to the concern that his current performance affects his future pay, managers would have an incentive to perform to their best. In order for the managerial labor market to exert effective control over managers, it has to be open and competitive so that wages reflect individual productivity. In addition, the movement of managers among different firms must be traceable.

The market for takeovers. External monitoring from a takeover market is less prevalent and more limited than that from the common stock market. Nevertheless, the threat of taking over the incumbent management team, either by a direct offer to purchase stock or by an appeal to shareholder votes for a new director, exerts pressure on the managers to act in the interests of residual claimants (Fama and Jensen, 1983a).

Internal monitoring. Internal monitoring refers to monitoring efforts within the organizational boundary in contrast to monitoring from outside markets. The modern corporation's internal structure is characterized as a decision and control hierarchy. The highest decision making organ is the board of directors – experts delegated by residual claimants with the rights to appoint and dismiss top-level managers, to set their remuneration, to ratify their decisions, and to oversee their performance. The board contains both internal and external members, where the internal members might be top-level managers.

Top-level managers delegate some decision making rights to lower-level agents in an organization. Decision initiatives of lower-level agents are passed back up to higher-level managers for ratification. In addition to the top-down monitoring, lower-level agents engage in collateral mutual monitoring (Fama and Jensen, 1983a). Due to their frequent daily interaction, lower-level agents can acquire information about their co-workers more easily than higher-level agents. This information serves as a basis for mutual monitoring.

The organizational structure includes a decision making hierarchy as well as an incentive and reward system. Because monitoring costs increase drastically with the complexity of the job, higher-level agents, who make complex decisions and control a wide range of subordinates, are less likely to be monitored directly and more likely to be paid according to performance. Holding the company's stock means agents are partly residual claimants; thus, to a certain degree, their interests are aligned with those of the shareholders. Lower-level agents performing simple and specific tasks can be monitored more easily without incurring large costs, and consequently they are more likely to be monitored directly and paid a fixed wage.

Optimal organizational structure

Since the control structure of a firm is an endogenous outcome of an equilibrium process that balances various costs and efficiency gains, there may not be a single optimal structure. Agency theory can be used to explain the prevalence and dominance of various organizational structures. Fama and Jensen (1983a, 1983b) applied the theory to explain organizations such as financial mutuals, professional partnerships,[7] and non-profit organizations.

In sum, the separation of ownership and decision making control in modern corporations thrives because of the demand for wealth from residual claimants to purchase stock and the risks they take in investing,[8] and because of the complex decision making structure of large corporations requiring specialized knowledge and skills. All these factors potentially result in greater efficiency gains than costs, even though the costs themselves are not negligible.

Implications of concentrated ownership

Agency theory has produced many predictions for empirical study. For example, if a company is owned by several large shareholders as opposed to numerous small shareholders, large shareholders can monitor managers more closely. Managers will be dismissed if they don't perform well, and thus will be less likely to engage in activities for personal benefit (Shleifer and Vishny, 1986). Managers would have less job security and greater turnover in firms controlled by large shareholders, and consequently, companies controlled by large shareholders may perform better and have greater value.

There has been some empirical evidence that supports these predictions. In the United States, most public firms are owned by many small shareholders, while in Germany and Japan, large blocks of shares are often owned by financial institutions and other large corporations. Several empirical studies have found that in Germany and Japan, companies with large shareholders are more likely to replace managers in response to poor performance (Kaplan, 1994a, 1994b; Kaplan and Minton, 1994; Franks and Mayer, 2001). Yafeh and Yosha (2003) also found that, in the chemical industry in Japan, large shareholding is associated with lower expenditure on activities conducted for managerial personal benefit. In the banking industry, evidence suggests that concentrated ownership increases banks' performance in Germany and Australia (Gorton and Schmid, 1999, 2000).

Chinese state enterprises' corporate governance and incentive issues

Any analysis of state enterprises in transitional economies would inevitably involve two streams of theories relevant to state ownership and corporate control. In this section, we apply the two sets of theories to analyze corporate governance of Chinese state enterprises at the different stages of the reform, which were described at the beginning of this chapter.

State ownership

Even in market economies, not all products and services are provided by private suppliers. There are public schools, hospitals, and utility and telecommunications companies. The size of the public sector varies across market economy countries[9] and has been rising and falling. It peaked during the Great Depression and World War II, and has declined radically since the 1980s.[10] Economists have striven to rationalize the very existence and the rise and fall of state firms in a market economy. Some researchers attributed the necessity of state firms in a market economy to various "market failures," such as externalities and non-excludability in certain markets (Atkinson and Stiglitz, 1980). Others, from a contractual perspective, have pointed out that state ownership was essentially the optimal outcome of a "make or buy" decision (Shleifer, 1998): the state may decide to have state firms to produce goods and services ("make") or contract them out to private firms ("buy").

Many of the above insights regarding state ownership may be applied to China. However, at least two modifications have to be made: (1) in a socialist country such as China, state ownership is not an endogenous outcome of the optimal decision of "make or buy" or simply a response to "market failures." State ownership or public ownership is politically imposed by Communist doctrine;[11] therefore, in an economic analysis of Chinese enterprises, state ownership has to be treated mostly as an exogenous condition; (2) over time, however, state ownership in a socialist country may be reduced.[12] When state ownership declines and state firms are privatized, the cost of privatization in a socialist country would be higher than in a capitalist country because of the additional efforts required to "reconcile" this with Communist doctrine.[13, 14] Therefore, in the long run, the scale of state ownership in a socialist country may not be as efficient as that in a market economy. The size of the state sector in a socialist country may be larger than the economically efficient size.

Despite these modifications, whether in a free market economy or a "socialist market" economy,[15] the motives of government bureaucrats are the same. It would be too naïve to believe that government bureaucrats simply represent the best interests of people and aim to maximize social welfare. With respect to state firms, the bureaucrats do not own the firms. Government bureaucrats are only agents, appointed by the state or the people, with the power to control and monitor state enterprises. This naturally gives rise to the agency cost associated with the principal-agent relationship between the people and bureaucrats.

A more realistic characterization of bureaucrats' motives is that bureaucrats are individuals who maximize utility. Social welfare considerations are only one aspect of bureaucrats' utility function. Shleifer (1998) and Shleifer and Vishny (1994) defined bureaucrats who only maximize social welfare as "benevolent." We argue that a "benevolent" bureaucrat by this definition is not the same as a good "monitor" or "manager" of state assets. Government has multiple functions which include economic functions to control state firms and social functions to promote full employment and provide affordable housing and pensions.[16] In addition, bureaucrats have their personal interests, which were vividly described as the "grabbing hand" by Frye and Shleifer (1997), and Shleifer and Vishny (1998). For example, in China, some politicians pressure firms to give donations to so-called "image" projects that drain a firm's profits, do not enhance social welfare, and only promote the politician's image and help him to advance his own career.

Thus, we characterize politicians' objectives by the following utility function, $U = U(e, s, \text{and } p)$, where e is economic efficiency, that is, the firm's profit or value maximization; s is social welfare considerations, and p is personal interests.

"Benevolent" government and corporate control

Unlike Russia and other former socialist countries in Eastern Europe, China's reform focused on transforming state enterprises' corporate control and changing the relationship between government and enterprise, rather than privatizing state ownership. It was only recently that reducing state ownership was endorsed for the first time. At the 16th CPC National Congress in 2002, the CPC publicized a new policy permitting the sale of small state firms, but in the meantime tightened control over large firms.[17] Shleifer and Vishny (1994) suggested that economic inefficiency associated with state ownership, such as the lack of incentives for innovation or cost control in state firms, would persist in large corporations in which the government holds all or the majority of shares. However, the "modern corporation reform" changed the corporate control and decision making structure. Here, we apply agency theory to discuss potential efficiency gains and problems associated with this type of organizational form, under the simplified assumption that government bureaucrats in charge of state firms are "benevolent." Then we will relax the assumption and address the complications arising from the government's "grabbing hand."

Inefficiency in the pre-reform period. In the pre-reform period, there was an entirely top-down authoritative and administrative relationship between the government and state firms and between different levels of agents within a firm. There was a lack of input, output, and labor market to determine factor price. Economic inefficiency in this kind of system can be attributed to "resource allocation distortion" (Samuelson 1948), "decision making inefficiency," and "insufficient monetary incentives."

First, the price mechanism is fundamental to efficient resource allocation. Inputs are best allocated in production, where the ratio of marginal product to the price of an input is equal for all inputs ($\frac{MP_1}{p_1} = \frac{MP_2}{p_2} = \frac{MP_3}{p_3} = \ldots$, input 1,2,3...). Since there is a lack of market to determine price, efficient resource allocation cannot be achieved. To allocate inputs efficiently, the central government must have complete information of the potential marginal gains and costs of allocating each input to each use. While in a small-scale economy this may be attainable, in a large, complex economy it is almost impossible.

Second, from the organizational economics perspective, the completely centralized decision making process suffers severe efficiency loss. Information is collected by lower-level agents and passed up to the central planner for decision making. Lower-level agents may intentionally conceal some information, or some information may be lost during transmission. After decisions are made, they are passed down to lower-level agents for execution. The outcome of executive decisions is then passed up to bureaucrats for evaluation. Afterwards, the policy may be changed and new decisions passed down again to be executed. With the decentralized decision making structure, decisions are made locally by lower-level agents and only the results need to be passed up to higher-level agents for evaluation. Thus, decision making is more efficient.

Finally, wages are set arbitrarily and do not reflect individual productivity. Specific reward systems create particular productivity responses. If pay is linked to productivity, workers are more productive; if pay and productivity are loosely correlated, incentives to perform are much smaller (Alchian and Demestz, 1972). A fixed salary is paid not only to the average worker in state firms but also to top-level managers. Top-level managers are responsible for monitoring a large number of subordinates; their job is more complex and difficult to be evaluated. They should thus be offered a flexible salary that rewards them based on performance. Moreover, the only form of reward that top-level managers may receive is being promoted to the government bureau. However, this kind of promotion opportunity is very limited and promotions are not based solely on managers' performance.[18]

Intermediate steps of the reform. Measures taken prior to the modern corporation reform can all be viewed as intermediate steps in restoring market and price mechanisms and decentralizing the decision making process. They include opening input and output markets and delegating to firms the authority to hire and fire workers, set employees' wage rates, purchase inputs, sell products, and set the price within the output target. The government bureau holds the power to set the output target and appoint top-level managers.

First of all, delegating to firms the authority to make decisions over internal structure and daily operation issues increases the decision making efficiency. Second, due to the reinstatement of the market mechanism, resource allocation efficiency has increased. With regard to the labor market, in the pre-reform period, high school, college and postgraduate school graduates were assigned to their jobs by the government. In the post-reform period, individuals compete for jobs and employers compete for workers. For the labor market to allocate workers efficiently, workers have to be able to move around at relatively little cost. Despite the *"Huko"* (residency registration and control) policy which is still in effect, labor mobility has increased considerably since the reform.

Moreover, since the reform, workers receive the guaranteed compensation (wages, bonuses, and all other types of monetary and non-monetary reward) set by the government, plus pay associated with their positions and bonuses that depend on enterprise performance. As a result, they have stronger incentives to perform. Despite the increase in income inequality in society due to increased pay differences across firms, labor productivity has increased. In contrast to the incentives restored for workers, there is still a lack of sufficient incentives for top managers, which does not correlate with their increased job complexity.

Completed form: "state corporations." Corporatization is the most recent policy of the reform. As a result, the relationship between government and state firms has changed from completely authoritative to mostly contractual.[19] The government has formed an independent agency, the State-owned Assets Supervision and Administration Commission. It is responsible for appointing, dismissing, and changing the board of directors and reviewing important business decisions. The Commission does not have control over other management issues and business decisions such as appointing managers. It is the board of directors that is responsible for hiring and firing top executives, while top executives appoint the lower-level managers.

Similar to corporations in Western market economies, China's "state corporation" would potentially gain efficiency from the separation of ownership (government) from decision making control (management). Since government holds large shares, it functions as a large shareholder in a western market economy. However, there is a crucial difference between them: unlike private large shareholders, government does not really own shares of state corporations, and it is the people or state that are the ultimate owners. Here, we apply agency theory and discuss the implications of this difference from the corporate control perspective.

Potential gains from separating decision making control from government (owners) include increased efficiency due to (a) separating government's social function from its function of supervising state corporations, (b) decentralized decision making, and (c) specialization of management tasks.

Separating government's social function from monitoring function: Although the Commission is not the real owner of state corporations and thus may lack incentives to perform the "monitoring job," separating social functions from its monitoring functions may increase efficiency because, to a certain degree, it prevents social welfare considerations from interfering with the Commission's objective of maximizing the firm's value.

Decentralized decision making: The Commission delegates routine supervising jobs to the board of directors. It is only responsible for selecting experts to form the board and evaluating their performance. The board further delegates to managers the right to make routine business decisions. This decision making structure best utilizes the specialized information and expertise possessed by the board and the managers.

Specialization of management: Managing large, complex corporations requires substantial specialist knowledge and skills. In China, prior to the reform, the management job was performed by "politician-like" managers whose ultimate goal was to be promoted into the government bureau. Management skills might not be the only or primary requirement for a manager. Being a party member and a loyal follower of Communist doctrine, and having a good relationship and reputation among employees and supervising bureaucrats, were also important factors, all of which are necessary characteristics for a politician but are not central to the performance of management tasks. Because of the specialization of management and decision making, managers are no longer required to possess political characters and so they can concentrate on acquiring and accumulating management knowledge and skills.

Our analysis suggests that efficiency may increase with the corporatization of state enterprises. However, because the government agency in charge of supervising state assets is not the owner of the assets, state corporations may not reach the same level of efficiency as their counterparts in Western market economies.

First, as suggested by Fama and Jensen (1983a), one of the potential efficiency gains is derived from the specialization of risk bearing. In the case of state corporations, because government bureaucrats are not the owners of assets they are supervising, they are prone to take more risks, such as influencing firms to invest in risky projects. For instance, it has been noted that state corporations often exhibit tremendously fast growth into multiple industries and invest in high-risk high-return projects such as real estate.

Second, agency costs rise with delegating decision making and control rights to managers. Despite the efficiency gains, if the agency cost cannot be controlled effectively, separating decision making from ownership may not result in a net gain. From the internal monitoring perspective, since government bureaucrats are not the *de facto* owners of state corporations and do not have residual claim rights, they may underperform in their role of supervising state corporations. For example, since the modern corporation reform, bureaucrats' responsibility has been reduced mainly to appointing the board of directors. However, bureaucrats may not make their best effort to find experts to form the board. Subsequently, the monitoring of managers by the board may not be adequate.

With internal monitoring being compromised, it is even more important to rely on the market as an independent external monitor of managers. External monitoring exerted by the stock market, the managerial labor market, and the market for takeovers, is largely free from bureaucrats' direction and influence. In China, the market for takeovers is very limited, if not completely absent. Stock exchanges were founded in the late 1980s and early 1990s, and experienced substantial growth only after the mid 1990s. Since large state shares are either not transferable or transferable but highly restricted,[20] it inevitably affects the accuracy of stock prices in reflecting management performance, and hence compromises its signaling function. Moreover, to date, an open, fair, and competitive managerial labor market does not exist – such a market is still under construction.[21]

In summary, corporatization results in efficiency gains from decentralizing decision-making, specializing the role of management, and separating government's function as a supervisor of state firms from its social functions. However, we argue that the agency cost may not be controlled as effectively in Chinese state corporations as in Western market economies, even if government bureaucrats are "benevolent." This is mainly because bureaucrats are not the actual owners of state assets and hence may underperform in their supervisory role. Specifically, internal monitoring in Chinese state corporations would not be comprehensive and strict as that in Western corporations. Moreover, because of the underdevelopment of the stock market and the managerial labor market, external monitoring would also be less adequate.

The "grabbing hand" and corporate control

The analysis in the previous section demonstrated that even "benevolent" government bureaucrats may underperform in their roles as supervisors of state corporations because the bureaucrats are not owners and do not have residual claim rights to enjoy "the fruit of their labors." As a consequence, government bureaucrats, as *de jure* large shareholders, may not respond effectively to poor performance by replacing managers. In contrast, private large shareholders in a market economy would monitor managers more closely and would be more likely to replace managers who perform badly. Thus, managers' job security may be greater and changes in management personnel less frequent in Chinese state corporations than in Western companies.

The "grabbing hand" model. Bureaucrats' motives are not always "benevolent." They take advantage of the control they have over state firms in exchange for personal benefits. These might be pecuniary (such as bribes) or non-pecuniary (such as "favors").[22] Under the "grabbing hand" model, bureaucrats give subsidies (*S*), such as special licenses to operate in an industry, protection of the firm's current monopolistic status, or generous bank loans, to firms, and extract personal benefits (*B*) from firms (Shleifer and Vishny, 1994).[23] In the worst case, bureaucrats may simply exert political pressure on managers and grab *B* without granting any *S*.

Assuming the firm's profit is π, in the worst case, profits become: $\pi - B$, so that welfare is transferred from firms to politicians secretly and illegally. The firm would bear the full loss if it operated in a competitive market, otherwise the firm may pass on some of its loss to consumers in the form of a higher price or lower quality if the firm has some market power.

If managers receive subsidies or favors from bureaucrats, these favors will likely increase profits, for example, in the form of monopoly rents. The size of monopoly rents probably depends on the nature or magnitude of the subsidy. In return, the firm gives part of its profits to the politician. The amount of *B* will likely depend on the scale of generated profits. So profits become: $\pi + \Delta\pi(S) - B(\Delta\pi(S))$. In this case, monopoly rent is transferred from consumers to the firm, and then some of the monopoly rent is transferred from the firm to politicians as a bribe or for other personal benefits. So consumers would bear a net loss. The firm bears a lesser loss than in the worst case scenario, but may still take a net loss if $\Delta\pi < B$. Politicians extract personal benefits directly from the firm and indirectly from consumers.

If *B* is collected in an open and legal manner, it would be similar to extra tax that adds to government revenue. Extra tax would not constitute a deadweight loss to society.[24] However, since *B* is illegal and secretive and contributes to politicians' undeclared "grey income", *B* is a loss in social welfare.

Implications of the "grabbing hand" for Chinese state corporations. If politicians threaten to take away *B* from a firm, the firm can only accept the loss. In China, since the economic reform, administrative decisions made on the orders of the Chinese government have been used less frequently. Firms and government have gradually evolved into a contractual relationship. In this case, managers and bureaucrats would both maximize utility and choose the optimal *S* and *B*. A somewhat surprising subsequent result is that the allocation of control rights or cashflow rights would not affect the equilibrium *S* and *B*. (Shleifer and Vishny, 1994).

If politicians have control rights and firms have cashflow, politicians would use *S* to induce firms to cooperate and pay *B*. If managers are given corporate control rights, they would use *B* to tempt politicians to give *S*. The equilibrium is that politicians and managers would fully cooperate and extract gains from consumers, which would result in a net loss in social welfare. An implication is that, with full corruption (that is, both politicians and firms' managers colluding fully in taking advantage of consumers), corporatization or privatization could not curb the "grabbing hand," especially if an industry is still highly regulated after the reform and politicians still have a lot of *S* to give out.

However, corruption is not without cost. After all, corruption is illegal. If it is not the full corruption case, politicians would be less likely to use their power to grab *B* from firms if they have less control over firms. However, bureaucrats would have no incentive to give up control. The economic reform has decentralized decision making and delegated many control rights in firms to managers. These measures have reduced bureaucrats' control and thus reduced the likelihood of resource allocation distortion due to *S* and *B*. But as long as politicians still have some control, the distortion may not be completely eliminated.

For example, after the reform, government bureaucrats maintain their personnel decision rights. Bureaucrats may appoint directors and influence the appointment of top executives. Bureaucrats may appoint their confidants to top managerial positions. A trusted manager, for example, can better support a government leader in his political career, give lucrative business contracts or high-level company jobs to a leader's family members and close friends, and/or directly pass on money to the leader, sometimes legally (for example, in the form of payment for services), and other times illegally (for example, a large bribe).

In recent years, there have been a number of cases in which top executives in large profit-making state enterprises have been replaced. The most prominent cases include Hongta Co. and Chu Shijian, ChangHong Co. and Ni Runfeng, and Jian Li Bao Co. and Li Jingwei. Honta Co., a tobacco company, is wholly owned by the state, as tobacco is one of the monopolistic industries exclusively controlled by the state. With regard to ChangHong, an electronics manufacturer well-known for making televisions, and Jian Li Bao, a sports beverage producer, the local government used to control the majority shares.[25] Since the government is the sole "owner" or large shareholder of these companies, it has considerable influence over personnel changes. Since these personnel changes are not a result of poor performance, it has raised suspicion that they may be related to bureaucrats' private interest in replacing incumbent managers with people they trust who are easy to control.

Politician-manager joint utility maximization produces three other results. First, with no collusion between politician and managers, control rights assigned to managers would increase the resource allocation efficiency (Shleifer and Vishny, 1994). The implication is that if China were corruption-free, corporatization would increase efficiency. This would be the ideal situation.

Second, if politicians maintain control over firms through political pressure or regulation, privatizing cashflows (that is, allowing a firm to manage its own cashflow) and giving managers autonomy both reduce efficiency and increase corruption. In fact, politicians would prefer privatizing cashflows as long as they maintain control over firms. Private ownership enables them to acquire more "grey income" by "bargaining" with firms, while previously all the revenue generated by state enterprises went directly to the Treasury (Shleifer and Vishny, 1994). This may explain why corruption hardly existed in China in the pre-reform period, while afterwards, it became a widespread problem.

Finally, imposing a decency constraint on politicians, which limits their power to give S to profitable companies, and managers acquiring more ownership would lead to restructuring in profitable firms and a reduction in B (Shleifer and Vishny, 1994). However, politicians would not want to relinquish ownership in profitable firms. This may explain why the Chinese government takes a tough line against management buyout offers in large state firms. It is typically managers in profitable companies who propose management buyouts. It may also explain why the government insists on maintaining sole state ownership in certain high-profit industries, such as tobacco, oil extraction and refinery, and telecommunications.

In sum, assuming the continued existence of bureaucrats who make decisions based on maximizing their own utility (welfare) and personal interests, rather than maximizing the benefit to society as a whole, corporatization or privatization may not curtail the "grabbing handing." However, reducing bureaucrats' control rights and deregulating industries would restrict bureaucrats' predatory behavior. These reform attempts may have to be imposed on the bureaucrats since they may have little incentive to adopt these efforts of their own accord.

Summary

In this chapter, we have reviewed the evolvement of Chinese state firms' corporate control and ownership structure during the reform. Then we have applied the agency theory and ownership theories to analyze potential efficiency gains and losses associated with state enterprises at different stages of the reform.

Our review has shown that the economic reform is a gradual process where the government loosens its control over state enterprises and the enterprises gain autonomy in business decision making. By 1994, enterprises, by law, have gained full independence in conducting business. The government withdrew from most business decision making, and only kept the right to appoint and dismiss the board of directors, and review and approve vital business decisions. In recent years, the government has also withdrawn the "helping hand," allowing unprofitable firms to lay off workers and file for bankruptcy, and tightening state banks' lending standards. Some former state firms have restructured their ownership and become limited liability companies and public corporations. The second section of the chapter was devoted to a comparative analysis of Chinese "state corporations" and public companies in Western market economies. Our analysis has reached two conclusions: first, corporatization leads to various efficiency gains due to the decentralization of decision making and management specialization. However, state corporations may not reach the efficiency level of Western corporations because bureaucrats in charge of supervising state corporations are not the real owners and may not perform their supervisory roles as well as private large shareholders. Second, bureaucrats' objectives may not be just to supervise state firms. A more realistic characterization is that bureaucrats maximize utility which depends on both social welfare and their personal benefits. Out of private interests, a bureaucrat might take advantage of his controlling power to coerce or collude with a firm, so that the firm would pass some profits to him in the form of a bribe or personal favor while the firm may or may not receive a "subsidy" in return. Given this characterization of bureaucrats, even corporatization or privatization could not cure the resource allocation distortion due to subsidies and bribe. On the contrary, privatizing cashflows to managers while politicians maintain control and regulatory power would only reduce efficiency and increase bribery. Although corporatization may not cure distortion or inefficiency, it reduces politicians' control over firms and thus limits their ability to exchange subsidies for personal benefits. The implication is that corporatization accompanied by sufficient deregulation may lead to a solution to the inefficiency and corruption resulting from the "grabbing hand."

Notes

1. We gratefully acknowledge helpful suggestions from Masao Nakamura, and other participants of the UBC-SASS workshop in Shanghai.

2. Traditionally, different levels of government in China demanded some form of payoff from the enterprises they own or govern. Such payoffs could be monetary in nature (such as straight cash payments) or non-monetary (such as the provision of labor services).
3. In our analysis, solely state-owned firms, or LLCs in which the state owns majority shares, are termed "state corporations." See also Groves et al. (1994).
4. "Input holders" refers to the owners of inputs that are used by firms for their production activities. Workers, for example, are input holders in that they provide their labor input to the firm.
5. "Joint input production" refers to all the separate inputs a firm must use simultaneously and in combination to produce its final product, and it needs to make optimum use of these inputs. In the context being discussed here, joint input production refers to all the inputs already within the firm, such as workers, engineers, managers, and so on.
6. "Residual claim rights" refers to the right to claim all or some of the firm's net profits. A firm's shareholders have residual claim rights by virtue of owning shares in the company. Workers or other employees who are given shares in their company thus also have residual claim rights, which may be an incentive for them to work harder.
7. A professional partnership is a special type of legally recognized organization, established by a group of professionals (such as accountants), that is suitable for that profession. They are different from ordinary stock companies, whose shareholders have limited liability, in that most partners in professional partnerships share unlimited liability but remain private.
8. Potential shareholders (potential investors) are willing to invest their own money in firms, hoping to make large amounts of profit in terms of capital gains and dividends from their investment. Because these investors (shareholders) are residual claimants, they are not entitled to any specific (known) cash payments beforehand. What they are entitled to is what is left after the firm has paid all bills and other legal obligations, so it is quite possible that they will get nothing in the end (which occurs when a firm's operating costs exceed its revenues). In this sense, these investors are facing the significant risk of losing their initial capital.
9. France, Italy and Spain had a large number of state firms, and even some in what are traditionally viewed as competitive industries ("Europe's Dirigiste Dinosaurs," *The Economist*, Vol. 317, No. 7681, November 17, 1990, pp. 83–4).
10. Shleifer (1998) has documented the history of the rise and decline in state firms in Western countries in the twentieth century.
11. See the Constitution of the People's Republic of China, Articles 6 and 7.
12. For instance, in China, the economic reform since 1979 has reduced state ownership in many competitive industries.
13. For example, in a socialist country, to justify privatizing state firms, constitutions have to be revised. These efforts add to the cost of privatization.
14. Frye and Shleifer (1997) compared privatization experiences in Poland and Russia and pointed out that the greater success of reforms in Poland were due to the better legal environment. We supply a further explanation: the better legal environment of Poland may be only one of the intermediate factors

that lead to Poland's success. Other intermediate factors include better market infrastructure, fairer competition, and less government interventions. These intermediate factors are ultimately explained by the lower transactional cost of privatizing state economy and constructing the private sector in Poland. Russia and Poland had the same political and economic systems prior to the reform. To be accurate, Poland copied Russian systems. However, Russia faced greater costs due to stronger political obstacles because communist doctrines and communist influences ran deeper and longer in Russia than in Poland.

15. The "socialist market economy" is the Chinese government's term defining a market economy in a socialist country such as in China.
16. In China, in the pre-reform period, state enterprises fulfilled many social functions, such as providing free housing, health insurance, pensions, and lifetime employment to workers. These activities were performed out of bureaucrats' social welfare considerations.
17. Experimentation with the privatization of small state firms had occurred in many places under the government's scrutiny since the late 1990s, but it was only after the 16th CPC National Congress in 2002 that the practice was legalized. The policy making process in China typically involves government-monitored small-scope experiments in selected firms first, then, if the experiments prove to be successful, the practice is legalized.
18. In the pre-reform period, managers in state firms were regarded as lower-level "bureaucrats"; they were evaluated and promoted in the same way as bureaucrats. Since important positions were always held by Communist Party members, evaluations were conducted within the party. High-level party members collected information about a lower-level member's job performance, personality, loyalty to the Communist doctrine, relationships with other people, and so on, and then made a promotion decision.
19. Administrative orders are still sometimes used by government, but much less frequently than before.
20. "Temporary Regulations on Trading or Transferring State Assets" of the State-owned Assets Supervision and Administration Commission, 2003.
21. See reports by Shao (2003a, 2003b), Associate Director of the State-Owned Assets Supervision and Administration Commission.
22. An example of a personal favor is a bureaucrat asking a firm to employ people it doesn't need, often the bureaucrat's own relatives and friends.
23. In their model, Shleifer and Vishny (1994) specified that politicians control employment. In this chapter, we generalize politicians' control so that it could be any control that politicians have over firms that is bestowed by virtue of their bureaucratic position.
24. That is, imposing the extra tax will benefit society to an amount greater than the cost of the tax. Deadweight loss occurs when, for example, some types of taxes to raise government revenue severely shrink the level of economic activity to the extent that the tax revenue and the benefits that the government gains from the taxation is less than the loss in the total economic activity.
25. Changhong Stock is listed on the Shanghai Stock Exchange. By June 2005, non-transferable state shares accounted for 56 percent of total shares. Jian Li Bao has not gone public. In 2002, SanShui city government in Guang Dong province sold the city's shares to a private investment company.

References

Alchian, A. A., and Demsetz, H. (1972) "Production, Information Costs and Economic Organization," *American Economic Review*, 62(5), 777–95.

Atkinson, A. B., and Stiglitz, J. E. (1980) *Lectures on Public Economics* (London: McGraw-Hill).

Coase, R. H. (1937) "The Nature of the Firm," *Economica*, 4, 386–405.

Berle, A. A., and Means, G. C. (1932) *The Modern Corporation and Property Rights* (New York: Macmillan Publishing Co.).

Fama, E. (1980) "Agency Problems and the Theory of the Firm," *Journal of Political Economy*, 88, 288–324.

Fama, E., and Jensen, M. (1983a) "Separation of Ownership and Control," *Journal of Law and Economics*, 26(2), 301–25.

Fama, E., and Jensen, M. (1983b) "Agency Problems and Residual Claims," *Journal of Law and Economics*, 26(2), 327–49.

Frye, T., and Shleifer, A. (1997) "The Invisible Hand and the Grabbing Hand," *American Economic Review*, 87(2), 354–8.

Demsetz, H. (1983) "The Structure of the Ownership and the theory of the Firm," *Journal of Law and Economics*, 26(2), 375-90.

Franks, J., and Mayer, C. (2001) "Ownership and Control of German Corporations," *Review of Financial Studies*, 14(4), 943–77.

Gorton, G., and Schmid, F. (1999) "Corporate Governance, Ownership Dispersion and Efficiency: Empirical Evidence from Austrian Cooperative Banking," *Journal of Corporate Finance*, 5(2), 119–40.

Gorton, G., and Schmid, F. (2000) "Universal Banking and the Performance of German Firms," *Journal of Financial Economics*, 58(1–2), 29–80.

Groves, T., Xiaoming, H., McMillan, J., and Naughton, B. (1994) "Autonomy and Incentives in Chinese State Enterprises," *Quarterly Journal of Economics*, 109(1), 183–209.

Jensen, M. C., and Meckling, W. H. (1976) "Theory of the Firm: Managerial Behavior, Agency Costs and Ownership Structure," *Journal of Financial Economics*, 3(4), 305–60.

Kaplan, S. (1994a) "Top Executive Rewards and Firm Performance: A Comparison of Japan and the U.S.," *Journal of Political Economy*, 102.

Kaplan, S. (1994b) "Top Executive, Turnover, and Firm Performance in Germany," *Journal of Law, Economics and Organization*, 10(1), 142–59.

Kaplan, S. N., and Minton, B. A. (1994) "Appointments of Outsiders to Japanese Boards: Determinants and Implications for Managers," *Journal of Financial Economics*, 36, 225–58.

Samuelson, P. A. (1948) *Economics* (New York: McGraw-Hill).

Shleifer, A. (1998) "State Versus Private Ownership," *Journal of Economic Perspectives*, 12(4), 133–50.

Shleifer, A., and Vishny, S. (1986) "Large Shareholders and Corporate Control," *Journal of Political Economy*, 94(3), 461–617.

Shleifer, A., and Vishny, S. (1994) "Politicians and Firms," Quarterly Journal of Economics, 109(4), 995–1025.

Shleifer, A., and Vishny, S. (1998) *The Grabbing Hand: Government Pathologies and their Cures* (Cambridge, MA: Harvard University Press).

Shao, N. (2003a) "Strengthening External Monitoring Over State Firms," Report to the State-owned Assets Supervision and Administration Commission of the State Council by the Associate Director of the Commission.

Shao, N. (2003b) "Advance State Firms Reform and Restructuring," Report to the State-owned Assets Supervision and Administration Commission of the State Council by the Associate Director of the Commission.

Williamson, O. E. (1964) *The Economics of Discretionary Behavior: Managerial Objectives in a Theory of the Firm* (Englewood Cliffs, N.J.: Prentice-Hall).

Yafeh, Y., and Yosha O. (2003) "Large Shareholders and Banks: Who Monitors and How?" *Economic Journal*, 113(484): 128–46.

"The Organic Law of the Central People's Government of the People's Republic of China," 1949

"Several Regulations on Increasing State Enterprise Operating and Management Autonomy," 1979

"Regulations on Increasing State Enterprise Retained Profits," 1979

"Permission to State Enterprises Changing from Submitting Profits to Paying Tax," 1983

"Temporary Regulations on State Enterprise Income Tax," 1983

"CPC Central Committee's Decision on Economic Reform," 1988

"Temporary Regulations on Delegating or Renting State Assets to Enterprises," 1988

"People Republic of China's State-Owned Enterprise Law," 1988

"Corporate Law," 1994

"Temporary Regulations on Trading or Transferring State Assets," 2003

"Temporary Regulations on Management Buyout of State Assets," 2005

7
Corporate Governance Practices in Post-Bubble Japan: Adapting to the Globalizing Economies of the Twenty-First Century

Masao Nakamura

Introduction

The burst of Japan's financial bubble in 1990 triggered a long recession in the Japanese economy. It lasted well into the early 2000s, and both Japanese firms and households suffered from the lack of economic growth for many years. Japanese banks' massive bad-loan problems limited their ability to finance business firms. Lacking the traditional source of bank financing and facing severe competition from abroad at the same time, the global competitiveness many Japanese firms enjoyed in the 1980s was all but lost.

In response to this, many Japanese firms began changing their business practices that used to be taken for granted. Many of these changes in business practices have been taking place throughout the 1990s and the 2000s and will likely have fundamental implications for the Japanese economy. Japanese firms' corporate governance practices are no exceptions. New Japanese reform laws in corporate governance and other related areas have prompted many industrial firms to undertake new business practices. In addition, failing Japanese banks became the target of the government reform. The new reform laws, some of which specifically addressed Japanese banks, were implemented to monitor banks' behavior after they were bailed out by the government. It is important to emphasize that Japanese banks traditionally shaped the corporate governance mechanisms of Japanese industrial firms. As we discuss below, Japan's financial deregulation laws and bank reform laws being implemented have had major impacts on Japanese bank behavior and, in particular, Japan's bank-based corporate governance mechanisms. However, to what degree Japanese banks' role in Japanese corporate governance has declined still remains to be seen.

Many of the changes in business practices that have been proposed or implemented so far are modeled after the corresponding U.S. (or more broadly the Anglo-American) practices. The establishment of (1) proper market-based mechanisms for corporate governance, and (2) mechanisms for monitoring to ensure smooth and transparent operations of such activities was emphasized by the Japanese government. This is also characterized as a process by which Japanese practices adapt to the Western standard (the *de facto* global standard). Since every aspect of today's Japanese economy is tied to the global economy in many ways, it is likely that significant adaptation of global practices by Japan will continue to take place.

Although it is premature to predict what types of patterns of corporate governance practices will result in equilibrium (or if such an equilibrium exists in the long run), it seems evident by now that the general approach to accomplishing many of the market-driven U.S.-style practices has been successful, though it has clearly been evolutionary and experimental in many ways.

We do not know yet how such an adaptation of Western practices will be mixed with the existing Japanese practices; for example, those practices involving interfirm (keiretsu) relationships.

We have argued that the Japanese government initiated a number of reform measures which they thought would help Japan to regain its global competitiveness. These measures are wide-ranging[1] and include new legal measures and institutional practices in such areas as: corporate governance, financial deregulation and monitoring; bank behavior, information disclosure and accounting; and the market for corporate control (M&As).[2] We briefly discuss these measures below.

Government initiatives

A significant number of new regulations and laws in corporate governance have been proposed and implemented throughout the 1990s and the early 2000s. Many of these changes will have a major impact on the corporate governance practices of many Japanese firms. For this reason it is noteworthy that these changes in the legal settings of Japanese corporate governance took place so promptly. It is generally agreed that the reason for this prompt acceptance of the major proposed changes in corporate governance practices is that the problems with the bank-based corporate governance mechanisms prevailing in Japan until the early 1990s were among the major causes of the demise of many Japanese corporations.[3] Even those who defend the benefits of the traditional bank-based corporate governance system concede that the time for such a system is gone. They also argue that a more market-based corporate governance system with proper incentive-based practices and disclosure clauses, particularly those of the Anglo-American system, should replace the old post-World War II Japanese practices. In order to achieve this goal, the Japanese government promptly introduced laws which bring transparency and market-based practices into corporate governance mechanisms, capital markets and bank behavior (for example, financial deregulation, monitoring), securities exchange and other areas related to corporate governance.

Capital market liberalization

Facing this circumstance and the near collapse of many of the major banks and industrial firms,[4] the Japanese government has implemented several capital market liberalization measures which would facilitate firms to access public capital markets. For example, firms can in principle issue straight corporate bonds without collateral. Until the early 1990s firms were free to issue unsecured bonds with equity nature (for example, convertible and warrant bonds) and secured bonds with collateral, but not (unsecured) straight corporate bonds. In order to force corporations to disclose relevant information to their investors, many aspects of the Commercial Code, the Securities Exchange Law and other laws have been revised. The primary objectives of these changes are to introduce Western standards in accounting transparency and protection of investors.

Accounting transparency

For example, Japanese corporations are now required to file quarterly consolidated financial statements with the Ministry of Finance which report activities for the parent company as well as its related firms (previous reporting was mostly for stand-alone firms.) Under these new reporting rules, many, if not all, of the transactions between the parent and subsidiary firms, which used to be hidden from the public, will have to be reflected in the reported accounting numbers.[5]

Under the new rules, the value of the financial securities (and also golf club memberships) a firm owns and their unrealized losses must be reported at market value under most circumstances. (Previously, no market value had to be reported so long as the securities remained unsold.) The new requirement implies that banks must disclose the state of their financial assets and loans at market value. This is expected to add previously non-existent transparency. This measure, combined with a new law limiting banks' equity ownership to the level of their own capital, has already had a major impact on Japanese banks.[6]

Another change took place in regard to how R&D expenditures were to be reported. Whereas previously, R&D expenses could be treated as either expenses or an item to be capitalized, now they must be treated as current expenses.[7]

Listing requirements and accounting transparency

Despite significant improvements in the transparency requirements in Japanese firms' reporting of their financial statements since the 1990s, several incidents of improper accounts reporting by some of the major listed corporations were reported in the last few years. These incidents include understating the extent of stock ownership by large shareholders, understating liabilities, and overstating profits. These fraudulent practices can imply the lack of protection of investors by Japan's stock exchanges and hence can lead to the loss of confidence and global competitiveness in Japanese stock markets. Serious concern was raised regarding the inadequate level of protection of individual investors provided by the current listing standards.[8] This suggests that further improvements in the design of institutions on corporate monitoring may be needed before Japan can attract more capital from global sources.

Corporate governance practices

In addition to the above measures to increase information disclosure and transparency, a number of measures have been implemented to improve firm performance and firm value by revising certain corporate governance practices and also market transactions (that is, mergers and acquisitions, M&As) involving corporations.[9] These include: options to use executive committees for management purposes; optional use of outside directors; legalizing holding companies;[10] legalizing Treasury stocks and warrants to new stocks; and legalizing issuing various classes of stocks previously not allowed (for example, tracking stock[11]). In addition, purchasing firms by exchanges of stocks became legal later in 2006. While takeover bids have been available since 1971, their effective use for M&As began only recently when other relevant tools for M&As (particularly hostile M&As) and legal settings became available. Also, the recent hostile takeover attempt by the Livedoor Corporation to acquire control of the Nippon Broadcasting System (NBS) prompted many other corporations to be prepared to defend hostile takeover attempts by implementing various anti-takeover measures, including "poison pills."[12] The Livedoor-NBS incident is summarized below.

Livedoor-Nippon Broadcasting-Fuji Television anti-takeover incident

A historical event involving a hostile takeover attempt by Livedoor Corporation took place in early 2005, giving the public an opportunity for a comprehensive case study of what could happen to Japanese corporations in a modern (Anglo-American?) era. This event was historical in that it made clear in the eyes of the public: (1) what is at stake (the incumbent management vs. the shareholders) in a hostile takeover; (2) that the Japanese courts accepted the rights of the firm's general shareholders as the owners of the firm (that is, the share value maximization principle), thus denying blind protection for incompetent management, as often occurred in the past; (3) that the incumbent management's anti-takeover efforts are justifiable only if they provide better expected future profits for the corporation; and (4) that there is a reasonable boundary within which poison pills and other anti-takeover devices are acceptable. The timing of the Livedoor incident coincided with the ongoing discussions of the revised (New) Company Law in the Japanese parliament, and the "lessons" from this incident were promptly incorporated into the New Company Law (subsequently enacted in May 2006).

In part prompted by the above incident, the Japanese government (the Ministry of Justice and METI in particular) has been revising both the Commercial Code and the Securities Exchange Law to delineate the legal extent of various poison pills being proposed by corporations.[13] One underlying issue, which was also highlighted recently by the court case involving Livedoor and NBS, is the protection of existing shareholders but not incompetent management while also allowing value-increasing takeovers to succeed.[14]

Japan has been vigorously implementing various market-based corporate governance practices and reporting requirements throughout the 1990s and 2000s. These new practices and the associated laws introduced are based mostly on the U.S. model. As discussed below, these reform measures have been accompanied by the considerable decline in status of Japanese banks as shareholders of Japanese industrial firms. Many of the shares sold by Japanese banks in the market have been purchased by both domestic and foreign individual and institutional investors. This has also resulted in an increased awareness of the importance of non-corporate shareholders such as individual and institutional shareholders by the management of many of Japan's listed corporations.[15]

Banks' role in corporate governance

Japanese banks were particularly influential in corporate governance as both the major creditors and the shareholders of many of their client firms until the mid 1990s. This dual role the Japanese banks have enjoyed is still allowed by the Japanese Anti-Monopoly (Anti-Trust) Law, by which banks can own up to 5 percent of the outstanding shares of any industrial firm for control purposes.[16] Since the late 1990s, their status as shareholders in Japanese firms has been significantly reduced, at least in the aggregate sense. Table 7.1 and Figure 7.1 show the shareholding patterns by stable shareholders of the listed firms in Japan.

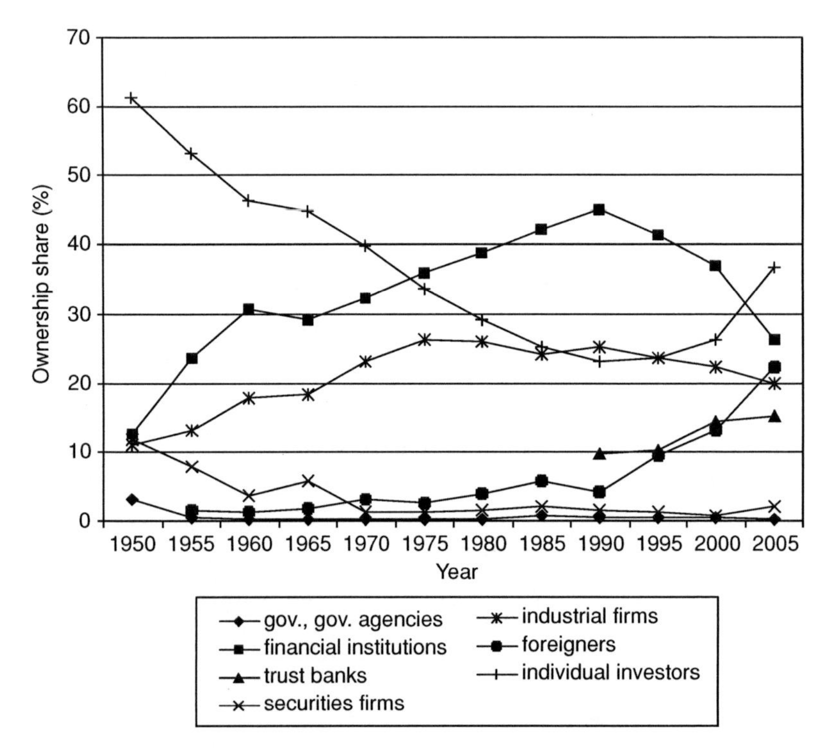

Figure 7.1 Long-term trends in the ownership structure of Japanese listed firms

Source: based on figures reported in the Tokyo Stock Exchange (2006).

Table 7.1 Changing patterns of stable shareholding: Japanese listed firms, 1987–2003 (%)

Year	*All stable share-holding*	*Financial institutions*	*Banks*	*Banks: cross-holding*	*Insurance firms*	*Insurance firms: cross-holding*	*Business firms*	*Business firms: cross-holding*	*Business firms: related firms owned*	*Cross-holding: securities firms*	*Cross-holding: total*
	(1)	*(2)*	*(3)*	*(4)*	*(5)*	*(6)*	*(7)*	*(8)*	*(9)*	*(10)*	*(11)*
1987	45.8	31.3	14.9	6.7	16.4	1.0	14.4	10.7	3.1	0.1	18.5
1988	45.7	32.3	15.6	7.1	16.6	0.9	13.3	10.0	2.8	0.1	18.1
1989	44.9	31.3	15.6	7.3	15.7	0.8	13.4	9.1	3.7	0.1	17.4
1990	45.6	31.5	15.7	7.5	15.8	0.9	14.0	9.7	3.7	0.1	18.1
1991	45.6	31.8	15.6	7.6	16.2	0.9	13.7	9.3	3.9	0.1	17.9
1992	45.7	31.8	15.6	7.5	16.2	0.9	13.8	9.4	3.8	0.1	17.8
1993	45.2	31.2	15.4	7.4	15.8	0.8	14.0	9.3	4.1	0.1	17.6
1994	44.9	31.1	15.4	7.4	15.8	0.8	13.7	9.1	4.0	0.1	17.4
1995	43.4	29.8	15.1	7.4	14.8	0.9	13.6	8.8	4.1	0.1	17.1
1996	42.2	29.8	15.1	7.9	14.7	0.9	12.2	7.5	4.5	0.1	16.3
1997	40.5	28.9	14.8	7.5	14.1	0.9	11.6	6.7	4.6	0.0	15.1
1998	39.9	26.7	13.7	6.5	13.0	0.7	13.2	6.0	7.0	0.0	13.3
1999	38.0	22.0	11.3	5.4	10.6	0.7	16.0	4.7	11.1	0.0	10.9
2000	33.1	20.7	9.8	5.4	10.9	0.7	12.4	4.3	7.9	0.0	10.4
2001	30.2	18.8	8.7	4.8	10.1	0.6	11.4	3.7	7.8	0.0	9.0
2002	27.2	17.0	7.7	4.0	9.3	0.6	10.1	3.3	6.9	0.0	7.9
2003	24.3	13.9	5.9	3.0	8.0	0.8	10.3	3.8	6.5	0.1	7.6

Note: these figures represent the fractions of ownership by the respective owners of the listed firms' outstanding shares (in share value); (1) = (2) + (7) + (10); (2) = (3) + (5); (3) > (4); (5) > (6); (7) > (8); (7) > (9); (11) = (4) + (6) + (8) + (10).

Source: compiled by the author using figures from Japanese Stock Exchanges (2005) and Nissei Kiso Kenkyusho (2004).

Table 7.1 shows the shares of stable ownership in Japan's listed firms by company shareholders such as banks, insurance companies and industrial firms. This type of stable ownership is intended for long-term control, business transaction benefits and other purposes. In most cases these corporate shareholders are considered "friendly" in that they do not sell their shares in an opportunistic manner and hence are typically called "stable shareholders." These stable shareholders include pairs of companies which cross-own each other's shares ("*mochiai*," or cross-shareholding).[17]

We see from Table 7.1 that the fraction of shares listed on Japanese stock exchanges that were held by stable shareholders declined from 45.8 percent in 1987 to 24.3 percent in 2003. In particular, the banks held 14.9 percent (of which 6.7 percent was in the form of *mochiai*) of the total stable shareholders' shares in 1987.[18] This share declined to 5.9% (3.0 percent *mochiai*) in 2003. The fraction of shares held by the financial institutions including banks and insurance companies declined from 31.3 percent in 1987 to 13.9 percent in 2003.

The substantial decline in shareholding by the banks started in 1998 when Japanese banks' massive non-performing loans prompted the Japanese government to force the banks to improve their financial performance. Two major government policy measures were implemented to achieve this: (1) an injection of public funds into the banks in financial distress; and (2) forcing banks to sell off the shares of other companies they owned. An injection of public funds came with severe government restrictions on bank management. One such restriction was to limit banks' shareholding. This, combined with the second policy measure, forced banks to reduce their holding of shares in other companies. We explain these in turn.

Injection of public funds

Japanese government's laws to stabilize the financial sector took the form of a series of cash injections in 1998 and 1999 into the troubled banks with the possibility of nationalizing them in case the banks could not recover and attain sound performance within certain specified periods. The first and second injections were budgeted, respectively, at ¥13 trillion and ¥25 trillion. All banks except the Tokyo-Mitsubishi Bank chose to apply for these government rescue cash injections. These cash injections took the form of preferred shares without voting rights which are convertible to common shares under certain bank performance conditions. For example, if a rescued bank fails to meet the government's performance criteria within a specified amount of time, then the government's shares will become common shares with voting rights and a government takeover of the bank will become possible.

Many of the banks were facing bankruptcy at that time, including major city banks. Injections of public funds came with many conditions that were imposed on the banks' management, including prompt disposition of the banks' bad assets (such as highly devalued financial securities in other firms) and non-performing loans which were increasing at a rapid rate. Non-performing bank loans that were disposed of in the period 1998–99 amounted to ¥10.4 trillion for the 14 largest banks.

In comparison, we also note that the total amount of public funds injected into Japan's large banks since 1998 amounted to ¥10.8 trillion, of which half had been returned by the banks to the Japanese government by early 2006. Upon payback, the government sold off the preferred shares that the banks owned in the market, making profits of at least ¥0.4 trillion yen (about US$3.8 billion).

Forcing banks to sell off other companies' shares

The continuing poor performance of stock prices during the recession periods since 1990 seriously hurt the banks which counted on capital appreciation over time in the shares they owned. For example, massive depreciation of bank-owned shares significantly reduced the ratio of banks' own capital to risky assets including loans, resulting in many Japanese banks' inability to satisfy the own-capital ratio requirement (8 percent or higher) set by the Basel Accord for conducting international operations.[19] Many Japanese banks, including some large banks, had to terminate their international banking operations, thus undermining their financing and investment capacity.[20]

It was at this time that the government (the Financial Supervisory Agency) adopted the policy that the banks must reduce their shareholding in order to lower their exposure to the fluctuations in stock prices.

Additional measures were taken by the Japanese government to reduce the banks' exposure to the stock market. One such measure was to set up the Banks' Shareholdings Purchase Corporation (BSPC) in 2002. The BCPS was created by the new law to limit Japanese banks' shareholding to the amount of their own capital. This law required the banks promptly to sell off the shares they held in other firms (including their own client firms) in order to meet the required capital target by the above-mentioned law. In order to avoid the anticipated negative impact on the stock market of such a mass sale of bank-owned shares, the BCPS was established for the purpose of purchasing bank-owned shares at market value. The banks were allowed to choose the shares to be sold off in the market.

The corporation was capitalized at ¥10 billion, which the member banks must provide. The Japanese government guaranteed all required financing which took the form of bonds issued by the corporation up to the value of ¥4 trillion (US$39 billion).

As it turned out, the rescue plan by the BSPC was not effective enough to induce the banks to sell the shares they owned. The banks argued that the transaction costs associated with the BSPC plan were in part to blame. Facing a further-deteriorating economy, the Bank of Japan (BoJ), under the pressure from the ruling political parties, decided to buy up the bank-held shares directly. (Under normal circumstances, such share purchases by the BoJ are prohibited.) In justifying this decision, the BoJ (2002) argued that:

> Japanese banks' non-performing loan problem reflects the structural problems of both Japanese industry and Japanese finance industry and hence both must be dealt with by policy; Japanese banks have either written off or set aside reserve for up to 90 trillion yen (about 890 billion dollars) of their bad loans in the previous 10 years (i.e. 1992–2001) and yet no improvement is in sight; these 90 trillion yen in bad loans accounts for almost 80% of the loans for Japanese industries' net investment provided by all Japanese banks during the bubble period 1986–1990, suggesting a serious structural problem in Japanese industry; in this circumstance, in order to prevent further deterioration in Japan's financial system and stabilize Japanese banks, it seems a viable alternative for the BoJ to buy up bank-held shares and also inject further public funds into Japanese banks.

The BoJ's plan was not to sell the acquired shares for at least ten years. It originally set aside ¥3 trillion for the purchase of banks' shares and actually bought ¥2.18 trillion (about US$20 billion) worth of shares from the Japanese banks during the period November 2002 to September 2004. The shares eligible for purchase were those of firms with BBB quality or above (i.e. firms able to pay back debt but whose ability to do so may deteriorate over time).[21]

This new bank capital law originally required all banks to limit the value of banks' shareholding to the level of their own capital by 2004, but the deadline was extended to 2006 because many of the banks could not make the 2004 deadline.[22]

Another factor which forced Japanese banks to reduce their shareholding was the new rule, discussed earlier, that states that the value of the financial securities (and also golf club memberships) that banks and firms own and their unrealized capital losses and gains must be reported at market value under most circumstances. Since continuing to hold poorly valued stocks in other firms did not help banks' financial reports under such market value-based reporting requirements, Japanese banks sold significant parts of their stock holdings.

To sum up, the massive purchases by the BoJ and the BSPC of the shares held by Japanese banks and the banks' own sale of their shares for the reasons given above, reduced the amounts of the shares they held rapidly, beginning in 1998, as shown in Table 7.1.

Keiretsu, shareholding among firms and holding companies

One characteristic of the industrial organization of Japanese firms is their tendency to use relatively small, but not negligible, amounts of equity ownership as a means of maintaining their interfirm (keiretsu) relationships, including business relationships.[23] In this section we discuss the recent developments in keiretsu relationships and the possible relationships of recently legalized holding companies to such relationships.

Bank-based horizontal keiretsu groups

Until the mid 1990s, the six horizontal keiretsu groups centered around the six major banks (Mitsui, Mitsubishi, Sumitomo, Daiichi-Kangin, Sanwa and Fuji Banks) were particularly prominent because of their large member firms representing most of the Japanese industries.[24] But the collective decision processes underlying their behavior as an industrial group were never transparent to the public and the groups themselves never took time to explain their decision processes. The economic effects, particularly the economic gains to the member firms due to their group memberships, have not been empirically demonstrated. These bank-based horizontal keiretsu group relationships have undoubtedly been going through significant reorganizations since the early 1990s for the following reasons.

First, the six banks had merged into three major bank groups by the early 2000s. These three bank groups are: the merged group of the Bank of Tokyo-Mitsubishi (resulting from the merger of the Mitsubishi Bank and the Bank of Tokyo) and the UFJ Bank (which resulted from the merger of the Sanwa and Tokai Banks); the merged group of the Mitsui and Sumitomo Banks; and the merged group of the Daiichi-Kangyo Bank, the Fuji Bank and the Industrial Bank of Japan. These three newly created bank groups are now represented by their respective (pure) holding companies.

At this time the relationships of these bank holding companies to the former six bank-based horizontal keiretsu groups is unclear.

Second, following the liberalization of access to the corporate bond markets in Japan in the 1990s, together with the existing access to certain global capital markets, many qualified and well-performing Japanese firms have chosen to depend more on outside capital markets for financing. As a result, the better firms significantly reduced their dependence on bank loans. At the same time, as stated above, the banks sold off many of the shares they held in these well-performing firms in order to raise cash and satisfy their capital requirements (see, for example, Rajan, 1997). The result is much-reduced equity ownership and bank debt-based relationships between the banks and their well-performing client firms.[25] In other words, the traditional main bank relationship (strong equity and bank loan-based relationships between the main bank in the center and member firms), which used to connect banks tightly to their client firms, whether inside or outside the bank's horizontal keiretsu group, has disintegrated significantly in the 1990s and 2000s (see, for example, Aoki, 1994; Sheard, 1994). It is also important to emphasize that poorly performing Japanese firms have not had any opportunity to raise outside capital on their own (for example, secured or unsecured corporate bonds), in part because Japanese bond markets are not yet able to deal with (or rank) high-risk bonds (such as junk bonds). Recent empirical studies (see, for example, Miyajima and Kuroki, 2007) suggest that the types of close relationships Japanese banks used to have with their client firms involving bank loans and equity ownership until the 1980s now tend to be, to a large extent, limited to Japanese firms with poor performance.

Following the reorganizations of Japanese major banks discussed above, we have not yet seen an equilibrium for the new patterns of financing for Japanese firms. Therefore, it is not clear what types of bank-based keiretsu groups will emerge once the current transitory circumstances resulting from the banks' non-performing loans, new corporate governance reform measures, and other factors, have been settled.

Production-based vertical keiretsu groups

Another main type of shareholding in Japan is shareholding among non-financial industrial firms. The typical objectives of such shareholding are to control supplier firms in vertical production relationships (called vertical or capital keiretsu) and also to exert influence on the business decisions of other firms. While it is not unusual for large Japanese manufacturers to own more than 50 percent of the outstanding shares of their key subsidiaries (often their former production divisions), particularly right after the spin-off of such divisions as new listed subsidiaries, it is also not unusual for large Japanese assembly firms (such as Toyota) to own relatively small amounts of the outstanding shares (for example, 20–30 percent) of many of their suppliers (see Table 7.2). Such assembly firms are able to exert much influence (on their suppliers' production decisions, for example) on an ongoing basis, in such strategic areas as quality control, just-in-time production systems and new product development.

Table 7.2 First-tier auto suppliers in the Toyota production keiretsu

Supplier company name	*Toyota's ownership share (%)*	*Is Toyota the largest shareholder?*	*Market value (in ¥ billion)*
Toyota Auto Body	50.0	Yes	242
Kanto Auto Works	50.0	Yes	89
Toyoda Gosei	42.7	Yes	248
Aisan Industry	34.7	Yes	59
Tokai Rica	27.0	Yes	147
Koyo Seiko	24.0	Yes	308
Toyoda Koki	23.6	Yes	140
Toyota Industries	23.5	Yes	955
Denso	23.2	Yes	2184
Aisin Seiki	22.2	Yes	713
Koito Manufacturing	20.0	Yes	188
Shiroki	16.9	No (Toyota is the second largest shareholder)	25
Akebono Brake	13.8	Yes	60
Futaba Industrial Co.	12.2	Yes	145
KYB (Kayaba)	8.8	Yes	81
Ichikoh (Ichimitsu) Industries	6.1	No (Toyota is the second largest shareholder)	26
Owari Precise Products	5.5	No (Toyota is the third largest shareholder)	4
T.Rad (Toyo Radiator)	4.9	Yes	36

Note: figures as at May 2005.

It is generally thought that production effectiveness of such a vertical keiretsu system relies not only on the business relationships such as customer–seller relationships between the assembler (customer) and their suppliers (sellers), but also the presence of the assembler firm's ownership in the suppliers. It is also not unusual for the assembly firm to send personnel as directors of their supplier firms' boards. In other words, equity ownership in these vertical relationships matters. The role of such equity ownership, however, has not been empirically well understood.

Right after its takeover in 1999 of Nissan Motor which was facing bankruptcy in Japan, Renault sent in Carlos Ghosn as Nissan's CEO. In his publicly announced plan to revive Nissan, Ghosn argued for the efficient and more profitable use of Nissan's assets and the selling off of those assets not generating enough returns. In particular, he declared his intention to sell most of the shares Nissan then owned in their suppliers (except for four suppliers' shares), arguing that this type of shareholding is mostly a drag on Nissan's performance and that Nissan can do well with its supplier relationships without resorting to such shareholding. Although he did not exactly rid Nissan of its supplier shareholding entirely, Nissan nevertheless sold off a large part of the shares it had in its suppliers. Table 7.3 shows some of the changes in Nissan's ownership in its former suppliers that took place between March 2001 and March 2002.

In the process of reviving Nissan, Ghosn reduced the number of suppliers by about 50 percent and brought competitive bidding into their parts procurement processes. Nevertheless, he subsequently conceded that supplier relations are important. In recent months Nissan has increased equity ownership in certain suppliers with the specific purpose of tightening up its supplier keiretsu. The impact of the keiretsu assembly firms like Toyota, Nissan and Honda on their keiretsu supplier firms' corporate governance is significant in many ways. But since these keiretsu supplier firms are not generally majority owned by their assembly firms, the assembly firms' influence on their suppliers' corporate governance and management decisions is complex, being limited and balanced against other factors such as the suppliers' competitiveness and ability to acquire customers other than their owner assembly firms.

Nevertheless, the assembly firm in a well-functioning vertical keiretsu can produce its final products at lower cost than a large, vertically integrated firm of corresponding size. The possible reasons for this are as follows. The group suppliers are usually much smaller than the assembly firm and hence pay lower wages. Furthermore, independently run supplier firms cause less agency cost than the parts divisions of a large, integrated assembly firm. On the other hand, the assembly firm operating a poorly coordinated supplier keiretsu cannot be an efficient producer of the final product. In order to run an efficient vertical keiretsu group the assembly firm must pour a substantial amount of effort into the management of its suppliers. Such know-how is a valuable managerial asset.

It is possible that, when Ghosn took over as Nissan's CEO, the Nissan keiretsu was in serious disarray and many of the Nissan keiretsu supplier firms were not contributing to the efficient production of Nissan vehicles.

Table 7.3 Nissan's suppliers who are owned at least 20 percent by Nissan

Supplier name	*Nissan's ownership (March 2001)*	*Nissan's ownership (March 2002)*
Tennex	56.7%	0%. Acquired by Mahle GmbH; became "Mahle Tennex," now fully owned by Mahle GmbH
Nissan Body	42.7%	42.6%
Aichi Machine Industry	41.4%	41.4%
Kiriu	36.7%	0%. MBO by Unison Capital. Now fully owned by Sumitomo Corp.
Calsonic Kansei	32.0%	32.0%. Now increased to 41.7%
Fuji Univance	31.1%	10.32%. Shares sold to I.S. Precision Machinery and Daido Steel. Will merge with I.S. Precision in 2005
Unipres	30.3%	14.89%. Shares sold to Nippon Steel and Mitsui Bussan
Ohi Manufacturer Co.	28.8%	0%. Became Mitsui Kinzoku's fully owned subsidiary; now merged into Mitsui Kinzoku
Hitachi Unisia Automotive	25.3%	0%. Now merged into Hitachi, Ltd.
Tsubakimoto Foaming Ind.	24.8%	24.8%
Nikki	23.8%	0%. Hitachi owns 7.39%.
Exedy	23.4%	0%. Shares sold to Aisin Seiki Companies
Jideco (Jidosha Denki Kogyo)	22.7%	0%. Now owned fully by Mtsuba
Nissan Diesel	22.5%	22.5%
Tochigi Fuji Sangyo	20.5%	0%. Now becoming fully owned by G.K.N. Automotive (Spain)
Kinugawa Rubber	20.3%	20.3%

Source: compiled by the author based on information published in the Japanese business press.

Ghosn may have brought the Nissan keiretsu back to where it should be in terms of overall efficiency.

Another example of interest is the role of the keiretsu suppliers for the Mitsubishi Motors Corporation (MMC). Facing severe financial distress, MMC was taken over by Daimler-Chrysler in 2000. Daimler-Chrysler dissolved MMC's supplier keiretsu group in 2002 (MMC Kashiwa kai)

which had 344 member firms. After MMC continued to suffer from poor performance and MMC's many scandals became public, Daimler-Chrysler decided to give up its control of MMC in April 2004 and sold its MMC shares to the Mitsubishi horizontal keiretsu group companies such as the Bank of Tokyo-Mitsubishi, the Mitsubishi Corporation and the Mitsubishi Heavy Industries. MMC's new management continued to have problems with its production operations. In early 2005, MMC announced that it would revive its supplier keiretsu group consisting of over 100 companies in order to solve the problems of quality control and cost reduction. Although Toyota, Japan's leading auto maker, has continued to strengthen its vertical keiretsu group throughout the 1990s and 2000s, Nissan and MMC have not. But both Nissan and MMC at this time appear to be focusing on their vertical keiretsu production groupings for improving their operational efficiency.

Implications of the legalizing of holding companies

Holding companies existed in Japan until the end of World War II. Typical examples of pre-war holding companies include Mitsui and Mitsubishi holding companies owned by the Mitsui and Mitsubishi zaibatsu[26] families. Following Japan's defeat in World War II, the Allied forces banned zaibatsu and holding companies in the newly instituted Anti-Monopoly (Anti-Trust) Law. This law banned pure holding companies (such as Mitsui and Mitsubishi holding companies) which exist only to control other firms owned by them. In addition, the law restricted large industrial holding firms, which own other firms for control while producing goods and services themselves, from owning excessively large amounts of equity in those industrial firms under their control. The law also prohibited banks from operating as holding companies to operate industrial firms.[27]

Since 1997, various measures to legalize holding companies have been introduced. The December 1997 revision of Japan's Anti-Monopoly Law legalized pure holding companies for industrial firms in Japan. In 1998, pure financial holding companies became legal. In 2002, industrial holding companies became legal and equity ownership restrictions for industrial holding companies were removed; and also restrictions on banks' equity ownership were relaxed and banks' owning of securities firms as subsidiaries became legal. In addition to these changes in the Anti-Monopoly Law, the Japanese government introduced various revisions in Japan's Commercial Code over time to allow firms to be able to take advantage of holding companies. These revisions include: unrestricted exchange and transfer of stocks in 1999; laws allowing firms to split operations into separate firms in 2000; and taxation based on consolidated financial statements in 2001. In addition, free reallocation and deployment of all the personnel of former companies under newly created holding companies became legal. This can in many ways override Japan's reasonably protective laws on employment of existing workers (see, for example, Nakamura, 1993), and in this sense is a major step forward for developing new company structures to maximize profit.

These revisions in Japan's Commercial Code, tax laws and other legal settings have now been incorporated into the New Company Law. These massive changes in the legal settings for company structures since the late 1990s have brought significant amounts of flexibility into Japan's industrial organization. In principle, industrial firms are free to merge and split firms' operations and workers into separate companies, while taking advantage of the liberal use of holding companies. While many of these practices are well-known in the West, they are new to Japan and have only just begun to be adopted.[28]

For example, under these new rules, Fuji Bank, Daiichi-Kangin Bank (DKB) and the Industrial Bank of Japan merged under the Mizuho Holding Company, a pure holding firm, and the Mizuho Holding Company in turn was able to reorganize the three former banks' operations and create new product and service-specific companies. Many Japanese firms began going through this type of reorganization exercise.

Keiretsu and holding companies

Keiretsu, as described above, and industrial holding companies have certain characteristics in common. For example, in a vertical keiretsu like that of Toyota, the assembly firm (Toyota) in the center owns some equity in its suppliers. Sometimes the assembly firm is the majority owner of supplier firms, but typically its equity ownership share in its keiretsu supplier firms is less than 50 percent. These supplier firms are usually listed and are not fully controlled by the assembly firm. Nevertheless, these supplier firms' management decisions are usually heavily influenced by their assembly firm's policies. In the U.S. this type of interfirm arrangement would be criticized for at least three reasons: (1) the assembly firm is usually much larger and much more powerful than its supplier firms, and hence whatever it tells its suppliers to do could be considered anti-competitive; (2) the policies that the assembly firm tries to impose on supplier firms might infringe the interests of the minority shareholders of the suppliers; and (3), on cultural grounds, American managers of such supplier firms might not tolerate the types of interference in their management decisions that many Japanese assembly firms impose on their keiretsu suppliers. In other words, Japanese-style vertical keiretsu would likely be declared illegal in the U.S. on anti-trust and shareholders' rights grounds. In fact, such keiretsu structures do not exist in the U.S.

This aspect of Japanese vertical keiretsu is different from the standard notion of industrial holding companies which typically fully own the firms under them. In this sense, the use of holding companies in Japan so far has been most prominent for reorganization of intra-firm and merged firms' existing operations. Newly created pure holding companies are found in both the financial and the industrial sectors. As of now there is no case of a vertical keiretsu group of firms that has been turned into a holding company structure.

We conclude that, unless two or more firms in a keiretsu group decide to merge, they are not likely to put themselves under a holding company's umbrella. Since keiretsu groups still exist in various forms in Japan, it is likely that they will continue to exploit production efficiency as their competitive edge and play their role in the Japanese economy. We also note that the demand for legalizing holding companies came mostly from the business sector, particularly the Nippon Keidanren, whose current thinking is clearly that holding companies can do a lot more than keiretsu in general. As we have argued, holding companies add a new degree of freedom to Japanese firms' organizational structures. It remains to be seen what, if any, impact holding companies will have on the evolution of Japanese keiretsu.

Non-corporate shareholders

A massive number of shares was made available to the Japanese stock market by Japanese banks when they sold off many of the shares they owned. Many of these shares were subsequently bought by domestic and foreign institutional shareholders (for example, mutual funds, pension funds, investment funds) as well as individual shareholders. The significant increase in the number of individual shareholders, in particular, has been accompanied by a substantial increase in the level of the shareholders' awareness of their rights as the owners of their corporations. As a result, many Japanese managers and executives now feel they need to respond seriously to their shareholders' inquiries. Initially driven largely by foreign fund managers in the mid 1990s, this trend of shareholders taking serious interest in various aspects of corporate decision making was unheard of in the past when large fractions of Japanese firms' shares were held by such stable shareholders as banks and other financial institutions, and many other corporations. In those days the general shareholders' meeting was never more than a formal ceremony taking little time, and ending without any substantive issues being discussed. Any objections raised by dissatisfied shareholders were suppressed by the *sokaiya*[29] hired by the management to keep the meeting short and quiet.

Japan's business press all noted that, in the general shareholders' meetings of many listed firms held in the latter two weeks of June 2005, many shareholders, both individual and institutional, raised issues with the firm's management about many aspects of management problems that affected their share prices. Many CEOs themselves responded to these questions. This was unthinkable just a few years ago.[30]

Foreign shareholders

We have noted above that banks and other corporate shareholders sold off many shares they used to own for the purposes of cross-shareholding (*mochiai*) and other stable shareholding relationships. These shares in turn were purchased by domestic and foreign pension and mutual funds as well as individual investors. Table 7.4 shows the change in the ownership patterns for Japanese firms' outstanding shares over time. Both domestic and foreign institutional shareholders more than doubled their shareholding in Japanese corporations between 1987 and 2002. Table 7.5 shows firms with high foreign ownership.[31] As of December 2004, the number of listed firms with more than 30 percent of foreign ownership share was 104 (the number for December 2003 was 75). Some of these firms had more than 50 percent of their outstanding shares held by foreign shareholders. In 2004, foreign investors bought US$65 billion more Japanese shares than they sold of the firms listed on the Tokyo, Osaka and Nagoya Stock Exchanges.

Table 7.4 Ownership patterns: Japanese listed firms (%)

	1987	*1992*	*1997*	*2002*
Institutional investors:				
Domestic	3.35	5.74	5.07	8.01
Foreign	3.62	4.45	6.83	6.66
Stable shareholders	30.54	30.34	27.61	16.67
Employee-owners	0.84	0.90	1.16	1.53
Sample size	977	1,079	1,164	1,369

Source: compiled by the author using figures from the Japanese Ministry of Economy, Trade and Industry (various years).

Table 7.5 Japanese firms with large foreign ownership, December 2004

	Company name	*Foreign ownership Dec 2004 (%)*	*Change from Dec 2003*	*Industry*	*Firm size (sales, total assets)*
1	Orix	57.2	6.5	Financial services	
2	Hoya	55.6	5.1	Optical	
3	Yamada Denki	55.6	5.5	Appliance retail	
4	Credit Saison	52.0	9.8	Financial services	
5	Canon	51.7	1.8	Precision	
6	Don Quijote	50.9	9.9	Retail	
7	Nitto Denko	49.5	4.0	Electrical mach.	
8	Meitech	49.5	9.7	Precision	
9	Fuji Photo Film	48.7	4.5	Chemicals	
10	Rohm	48.7	1.7	Semi-conductors	
11	Sony	48.1	8.7	Electronics/entmt.	
12	eAccess	48.1	–	Broadband serv.	
13	Kao	47.1	8.5	Chemicals	
14	SMC	45.2	7.0	Machinery	
15	Astellas	44.5	3.4	Pharmaceutical	
16	Fanuc	43.7	9.1	Numerical mach.	
17	Aderance	41.6	17.7	Wig mnfg.	
18	Tokyo Electron	41.5	4.6	Semi-con. equip.	
19	Shimachu	41.5	7.3	Furniture retail	
20	Takeda Pharmaceutical	41.0	2.9	Pharmaceutical	
21	TDK	41.0	–1.0	Electronics	
22	Secom	40.8	3.6	Security service	
23	Mitsui Sumitomo Insur.	38.8	–1.7	Insurance	
24	Osaka Stock Exchange	38.6	19.2	Stock exchange	
25	Murata Pharmaceutical	38.1	2.1	Pharmaceutical	
26	Santen Pharmaceutical	37.9	2.3	Pharmaceutical	
27	Kurita	37.9	5.4	Build. equip.	
28	Nintendo	37.9	–1.4	Entertainment	
29	Nomura Securities	37.9	–2.3	Securities	
30	Eisai	37.7	2.2	Pharmaceutical	
31	Ryohin keikaku	37.7	4.7	Retail	
32	Shimano	37.6	8.3	Precision	
33	Mitsui Fudosan	37.6	3.2	Real estate, dev.	
34	Hirose Denki	37.4	0.1	Appliance retail.	
35	Nippon Koa	37.3	6.5	Auto insurance	
36	Mandom	37.2	11.1	Consumer prod.	
37	Daito Kensetsu	37.1	2.1	Real estate, dev.	
38	Daikin	37.0	4.2	General mach.	
39	Olympus	37.0	6.9	Precision	
40	Sumitomo Trust Bank	37.0	6.1	Trust banking	
41	Pioneer	36.9	0.2	Electronics	
42	Sompo Japan	36.7	1.8	Insurance	
43	Keyence	36.6	3.9	Precision	
44	Hitachi, Ltd.	36.5	1.8	Electrical mach.	
45	Millea Holdings	36.5	4.5	Insurance	
46	UFJ	36.4	4.9	Banking	
47	Konica Minolta	36.3	0.0	Precision	
48	Advantest	36.2	7.9	Precision	
49	Mitsubishi Estate	36.2	4.2	Real estate, dev.	
50	Nittan Valve	36.1	8.2	Machinery	

Note: Foreign ownership by institutional investors (pension and mutual funds) and individual investors only.

Source: Sample: firms listed on the major Japanese stock exchanges, excluding those listed on the stock markets for emerging firms (that is, JASDAQ, TSE Mothers, OSE Hercules).

It has also been pointed out that firms with a high level of foreign ownership tend to be the firms with better (industry-adjusted) performance than others. It is possible that foreign shareholders are better able to identify undervalued firms while being vocal in demanding improvement in the firms' management. In this sense, foreign shareholders have contributed to improving the performance of the firms they own. It is also possible that they may have invested in already well-known high-performance firms with high growth prospects. As Japanese domestic shareholders are becoming more sophisticated and more vocal about firm managers' performance, it is possible that the present foreign shareholder effects may erode over time. Nevertheless, it seems clear that the increasing presence of foreign shareholders in the Japanese stock markets, particularly large pension and mutual funds from the U.S. and elsewhere, has played a significant role in modernizing the Japanese corporate governance practices in the 1990s. Those fund managers' questioning of corporate management decisions prompted many Japanese firms to pay more attention to share value maximization and better utilization of their firms' assets.

For example, foreign shareholders expressed serious objections to many of the items on the agenda to be discussed at their firms' general shareholders' meetings held in June 2005. Foreign shareholders voted negatively on more than 1,800 items at the general shareholders' meetings of Japanese listed firms. In particular they have objected strongly to management's proposals to introduce poison pills which would allow the management to expand the firm's share base in response to hostile takeovers.

The management's proposals to set up a poison pill for deluding the share base was voted negatively in more than 200 cases (more than 85 percent of all cases) at the listed firms' general shareholders' meetings. It is believed that many foreign shareholders followed the advice of the Institutional Shareholder Service (ISS) to accept or reject each of the specific agenda items proposed for approval by the management at each of the 2,000 firms listed on the Japanese stock exchanges. The ISS was commissioned by U.S. and European pension and mutual funds to make recommendations on each of the 1,830 agenda items proposed by the management of the 2,000 listed firms for approval by their shareholders.[32]

In the next section we summarize recent developments in M&A-related activities which are of particular interest to Japanese corporations in the new legal environment.

Recent developments in the market for corporate control: M&As in Japan

The Livedoor incident prompted vigorous discussions on possible government policy alternatives which would define the legal environment for M&A activities. The New Company Law, which implements changes on almost all aspects of Japan's antiquated Commercial Code, stipulates the new rules about M&As in two parts: on poison pills, which took effect in 2006; and on the provisions for facilitating M&As, which took effect in 2007. For example, in anticipating hostile takeover attempts, a firm's management is allowed to give equity warrants to shareholders in advance and to issue new shares to the holders of the warrants when a hostile bidder acquires a predetermined fraction of the firm's outstanding shares. The new law also allows management to change their corporate charters to make stricter the conditions under which the shareholders can approve of mergers at their general meetings. A major change in the New Company Law and the Commercial Code regarding the rules about M&As, which took effect in May 2007, allows triangular mergers by which foreign companies can buy Japanese firms with exchanges of their shares using their Japanese units. One of the last issues on this was that of taxation. Japanese tax rules meant that the shareholders of the acquired company must pay taxes on relevant capital gains at the time when their shares are sold in exchange for the acquirer's shares. The Japanese Ministry of Finance's new decision in April 2007 now allows the deferral of taxes from such capital gains until the acquired company's shareholders sell the shares of the acquired company. We expect to see an increase in foreign companies taking over Japanese companies as a result of this new legal change.

Another change in the law regarding M&As in Japan will likely be implemented by Japan's Fair Trade Commission (FTC). The FTC introduced a new rule, yet to be passed by the parliament, that would allow the FTC to use global, rather than domestic, market shares and state of competition as a basis of approving proposed mergers.[33] Once passed, we expect this to facilitate further large-scale mergers involving Japanese corporations.

Another related legal revision made in response to the Livedoor incident is the more active enforcement of the takeover bid (TOB) clause. Japan's parliament passed the revised Securities Exchange Law, and one of the new provisions of the revised law states that the purchaser of more than one-third of a listed firm's outstanding shares from the existing large shareholders outside the stock exchange system must use the TOB mechanism all the time. Livedoor used a loophole of the previous law which required TOBs only for such purchases of outstanding shares during the hours of operation of the open market of the Japanese stock exchange system. Once the Tokyo Stock Exchange (TSE) closes, the open market closes, but the TSE system continues to operate off-hours, and transactions using the TSE system during off-hours are registered as market transactions, which did not violate the previous law on TOBs. The new provision on TOBs of the Securities Exchange Law was enacted in July 2005 and closed the loophole Livedoor used in its hostile takeover attempt for the Nippon Broadcasting System.[34]

In response to the increased possibility of hostile takeovers many firms have expressed interest in implementing poison pills. The Japanese government (METI and the Ministry of Justice) responded to this by setting guidelines by which poison pills may be justified.

Poison pills

The types of poison pills which caused the shareholders' revolts discussed above are those that are well known in the U.S. However, the following anti-takeover devices have special implications for Japanese firms and deserve attention.

First, promoting cross-shareholding and other stable shareholding would reduce the number of outstanding shares the potential hostile takeover bidders could buy up[35] and hence would work as a poison pill. This method has been historically the cornerstone of Japanese firms' anti-takeover mechanisms since the 1960s and its effectiveness has been unquestionable. While this will continue to be potentially effective in Japanese corporate governance, the actual extent of stable shareholding including cross-shareholding, as we discussed above (Table 7.1), declined significantly during the 1990s. For this reason, despite its popularity among many Japanese firms, prospects for its success are unclear.

Another anti-takeover method, delisting the shares of the subsidiaries which are owned by a parent firm, is a standard method in the U.S. This would eliminate the possibility that the parent firm gets greenmail[36] from the firms buying up the outstanding shares of their listed subsidiary firms. We explain here that Japanese firms, unlike U.S. firms, may suffer certain economic efficiency loss from instituting this poison pill. This is likely to occur in Japan because, unlike in the U.S., many Japanese firms list their subsidiary firms' shares in stock exchanges while owning only a block of shares (sometimes more than 50 percent, but not always so) in these subsidiaries. Recall that many production (vertical) keiretsu groups have this type of shareholding pattern. For example, Table 7.2 shows that

Toyota Motors owns less than 50 percent of most of its first-tier Toyota group suppliers.[37] Toyota is known to be seriously concerned about the possible hostile takeover of any one of these suppliers.

Using this poison pill implies reorganizing these partially owned subsidiaries as fully owned subsidiaries. This would eliminate the anti-takeover/greenmailing possibilities via these subsidiary firms. However, a potentially serious management problem associated with this method is the loss of production efficiency resulting from the parent firm fully consolidating its supplier divisions. To the extent that Japanese supplier keiretsu is known to have its own economic merit, large assembly firms which rely on such keiretsu efficiency might be reluctant to consolidate their subsidiaries. For example, such full consolidation might result in higher wages and the loss of production efficiency (for example, due to the agency costs associated with large firms and the lack of plant-level incentives) at the subsidiary's plant operations.[38] But the present vertical keiretsu system, as argued above, is inevitably susceptible to hostile takeover attempts and greenmailing.

A well-known example is the case of T. Boone Pickens, a corporate raider, who, despite being the largest single stockholder of a Japanese auto supplier, the Koito Manufacturing, in 1990 was denied a seat on its board of directors. Koito is a member of the Toyota keiretsu (Table 7.2), and Toyota, Koito's second largest shareholder, had three seats. The Koito management was able to deny Pickens a directorship because Koito's stable shareholders, including Toyota, other group firms and financial institutions, held more than 70 percent of Koito's outstanding shares. Pickens complained to the U.S. Justice Department that "If the Japanese want to operate in this country, they should do so only in complete compliance with all of our laws. If they refuse, then they should face the same civil and criminal penalties as other antitrust violators" (quoted in Common Cause, 1992). Pickens pulled out of Koito in 1991. It is well known that Toyota has been strengthening its keiretsu relationships with its suppliers, including heavily guarded stable shareholding patterns. Such patterns are not easy to maintain for many other Japanese manufacturers who also depend on their traditional keiretsu suppliers. For them, it may only be a matter of time before some of their suppliers experience successful hostile takeovers.

Implementing poison pills

Recent surveys by Nikkei in December 2005 and by Nomura Securities in May 2006 found that the fraction of Japanese firms which have poison pills and other anti-takeover devices installed is relatively small (6.7

percent for firms with fewer than 1,000 employees vs. 7.0 percent for firms with at least 1,000 employees). For large firms with a market value greater than ¥100 billion, this fraction is 8.5 percent.[39] Of the anti-takeover devices used, poison pills appear to be the most popular. The triggering point at which the poison pill kicks in tends to be 20 percent of ownership for many industrial companies (for example, Matsushita Electric Industries), but recently Eisai Pharmaceutical chose 15 percent, a more popular level in the U.S. and Europe.

Given the possibility that these poison pills potentially benefit the existing management of the firm proposing them, many objections have been raised regarding plans to implementing them. For example, Steel Partners, the largest shareholders of Sapporo Beer and Aderans (a producer of wigs) has objected to both companies' management decisions to introduce poison pills. Sapporo Beer, however, passed its resolution to implement poison pills at its general shareholders' meeting on March 29, 2007. At the time of writing, Aderans was yet to hold its general shareholders' meeting. We expect to see Japanese and foreign shareholders' involvement in corporations' management decisions such as the ones discussed above to continue. However, it remains to be seen how successful their efforts will be in terms of improving the performance of the firms.[40]

A perspective on M&As in Japan

In Japan until the mid 1990s, up to 70 percent of the outstanding shares of most listed firms were owned by "friendly" shareholders: banks, other financial corporations and other firms. Hence it was impossible to gain support for a hostile takeover.[41] Consequently, virtually all large-scale mergers that took place in Japan until the 1980s were friendly mergers involving domestic companies. They did not involve major changes in the management personnel. In some exceptional cases foreign firms were able to acquire some or the entire ownership of existing Japanese firms in friendly negotiations. In particular, foreign firms were able to take over some of the failing firms which no Japanese firms would want to acquire.

For example, Mazda Motor experienced such takeovers twice (25 percent by Ford in 1979, which was increased to the controlling ownership level of 33.4 percent in 1996). Two previously discussed examples are: Nissan Motor, facing bankruptcy in 1999, was taken over by Renault (ownership 36.8 percent, which was increased to 44.4 percent in 2001); and Mitsubishi Motor Corporation, whose control was acquired by Daimler-Chrysler in 1999 (ownership 37 percent), though this relationship was entirely abandoned by Daimler-Chrysler and all of MMC's shares abandoned by Daimler-Chrysler were purchased by Mitsubishi keiretsu companies.

As the MMC example shows, Japan's keiretsu groups of various types are heavily involved in M&As. While less than 20 percent of Japan's M&As involved intra-keiretsu group firms until 1992, the proportion of intra-group M&As has increased rapidly since then. Since 1996, intra-group M&As accounted for more than half of all Japan's M&As. These M&As are between group firms, and, by definition, no group M&As are hostile. It is of interest to compare the implications for economic efficiency between intra-group and non-intra-group M&As (see, for example, Bradley et al., 1988).

We also note that, despite a number of well-publicized foreign takeovers of failing Japanese firms in recent years, the overwhelming majority (more than 80 percent) of M&As of Japanese firms are between Japanese firms. Japanese firms' acquisitions of foreign firms constitutes about 15 percent of all M&As, while the remaining 5 percent involve foreign firms acquiring Japanese firms. The numbers of M&As using takeover bids in 2005 and 2006 were around 50 and 60, respectively.[42] The use of TOBs was rare in Japan until 1997, but then began to increase gradually. Another trend in the recent M&As is the involvement of investment funds (mostly of U.S. and European origin) as acquirers of Japanese firms. Acquisitions by these investment funds were almost non-existent until 1998 but have become very visible in the last few years. They are estimated to be involved in about 300–400 M&As annually in Japan.

Globally, the size of Japan's M&A market is quite small by comparison. For example, the total amount involved in global M&As 2004 was US$1,500 billion, of which Japan's share was only 4.4 percent (US$65 billion).[43] Most of these M&As took place in the U.S. and Europe. In this sense the market for corporate control in Japan is not yet as fully developed as that in the U.S. But Japan's current attempts to deregulate all areas of M&A activities have had a positive impact on expanding the market, as the above figures suggest.

M&As, particularly those involving foreign firms, can potentially have significant impacts on the real economy in the form of higher productivity. Murakami and Fukao (2006) report that M&As where foreign firms purchase domestic firms tend to increase the productivity of the acquired firm (primarily because these M&As are typically accompanied with some reductions (for example, layoffs) in employment). On the other hand, M&As between two domestic Japanese firms tend to be characterized as stronger firms absorbing weaker and struggling firms, resulting in somewhat lower productivity increase, if at all, for the acquiring firm.

The amounts of Japan's inward foreign direct investment (FDI) continue to be quite small compared to the amounts of Japan's outward FDI. But foreign firms often bring in new technology and management methods, for example, which contribute to increasing Japanese productivity. For this reason we would expect that deregulation of M&As involving foreign firms will result in visible increases in Japan's productivity.

The state of corporate governance

The prolonged recession, the massive non-performing loan problems of banks, globalizing trends in business operations, and other factors, have faced Japanese corporations since the burst of the bubble in the 1990s. The financially weakened Japanese banks and industrial firms have sold off many of the shares they held in other firms. In this process Japanese banks seemed, in particular, to have reduced their capacity to influence firms' corporate governance. Strong industrial firms are now able to depend more than ever on debt capital directly raised in public capital markets. Individual and institutional shareholders, many of whom are foreign, have acquired the shares Japanese banks and firms used to hold as stable shareholders. The reduced presence of stable shareholders and the presence of substantially increased and vocal foreign and domestic shareholders are forcing many Japanese corporations to pay more attention to their corporate governance. This became particularly evident in the late 1990s and the 2000s.

In response to public opinion that the bank-based Japanese corporate governance practices prevailing in the 1980s reduced the competitiveness of Japanese industrial firms and the Japanese economy in general, the Japanese government promptly introduced a series of new reform measures in the 1990s and 2000s for revising the laws underlying Japanese corporate governance practices. These new measures emphasize information disclosure and transparency of corporate decisions, among other things, so that Japanese shares become more attractive to increasing numbers of individual shareholders in Japan. These measures are, to a large extent, based on the Anglo-American practices of corporate governance. One implication of this is litigation against corporations and their directors by their shareholders. Such litigation has been common in the U.S. but is only beginning to be more fully appreciated by shareholders for protecting their rights as shareholders.[44]

In part because of zero-interest policy many individuals have been shifting their savings from bank deposits to stocks in large numbers in the last ten years. Some of them have brought class action suits against corporations in which they hold shares, with some success. The reasons for these legal suits include lack of information disclosure, misrepresentation of information, illegal business practices and questionable use of corporate funds. For example, Kabunushi (Shareholders) Ombudsman, a Japanese not-for-profit organization owned by individual shareholders, brought class action suits against the following corporations: Kumagaigumi Construction (for inappropriate political contributions, being appealed, May 2006); and Mitsubishi Heavy Industries and six other companies for so-called "*dango*," bid-rigging on public works projects (bridge construction, July 2005). Another class action suit by shareholders in progress is that against Livedoor Corporation for misrepresentation of information. While the likelihood of such legal actions by shareholders is still limited in Japan, partly because punitive damage is not available for many types of civil dispute in Japan, the recent public awareness in corporate governance and corporate social responsibility means that such legal actions will continue to increase.

A noteworthy aspect of Japan's corporate governance reform measures is that, unlike U.S. practices, Japanese corporations are given a choice, in some essential aspects of their corporate governance mechanisms, between the U.S. and the Japanese systems. Another noteworthy aspect is that, while holding companies are now legal, the Anti-Monopoly Law was not changed in other essential areas of corporate governance; that is, banks' shareholding in other firms and also shareholding among industrial firms, particularly in vertical keiretsu formats. Thus, legalization of holding companies has expanded the set of possible corporate structures for Japanese firms.

At this time it seems premature to predict what types of corporate governance practices will prevail in Japan. Gilson and Milhaupt (2004), for example, find that, as of March 2003, no firm which is a member of a bank-centered horizontal keiretsu group had adopted the executive committee system of governance. On the other hand, Nomura financial holding company and its 13 privately held subsidiaries, as well as Hitachi Ltd. and 21 of its affiliates, had adopted the executive committee system. They also note that many of the adopting firms are in the electronics industry and are largely characterized as being free of keiretsu influence and having more than average foreign ownership.

The executive committee system would require at least two outside board members. One-third to two-thirds of the adopting firms' board members are outside members. In contrast, only one-quarter of the firms listed on the Tokyo Stock Exchange have outside board members, and outside members constitute less than 20 percent of all board members of the listed firms. The definition of "outside" board member is also questionable since many of these outside members are sent from the firms' affiliated firms (such as parent firms). For example, all outside members of the Hitachi affiliated firms come from Hitachi Ltd. This may reflect the strategic necessity on the part of the parent firm to make sure that the production activities of both the parent and affiliated firms are coordinated. Outside members of affiliated firms may be delegated such tasks of production coordination.[45, 46]

We should also point out that some of the indeterminacy we have found with respect to possible future configurations of Japan's corporate governance mechanisms is due to the fact that the New Company Law gives Japanese corporations little guidance on the design of corporate governance practices. This is in part a consequence of the frequent revisions of the Commercial Code by the Japanese government in recent years. (In order to prop up Japanese firms' performance, the Japanese government has revised Japan's Commercial Code 13 times since 1990, sometimes three times within a year.)[47] Many characterize this process a transition Japan is going through in company laws from the continental civil law (Japanese commercial code) based approach to the Anglo-American common law (new Japanese company law) approach. If this turns out to be the case, it will be essential that Japanese stock exchanges and the associated securities exchange laws will play a much stronger role of governance in overseeing securities transactions as is done, for example, by the SEC and stock exchanges in the U.S.

Conclusion

There are few who would predict a revival in dominance of the old-style bank-based corporate governance system. Japan has already adopted many market-based Anglo-American-style corporate governance practices, albeit in somewhat modified ways. What type of role Japanese banks will play in corporate governance once their financial problems have been cleared is of interest.[48, 49] Good Japanese firms have many choices in designing their corporate governance system based on the new laws, new financing realities, more vocal shareholders, the new employment practices and the production keiretsu relationships which can improve their efficiency. But firms whose performance is poor continue to face rather limited choice in financing, management and corporate governance practices and will most likely rely on bank financing.

We have noted that the recent changes in the laws and business practices related to corporate governance will be significant in many ways once they become fully implemented. These changes have legitimized the presence of institutional speculators in the market for corporate control in the eyes of the public, the government and the business communities. To the public, the primary objective of Takahumi Horie and Yoshiaki Murakami, the founders of Livedoor and the Murakami Fund, respectively, appeared to be to buy the shares of undervalued firms and sell them for profit in the short run. In this process of profit making both Murakami and Horie were heavily involved in the corporate governance issues of the companies whose value they tried to increase. In this regard their behavior seems little different from that of the foreign institutional investors who have been active in corporate governance of many Japanese firms as large shareholders.

Facing the possibility of potential hostile takeovers, the management of many listed firms has expressed interest in implementing U.S.-style poison pills and other anti-takeover devices. One additional mechanism many Japanese firms are proposing as an anti-takeover device is strengthening their keiretsu, cross-shareholding and other equity-based interfirm relationships.[50]

Ironically, this process of keiretsu formation as an anti-takeover device resembles very much that found in Japan in the early 1950s. Following the zaibatsu dissolution by the Allied forces at the end of World War II, the shares of all former zaibatsu firms were dumped in large quantities in the stock market. Stock prices collapsed, and many of these firms with valuable assets such as land and production and management skill became ideal targets for post-World War II Japanese greenmailers. These greenmailers were successful in making huge profits and also in taking control of some companies. In response to their experience of being exposed to many hostile takeover attempts which turned out to be highly costly, former zaibatsu firms created their bank-based keiretsu to lock in their control shares within their group of companies. This took place over a few years following the end of the Allied occupation of Japan in 1952.[51]

Unlike the 1950s, however, Japanese banks may no longer be willing or able to become influential players in the corporate governance of Japanese firms. It may therefore be possible that forms of strengthened keiretsu groupings, which some Japanese firms clearly want to achieve, will emerge as an anti-takeover device to protect incumbent management from hostile takeovers.[52] We conclude that, in order for Japan to continue competing in a globalizing world, it has no choice but to continue working towards making the Japanese corporate governance system more closely resemble that of the market-based Anglo-American system, with greater transparency in accounting, increased disclosure, and greater reliance on outside directors.

Notes

1. Even though some aspects of the reform (that is, capital markets liberalization) began in the 1980s, most of the essential parts of the reform measures were taken up by the Japanese government after the burst of the bubble.
2. Another important reform undertaken by the Koizumi government was the privatization of Japan Post, a government corporation providing a postal service, financial and other services to the public. Japan Post has extraordinarily large amounts of cash reserves held in the savings accounts of client households. (As of 2004, of the total Japanese personal financial assets of US$13 trillion, US$2 trillion is in postal savings accounts, and US$3.3 trillion of personal savings and insurance business go to various postal accounts annually.) Cash from this source has been invested in numerous public projects with little or negative returns by many government agencies and is often the source of corruption and political patronage. Japanese banks also want to be able to tap into these accounts currently held by Japan Post, arguing that the cash reserve held by Japan Post is a source of economic inefficiency and should be invested by the private sector. Despite significant opposition from the political and bureaucratic sectors, the lower house of the Japanese parliament passed the government's bill for the privatization of Japan Post in early July 2005. After the defeat of the bill in the upper house, Koizumi had a surprise general election of the lower house of the parliament seeking approval of the bill from Japanese voters. After an overwhelming victory of Koizumi's Liberal Democratic Party in the election, Koizumi sent the same bill back to both houses of the parliament. The bill easily passed this time and the privatization of Japan Post began.
3. See, for example, Morck and Nakamura (2001), Nakamura (2006).
4. Throughout the 1990s many banks and industrial firms were suffering, respectively, from massive bad loans and excess capacity. Most of the industrial firms' excess capacity was financed by bank loans.
5. Many business researchers raised concern, however, that consolidation of the financial statements of a parent firm and related firms under its control masks subsidiary-specific information that used to be available to investors. For example, listed subsidiary firms used to be required to report their financial statements on their own (stand-alone) operations. Such information is no longer available, even though firms may still choose to disclose certain information; for example, on their operation and performance by geographic area and line of business. This type of problem is more serious for Japanese than Western firms, because many Japanese firms are connected to their keiretsu firms in a complex manner. Parent firms have some flexibility in

deciding which of their related firms are to be financially consolidated. New Japanese laws require parent firms to use their control status and equity ownership to decide how they consolidate their related firms.

6. Japanese banks' shareholding of other firms was at its height in the late 1980s. They owned a large number of shares in industrial firms (up to 16 percent of all listed firms' outstanding shares) for a variety of control and business purposes. In most cases the banks paid little attention to the value of the shares they owned. Their primary interest was to secure their income from their loans to the firms whose shares they owned. For this purpose, owning large chunks of shares in the firms to which they were creditors worked very well (see, for example, Morck and Nakamura, 1999). Following the burst of the bubble, Japanese banks faced the sluggish Japanese economy and the reality of massive non-performing loans in the 1990s. The general consensus was formed that the traditional Japanese corporate governance practices were to blame. The Japanese government reacted promptly and introduced new measures to reform all aspects of the corporate governance behaviors of Japanese firms and banks. These legal measures rewrote many parts of Japan's Commercial Code in the areas of company and bank laws, as well as other related laws which govern corporate behavior. One such measure introduced forces Japanese banks to limit their holding of other firms' shares to the level of their own capital. This law was introduced to insulate Japanese banks from being hit excessively by stock market fluctuations. (It should be noted, however, that, unlike U.S. banks, Japanese banks are still allowed by Japan's Anti-Monopoly Law to own up to 5 percent of any firm's outstanding shares for control purposes.) Since all Japanese banks' shareholding exceeded their capital level by a big margin in the early 1990s, they all sold many of the shares they held, destroying many of their stable shareholding practices with their client firms. Such share selling was also done in part to raise cash to cope with their massive and steadily increasing non-performing loans. By the early 2000s, Japanese banks owned less than 6 percent of the outstanding shares of Japan's listed firms. This has significantly reduced the role of Japanese banks' in the governance of Japanese corporations.
7. Unlike the Securities and Exchange Commission (SEC) in the U.S., the Tokyo Stock Exchange (TSE) has no disclosure requirement on the annual compensation (salaries and benefits) its listed firms' top five executives earn. Accordingly, few Japanese firms disclose their executives' compensation amounts. (Nikko Cordial Group, a securities firm, is an exception in this regard and publishes its top executives' total compensation.) Despite the important role executive compensation plays in firms' corporate governance, neither the Japanese government nor the TSE seems to be interested in instituting the disclosure requirement in this area.
8. Three major cases of improper accounts reporting are: (1) Seibu Railways for false reporting, non-protection of public and investors' interests, underreporting of the extent of stock ownership by large shareholders (a practice which lasted for more than 40 years); (2) Kanebo for false reporting, overstating profits, and concealing liabilities exceeding assets; and (3) Nikko Securities for false reporting and overstating profits. The stocks of Seibu Railways, Kanebo, and Nikko Securities were placed on the Tokyo Stock Exchange's supervision post, respectively, on October 13, 2004, October 28, 2008, and December 18,

2006. Subsequently, Seibu Railways was delisted on December 17, 2004, and Kanebo on June 13, 2005, but Nikko was not delisted (*Nikkei*, February 24, 2007).

9. After these government and private sector measures were introduced to increase activities in the market for corporate control, the number of M&As in Japan increased substantially, as discussed later.
10. During the corporate governance reform negotiations in the mid 1990s, the Japanese government promptly accepted industrial firms' argument that reorganizing their groups of divisions and firms under a holding company umbrella would allow these firms to improve their financial performance (due to consolidation of money-losing and money-making subsidiaries' financial statements).
11. A multi-division firm may issue a tracking stock which reflects only the value of a particular division or a particular subsidiary. Tracking stock shareholders have the same voting rights as the parent firm's common shareholders. In comparison, shareholders of a listed subsidiary firm have voting rights for the subsidiary but not for its parent firm. Also, the parent firm continues fully to own the particular division or subsidiary for which tracking stock shares are issued. On the other hand, the parent firm's ownership shares in its subsidiary firms decline when the subsidiaries are listed. In the U.S., General Motors was the first to issue tracking stock, to be followed by USX's tracking stock on USX Marathon, AT&T's tracking stock on wireless lines of business, and others. Conglomerate firms which tend to suffer from conglomerate discounts may find merit in such tracking stock. Nevertheless, only a limited number of firms have used tracking stock so far. In Japan, Sony issued tracking stock in 2001 on its subsidiary firm, Sony Communication Network (SCN). SCN's tracking stock was then listed in the first section of the Tokyo Stock Exchange. However, Sony terminated this tracking stock in December 2005 when SCN went public on the Tokyo Stock Exchange Mothers Section. Sony is the only Japanese company which has issued tracking stock so far.
12. "Poison pill" is a term referring to a business strategy designed to increase the likelihood of negative results over positive ones for a party that attempts a hostile takeover. As discussed below, the recent demise of Livedoor Corporation and its founder Takahumi Horie has not diminished the impact on Japan's corporate governance practices that Livedoor caused when it tried to take over NBS.
13. In May 2005 the Japanese government (Ministry of Economy, Trade, and Industry (METI) and the Ministry of Justice) did announce the guidelines for corporations attempting to introduce poison pills. These guidelines delineate the conditions under which poison pills may be introduced either by firms' general stockholders' meetings or by firms' boards of directors. These guidelines will be used together with the revised Company Law in the Commercial Code which took effect in June 2005.
14. This issue is discussed further in the fifth section of this chapter.
15. In order to enhance securities exchange transparency, the Securities and Exchange Surveillance Commission (SESC), a government agency, and the Japan Securities Dealers Association (JSDA), a voluntary industry group, both have formal mechanisms for policing exchange activities. Both the SESC and the JSDA report the number of abnormal activities which have violated the

securities exchange guidelines in areas such as securities pricing and insider trading clauses (see SESC, 2003). The effectiveness of the SESC's monitoring ability has been seriously questioned. One reason for its lack of effectiveness is that the agency is underfunded and understaffed, with only 217 specialists as of 2003. In comparison, the U.S. SEC has about 3,100 professional staff.

16. The limit was 10 percent until 1987, when it was reduced to 5 percent. Banks' possible conflicts of interest in this dual role are thought to cause economic inefficiency (Morck, Nakamura and Shivdasani, 2000).
17. The most prominent examples of cross-shareholding are found in companies belonging to the so-called six bank-based horizontal keiretsu groups. These keiretsu will be discussed in detail in the next section.
18. See, for example, Fruin (1983), Miyajima (2004) and Morck and Nakamura (2005) for the history of corporate governance in Japan. Miyajima and Kuroki (2005) also analyze the recent trend in cross-shareholding in Japan.
19. In 1988, the Basel Committee on Banking Supervision of the Bank of International Settlements (BIS) developed the Basel Accord capital ratio requirement for G10 banks which have significant international banking activities. It has been subsequently accepted by more than 40 countries. The BIS rule allows banks to include 45 percent of unrealized capital gains from the stocks they own as part of the banks' own capital. Revised BIS rules for determining the items used for calculating the capital ratio became operational in 2007. Note also that Japan allows banks with only domestic operations to continue operations so long as the banks' BIS capital ratio is above 4 percent.
20. The Nikkei Index peaked in January 1990 at around 38,922, dropped to as low as 7,804 in May 2003 and then came back to around 11,600 (July 6, 2005). The massive supply of shares dumped in the market by all Japanese banks and other financial institutions in financial distress since the late 1990s dampened the market which had never recovered from the collapse of stock prices immediately after the bubble burst in 1990. By early 2007, the Nikkei Index gained somewhat to reach the mid 17,000s.
21. As of March 2004, the market value of the shares the BoJ purchased collectively registered a net gain of about ¥646.4 billion. A significant rise in Japanese stock prices in recent years has allowed the BoJ to be able to sell back to Japanese banks, for a profit, the shares it purchased from them. For example, the BoJ reported a profit of US$4 billion from selling back the bank shares in 2005.
22. For example, as of March 1998, the total amount of other firms' shares that Japanese banks owned amounted to about ¥50 trillion (US$385 billion in 1998 dollars), which was twice as much as the banks' own capital (Fukao, 1999).
23. See, for example, Aoki (1988, 1990), Gilson and Milhapt (2004) and Gilson and Roe (1993). For example, Japanese supplier-assembler groups of firms in such equity relationships are neither independent nor fully vertically integrated. Rather, they are in between. As discussed below, the legality of equity-based partially vertically integrated relationships like those found in Japan is often questioned in the U.S. anti-trust context.
24. Each of these horizontal groups typically includes one major firm from each of the industries. For example, Honda, a successful auto firm which has always had a significant relationship with the Mitsubishi Bank, does not belong

to the Mitsubishi Bank group because the Mitsubishi Motor Corporation is the auto maker in the group. Business history is generally an important factor of the firms' membership of the groups (see, for example, Fruin, 1992). From the beginning of their operations, Toshiba and Toyota both had major relationships with the Mitsui Bank and hence are significant members of the Mitsui group. It is of interest also to note that Toyota, a bank debt-free company, continues to be a willing member of the Mitsui group. On the other hand, Hitachi Ltd. belongs to multiple bank-based groups.

25. It is not clear yet if the banks followed a systematic decision rule in choosing which other firms' shares to sell. While selling off the shares of well-performing firms takes little time and would help the banks' cash positions, from a strategic perspective the banks may prefer sell off the shares of poorly performing firms.
26. "Zaibatsu" is a Japanese term referring to family-owned industrial and financial business conglomerates that began to emerge in Japan in the late 1800s. Well-known zaibatsu families included Mitsui, Mitsubishi, Sumitomo, and Nissan, whose holding companies controlled a significant portion of Japan's key industries by the mid 1900s. The Allied forces disbanded the zaibatsu at the end of World War II. See Morck and Nakamura (2005, 2007) for further details.
27. Recall that banks have always been allowed to own, up to certain limits, equity for control purposes in other industrial firms including their client firms. These limits have changed over time. Since 1988, banks have been allowed to own up to 5 percent of equity in other industrial firms.
28. These changes were enacted promptly, while the Japanese government accepted most of the recommendations made by Nippon Keidanren (the Japan Business Federation) who argued that these changes were required for regaining Japan's global competitiveness (see also Ginsberg, 2002).
29. "*Sokaiya*" is the term for a type of corporate blackmailer in Japan (usually members of Japan's organized crime syndicates). *Sokaiya* demand huge cash payoffs in return for not publicly humiliating a company and its management by disrupting the company's annual general shareholders' meeting and revealing to the shareholders information that the company would prefer to keep under wraps. Until a decade or two ago, many companies, including well-known ones, chose to pay off the *sokaiya* rather than face such action.
30. It should also be pointed out that some firms (for example, Mitsubishi Material, Mitsubishi Real Estate, Mitsubishi Heavy Industries) are not yet willing to adopt the practice of information disclosure that more progressive and better-performing Japanese firms have already adopted. The business press argues that this is the reason why these three Mitsubishi companies continue to run closed-door general shareholders' meetings (*Sankei Shinbun*, June 30, 2005).
31. By "foreign shareholders" we mean both individual shareholders and institutional investors (for example, mutual and pension funds) who reside outside Japan.
32. Another example of foreign shareholders-driven rejection of a management's proposal occurred in late February, 2007, when Tokyo Steel Industrial Co. had its general shareholders meeting to discuss the management's proposal on the agreed-on acquisition of Tokyo Steel Industrial by Osaka Steel. Arguing

that the proposed purchase price by Osaka Steel of Tokyo Steel Industrial's shares was too low, a Japanese investment fund, Ichigo Asset Management, asked other shareholders to oppose the management plan of the acquisition by Osaka Steel. 42% of shareholders voted against the management and the proposal was rejected. (*Yomiuri Shinbun*, Tokyo, March 26, 2007.)

33. This was passed in the May 2007 session of the parliament, and immediately affected firm combinations in industries such as iron and steel and semiconductor firms in Japan.
34. It has been pointed out that this revision on the TOB clause still contains a loophole because a hostile bidder could purchase less than one-third of a firm's outstanding shares during off-hours and buy the remaining shares needed for the controlling interest in the firm in the open market. The government argues that such a case will still be subject to the new TOB provision.
35. An implication of cross-holding for the Japanese stock market capitalization is discussed by McDonald (1989).
36. Greenmailing is the practice of buying enough of a company's stock to threaten a hostile takeover and then reselling it to the company at above market value.
37. Toyota's ownership shares, shown in Table 7.1, affect how these suppliers are dealt with in Toyota's consolidated financial statements. Japanese Commercial Code rules on this are as follows: firms (that is, suppliers) in which the parent firm (that is, Toyota) owns more than 50 percent of the equity must be consolidated into Toyota's financial statements; for 40–50 percent ownership, consolidation is required only if Toyota controls the supplier, otherwise Toyota's financial statements must reflect only the supplier's financial figures in proportion to Toyota's ownership (the proportionality principle); for 20–40 percent ownership, the proportionality principle applies. Another Commercial Code rule on voting rights states, however, that if Toyota increases its ownership in a supplier to more than 25 percent, and if the supplier owns some equity in Toyota, then the supplier's voting rights in Toyota disappear. That is, beyond 25 percent ownership by Toyota, the supplier's voting rights in Toyota associated with its cross-holding arrangements with Toyota are lost. This explains the bunching of ownership shares between 20 percent and 25 percent in Table 7.2. We also note that a block holder with more than one-third of the total outstanding shares can reject any proposal in the general shareholders' meeting.
38. It is often said that GM produces 70 percent of its parts internally while Toyota outsources 70 percent of its parts. Many Japanese assembly-based manufacturers rely heavily on their production keiretsu structures for maintaining efficient production. However, the merit of this system was seriously questioned in the 1990s when critics argued that this kind of keiretsu system prevented Japanese manufacturers from using the lowest-cost suppliers on a global scale. Nevertheless, this system still exists to a large extent in Japanese manufacturing industries.
39. Nikkei (2008) reports that, by the end of February 2008, more than 10 percent of Japan's listed firms have adopted poison pills, and more are considering doing so.
40. One obstacle will continue to be the presence of keiretsu and other corporate shareholders who usually support the management.

41. When Japan's Daiichi Bank and Kangyo Bank merged in 1971 to become the Daiichi Kangyo Bank (DKB), one of the adopted rules for the merger was to maintain the original personnel management systems of both Daiichi and Kangyo Banks for the following ten years. Because of this, the DKB's performance continued to lag behind its competitors for the next two decades. However, this type of expensive and inefficient personnel management for merged firms is still commonly adopted in Japan. It is abandoned only when poor firm performance requires the firm to do so.
42. The estimated numbers of publicly announced M&As involving Japanese firms are: 1,728 in 2003, 2,211 in 2004), 2,725 in 2005, and 2,775 in 2006. Most of these M&As took place in non-manufacturing industries. For example, the industrial breakdown of 2,775 M&As in 2006 is: distribution (603 M&As), service (585), information technology (470), other (445), finance (382), biotechnology (178), and real estate (112). Total amounts involved in these M&As are estimated to be ¥15,000 billion (approximately US$130 billion) (see, for example, Recof, 2007).
43. In comparison, M&As in Canada amounted to about US$160 billion.
44. While litigation against corporations and their directors is still new in Japan, legal cases against brokers selling complex investment without adequate disclosure (for example, currency and commodity futures) have occurred numerously. A historical example of litigation against directors of all major securities firms took place in the early 1990s when these firms, under comprehensive investment agreement with large corporations, incurred massive capital losses in these corporations' investment accounts when the securities firm-managed investment went sour as a result of the Japanese bubble burst in 1991. All major securities firms paid back the losses, at least partially, and the amount of this loss compensation (called "*hoten*") amounted to more than US$2 billion in total in 1991. Individual shareholders brought legal suits against directors of these securities firms for their inappropriate use of corporate funds. Although the courts partially sided with the shareholders, no securities firm directors received any penalty. Such capital loss compensation practice was made illegal by the revised Securities Exchange Law in 1992.
45. The role of the outside directors sent by parent firms to their affiliates is in some ways similar to the role of the outside directors Japanese banks often send to their client firms. The bank-appointed outside directors are primarily concerned with their client firms' financial matters.
46. The connection between the adoption of the executive committee system and the coordination of production activities within a production keiretsu group such as the Hitachi group using the directors sent to the parent firm's affiliates is probably irrelevant since such coordinating activities can be done without adopting the executive committee system.
47. Certain inconsistencies and dysfunctionalities that inevitably exist in many revisions of Japanese laws on corporate governance may add to the current state of ambiguity in Japanese corporate governance.
48. There is some evidence that Japanese banks facilitate their client firms' issuances, for example, of corporate bonds in capital markets (see, for example, Campbell and Hamao, 1994; Nakamura, 2002). However, it is not clear how this will fit in with the emerging new corporate governance system.

49. The issues associated with the possible transfer of Japanese-style corporate governance systems to the U.S. are discussed, for example, in Morck and Nakamura (1995) and Romano (1995).
50. This device either does not exist or is impractical as an anti-takeover device in Anglo-American countries.
51. See, for example, Morck and Nakamura (2005).
52. One basic issue is the relationship between the alliance capitalism characterized by various types of keiretsu (see, for example, Gerlach, 1992: Lincoln et al., 1996; Lincoln and Gerlach, 2004; Lincoln et al., 1992) and economic efficiency in the new economic environment now operating in Japan. The supporters of the Anglo-American system of corporate governance thought that the Japanese economy was greatly underperforming in the 1990s and predicted a potentially substantial efficiency gain under the Anglo-American system.

References

Aoki, M. (1988) *Information, Incentives, and Bargaining in the Japanese Economy* (New York: Cambridge University Press).

Aoki, M. (1990) "Toward an Economic Model of the Japanese Firm," *Journal of Economic Literature*, March, 1–27.

Aoki, M. (1994) "Monitoring Characteristics of the Main Bank System: An Analytical and Developmental View," in M. Aoki and H. Patrick (eds.), *The Japanese Main Bank System: It's Relevancy for Developing and Transforming Economies* (Cary, N.C.: Oxford University Press).

Bank of Japan (2002) *Huryo saiken mondai no kihontekina kangaekata (Basic thinking about the Non-performing Loan Problem)* (in Japanese) (Tokyo: Bank of Japan), October 11.

Bradley, M., Desai, A., and Kim, E. H. (1988) "Synergistic Gains from Corporate Acquisitions and Their Division between the Stockholders of Target and Acquiring Firms," *Journal of Financial Economics*, 21, 3–40.

Campbell, J., and Hamao, Y. (1994) "Changing Patterns of Corporate Financing and the Main Bank System in Japan," in M. Aoki and H. Patrick (eds.), *The Japanese Main Bank System: Its Relevancy for Developing and Transforming Economies* (Cary, N.C.: Oxford University Press), pp. 325–52.

Common Cause (1992) "The Bushes' Ruling Class (Bush I)," *Common Cause* magazine, available at http://www.bestcyrano.org/cCcauseBushesRulingClass.htm.

Fruin, W. M. (1983) *Kikkoman: Company, Clan, and Community* (Cambridge, MA: Harvard University Press).

Fruin, W. M. (1992) *The Japanese Enterprise System: Competitive Strategies and Cooperative Structures* (New York: Oxford University Press).

Fukao, M. (1999) *Corporate governance nyumon (Introduction to corporate governance)* (in Japanese) (Tokyo: Chikuma Shobo).

Gerlach, M. L. (1992) *Alliance Capitalism: The Social Organization of Japanese Business* (Berkeley: University of California Press).

Gilson, R. J., and Malhaupt, C. (2004) *Choice as Regulatory Reform: The Case of Japanese Corporate Governance*, Columbia Law and Economics Working Paper No. 251.

Gilson, R. J., and Roe, M. (1993) "Understanding the Japanese Keiretsu: Overlaps between Corporate Governance and Industrial Organization," *Yale Law Journal,* 102(4), 871–906.

Ginsberg, T. (2002) "Japanese Legal Reform in Historical Perspective." Paper presented at the American Society for Legal History Annual Meeting, San Diego, California, November 7–9, 2002.

Japanese Ministry of Economy, Trade and Industry (various years, 1987–2003) *White Paper on International Trade* (in Japanese).

Japanese Stock Exchanges (2005) *2005 Survey of Shareholding Patterns* (in Japanese) (Tokyo: Japanese Stock Exchanges).

Lincoln, J. R., and Gerlach, M. L. (2004) *Japan's Network Economy: Structure, Persistence, and Change* (New York: Cambridge University Press).

Lincoln, J., Gerlach, M., and Ahmadjian, C. (1996) "Keiretsu Networks and Corporate Performance in Japan," *American Sociological Review*, 61, 67–88.

Lincoln, J., Gerlach, M., and Takahashi, P. (1992) "Keiretsu Networks in the Japanese Economy: A Dyad Analysis of Intercorporate Ties," *American Sociological Review*, 57, 561–85.

McDonald, J. (1989) "The Mochiai Effect: The Japanese Corporate Cross-holdings," *Journal of Portfolio Management*, Fall, 90–4.

Miyajima, H. (2004) *Economic History on Industrial Policy and Corporate Governance (Sangyo seisaku to kigyotouchi no keizaishi)* (in Japanese) (Tokyo: Yuhikaku).

Miyajima, H., and Kuroki, F. (2007) "The Unwinding of Cross-shareholding: Causes, Effects, and Implications," in M. Aoki, G. Jackson and H. Miyajima (eds.), *Corporate Governance in Japan: Institutional Change and Organizational Diversity* (Oxford: Oxford University Press), pp. 79–123.

Morck, R., and Nakamura, M. (1995) "Banks and Corporate Governance in Canada," in R. Daniels and R. Morck (eds.), *Corporate Decision-Making in Canada*, Industry Canada Research Series (Calgary: University of Calgary Press), pp. 481–501.

Morck, R., and Nakamura, M. (1999) "Banks and Corporate Control in Japan," *Journal of Finance*, 54, 319–39.

Morck, R., and Nakamura, M. (2001) "Japanese Corporate Governance and Macroeconomic Problems," in M. Nakamura (ed.), *The Japanese Business and Economic System: History and Prospects for the 21st Century* (London and New York: Palgrave Macmillan/St. Martin's Press), pp. 325–49.

Morck, R., and Nakamura, M. (2005) "A Frog in a Well Knows Nothing of the Ocean: A History of Corporate Ownership in Japan," in R. Morck (ed.), *A History of Corporate Governance around the World: Family Business Groups to Professional Managers* (Chicago: NBER/University of Chicago Press), pp. 367–59.

Morck, R., and Nakamura, M. (2007) "Business Groups and the Big Push: Meiji Japan's Mass Privatization and Subsequent Growth," *Enterprise and Society*, 8, 543–601.

Morck, R., Nakamura, M., and Shivdasani, A. (2000) "Banks, Ownership Structure, and Firm Value in Japan," *Journal of Business*,73, 539–69.

Murakami, Y., and Fukao, K. (2006) "Inward Foreign Direct Investments and Productivity Growth in Japan," Hi-Stat DP Series, No. 143, Institute of Economic Research, Hitotsubashi University, Tokyo, February.

Nakamura, M. (1993) "Japanese Industrial Relations in an International Business Environment," *North American Journal of Economics and Finance*, 4, 225–51.

Nakamura, M. (2002) "Mixed Ownership of Industrial Firms in Japan: Debt Financing, Banks and Vertical Keiretsu Groups," *Economic Systems*, 26, 231–47.

Nakamura, M. (2006) "Japanese Corporate Governance Practices in the Post-Bubble Era: Implications of Institutional and Legal Reforms in the 1990s and Early 2000s," *International Journal of Disclosure and Governance*, 3, 233–61.

Nikkei, (2008) "Cold Criticisms Towards Poison Pills" ("*Baishu boeisaku eno tsumetai shisen*"), (in Japanese) (Tokyo: Nihon Keizai Shinbun), March 12.

Nissei Kiso Kenkyusho (2004) *Cross-holding Survey* (in Japanese) (Tokyo: Nissei Kiso Kenkyusho).

Rajan, R. (1997) "Insiders and Outsiders: The Choice between Informed and Arm's-length Debt," *Journal of Finance*, 47, 1367–406.

Recof (2007) *M&A Database*, Tokyo, http://www.recof.co.jp/ma/index.html.

Romano, R. (1995) "Commentary on Part V, International Aspects of Corporate Governance," in R. Daniels and R. Morck (eds.), *Corporate Decision-Making in Canada*, Industry Canada Research Series (Calgary: University of Calgary Press).

Securities and Exchange Surveillance Commission (SESC) (2003) *Shoken torihiki kanshi iinkaino katsudou joukyo* (*Recent Activities of Securities and Exchange Surveillance Commission*) (in Japanese) (Tokyo: SESC).

Sheard, P. (1994) "Interlocking Shareholdings and Corporate Governance," in M. Aoki and R. Dore (eds.), *The Japanese Firm: Sources of Competitive Strength* (Oxford: Clarendon Press), pp. 310–49.

Tokyo Stock Exchange (2006) *2005 Survey of Japanese Listed Firms* (Tokyo: Tokyo Stock Exchange).

8
Understanding the M&A Wave in Japan: What Drives Japanese M&As?[1]

Yasuhiro Arikawa and Hideaki Miyajima

Introduction

Mergers and acquisitions (M&As) between Japanese corporations began to increase rapidly during the late 1990s. The pace of merger activity in Japan, which had been hovering at around 500 transactions a year in the 1990s, began to pick up from around the end of that decade to reach an annual volume of 2,725 transactions in 2005. The increase in M&A transactions represented a fivefold increase over a ten-year period (Figure 8.1). The value of the transactions totaled US$25.3 billion between 1991 and 1997, and US$138.1 billion between 1998 and 2005. Hence, the value of M&A transactions also experienced a fivefold increase during this time period.[2]

For most of the postwar era, Japanese firms rarely resorted to M&As as a growth strategy or as a means of corporate restructuring. In contrast, M&A activity in the form of deals between domestic corporations and foreign takeovers of Japanese firms surged from the late 1990s. Moreover, the merger activity did not affect all sectors evenly, but tended to cluster in the following sectors: paper and pulp, oil refining and other material industries, finance, telecommunications and information, and distribution. The main purpose of this chapter is to analyze the key factors contributing to the Japanese M&A wave that began in the late 1990s.

Research into the causes of M&A waves has made great strides in the U.S., which has experienced five such waves since the late 1890s. The key forces behind these waves can be divided into two categories: (1) real-economy (neoclassical) forces; and (2) financial forces.[3]

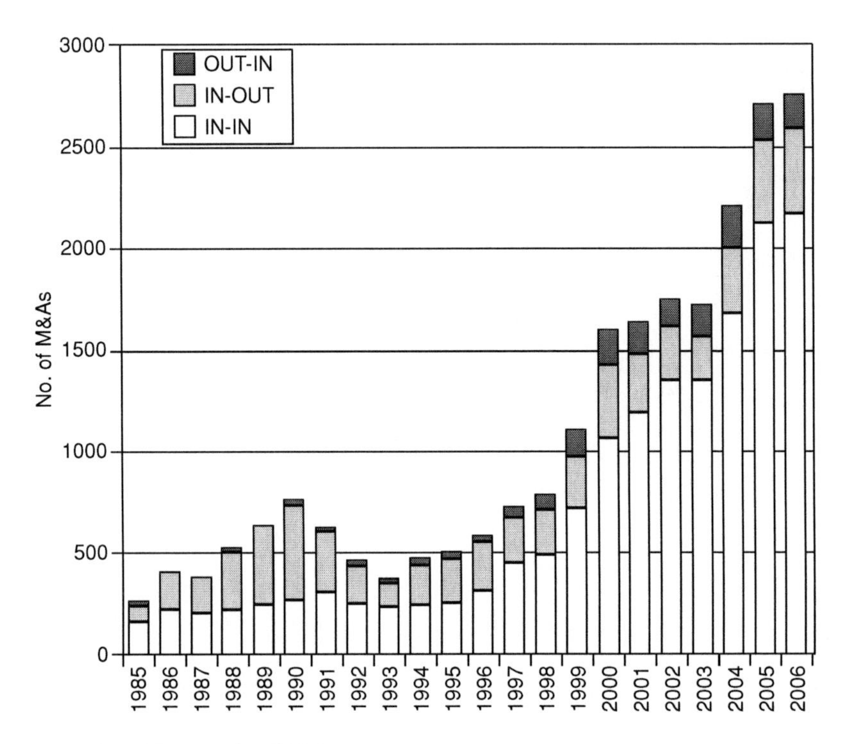

Figure 8.1 The trend in M&As

Source: authors' calculations.

Real-economy forces exert both positive and negative shocks on productivity and profitability. Examples of forces that have been identified as triggering M&A activity through their positive effects on the economy include technical advances that facilitate economies of scale and scope, and deregulatory measures that encourage entry into more profitable sectors. Other scholars such as Jensen (1993) put an emphasis on real-economy forces that create negative shocks to the economy. These include surges in the cost of primary goods due to political uncertainty, the rising cost of raw materials due to the reorganization of upstream or downstream industries, the rapid decline in demand due to catch-up development by developing countries, and other shocks that force marginal corporations in certain industries into the red (Shleifer and Vishny, 2003; Rhodes-Kropf and Viswanathan, 2004). M&As are an effective means of reallocating resources, when real-economy shocks give rise to excess productive capacity.

Representative examples of financial forces that promote M&A activity are the volume of funds available for acquiring firms and the stock price of the acquiring firms. Shleifer and Vishny (1992) hypothesize that when increased cashflow leads to rising stock prices, the financial constraint on the acquiring firm is relaxed. As a result, as the offered price to the target firm goes up, so does the supply of target firms to the M&A market. Empirically, it is clear that the increase of M&A activity in the U.S. from the second half of the 1990s was fueled by the increase in capital liquidity as indicated by the decline in the interest rate spread (Harford, 2005).

As for the relationship between stock price and mergers, it has been pointed out that all five waves of merger activity have occurred during booms in the stock market (Golbe and White, 1988). Theoretically, an M&A boom induced by a rise in the stock market leads to both positive and negative welfare effects. If the stock market is efficient and accurately evaluates the high growth potential of a particular industry or firm, rising stock prices make it easier to raise funds for M&A activity. This promotes M&A in that industry and contributes to a more efficient allocation of resources in the economy as a whole. However, when the stock market overvalues the stock of a firm in a particular industry for one reason or another (in comparison to its fundamental value), the welfare effect of the stock market boom on the M&A boom will vary.[4] For example, suppose that the stock market has overvalued firms in the information technology (IT) industry, which has been experiencing rapid technical innovation.[5] Managers who know that their own firm's stock is overvalued have a strong incentive to carry out M&As using their own firm's stock to pay for assets from other firms. This perspective was put forth as a way to explain the late 1990s M&A wave in the U.S. that was characterized by friendly takeovers and stock swaps. Of course, the Japanese stock market had been in a slump in the late 1990s, so the problems of bias caused by overvalued stock prices would not have been important. However, even if the market as a whole is not in the midst of a boom, soaring stock prices in a certain sector, as was the case during the IT bubble, could prompt a merger boom.

The first aim of this chapter is to analyze whether the M&A boom in the late 1990s, the first such boom in Japan in the postwar era, can be explained by real-economy (neoclassical) forces and financial forces.

The second aim is to identify the key characteristics of acquiring firms and target firms. Various factors can be considered worthy of consideration, such as the scale of a firm and the level of competition within the industry. A specific focus here will be the question of whether firms with high growth opportunity can improve their efficiency by taking over firms with diminished growth opportunity. Jovanovic and Rousseau (2002) assert that M&As are a form of investment undertaken by firms that can be explained by Tobin's *q*.[6] In other words, a higher Tobin's *q*, which is the ratio of firm's value to asset reacquisition costs, indicates a greater potential for M&As. If this relationship can be confirmed, by stipulating that a highly profitable firm with a high Tobin's *q* has a higher level of managerial and operational know-how compared to a low-profitability firm with a low Tobin's *q*, then M&As probably contributed to an improvement in organizational efficiency.

On the other hand, if a firm in a mature industry attempts a merger despite having exhausted its growth opportunity, the risk that the merger will not contribute to an improvement in the organizational efficiency is relatively higher. Similarly, if firms with low growth potential are more likely to become M&A targets, then we can assume that M&As have become an effective tool for corporate restructuring in Japan. Furthermore, debt would appear to have a disciplining effect on management in the event that firms with higher leverage are more likely to become M&A targets. This chapter seeks to identify the characteristics of acquiring and targeted firms during the M&A boom in Japan since the late 1990s.

The chapter is organized as follows. The next section describes the institutional factors that greatly influenced M&As since the late 1990s. The third section discusses how M&As between domestic firms were concentrated in a handful of industries. The fourth section analyzes the real-economy and financial factors that contributed to M&As in certain industries. The fifth section estimates a decision model for M&As for a particular firm, and asks, who buys whom? The final section offers some concluding remarks.

Legal reforms promoting M&As[7]

The impact of lifting the ban on holding companies and the stock transfer system

The laws for corporate integration and other institutional changes created an infrastructure for M&A activity and played an important role in the increase in M&As from 1999. Although it is not possible to explain the rapid increase in M&As from the late 1990s solely in terms of institutional changes, it cannot be denied that legal changes have played a crucial role. Therefore, before conducting a quantitative analysis of the increase in M&A activity, a simple overview of the rapid implementation of a legal framework for M&As will be discussed.

The first important legal change was the June 1997 revision to the Anti-Monopoly Law, which lifted the ban on holding companies. As is well known, the 1947 Anti-Monopoly Law prohibited the formation of holding companies and restricted corporate organizational choices. Holding companies are companies whose purpose is to hold stock, to formulate strategies for business groups, to coordinate and monitor group companies, and to conduct audits without engaging in line business activities. Lifting the ban on holding companies carried the following benefits: it turned line businesses into joint stock companies, made it easier to buy and sell these operations; and allowed an acquirer to reduce the cost of rationalizing the merged back-office.

The ability to transfer the former corporation's stock at low cost to the newly established holding company is essential to a successful corporate integration through this organizational approach. This hurdle was cleared in October 1999 with the introduction of the stock transfer system under an amendment to the Commercial Code. This system creates an integrated approach that allows a firm to create a parent (holding) company holding 100 percent of its stock. It also allows the parent company to issue shares to the existing shareholders. Stock in the newly established parent company would be exchanged for stock in the original company. This approach promoted consolidations as multiple corporations exchanged stock to jointly come under the umbrella of a newly established parent company (Table 8.1).

Table 8.1 Number of deals using a stock transfer system, stock swap, and company divestiture system

Stock transfer and swap system				*Company divestiture system*			
Merger (stock transfer system)	*Merger (stock swap system)*	*Acquisition (stock swap system)*	*Total*	*M&As*	*Intra-group*	*Holding company*	*Foreign company*
4	0	10	14	–	–	–	–
10	0	21	31	–	–	-	–
8	1	18	27	29	68	9	0
7	1	29	37	37	93	15	0
7	2	13	22	31	86	14	1
8	2	69	79	57	85	25	1
9	3	68	80	54	97	41	3
53	9	228	290	208	429	104	5

Note: Each number in the table indicates the number of the deals using each newly introduced measure. The number of spin-off deals are excluded.

Source: Compiled by the authors using figures from Recof (2006).

The holding company system has been used in place of previous merger procedures in the financial and manufacturing sectors since 1999. The first major merger to take place under the new holding company system was the formation of Mizuho Bank from Fuji Bank, Dai-Ichi Bank, and the Industrial Bank of Japan. The merger was announced in the summer of 1999, and finalized in April 2001. The first case that attracted attention in the manufacturing sector was the formation of Nippon Unipac Holding by Nihon Paper Industries and Daishowa Paper Manufacturing. In the steel industry, the merger of NKK and Kawasaki Steel was the first under the new procedures. Once these two companies came under the umbrella of the holding company, JFE Holdings, as wholly owned subsidiaries in September 2002, their steel and engineering operations then were combined to form two separate companies.

The introduction of the holding company system is believed to have had several important implications for the promotion of consolidation. First, since only one of the partners in a merger survived as an ongoing concern in the past, mergers were often opposed and blocked by target company employees. Often these suffered from lack of motivation after being taken over.[8] Under the new holding company system, the targeted corporate entities continue to survive as separate corporate entities. Since friction in personnel and organizational matters is avoided, a smoother integration of the businesses is possible. Second, wage and employment structures between the acquiring firm and the targeted firm are not required to be equalized after integration, thus making it easier to merge corporations with different organizational structures.

The surge in stock swaps and takeovers

The introduction of the stock swap system also facilitated takeovers. Stock swapping is the mandatory exchange of parent-company and subsidiary-company shares. This system makes it possible to exclude minority shareholders with a special resolution by the shareholders' meeting of the target company. Whereas stock swaps could previously only occur under mergers, they could now be employed in takeovers. This had two major implications. It was now possible to (1) buy all the stock from a large number of shareholders, and (2) pay for the shares of a subsidiary company using the shares of the parent company and not cash. As seen in Table 8.1, introducing the stock swap system led to an increase in the use of stock swaps, which was particularly striking in 2004 and 2005.

There are two main features to the stock swap system. First, it can be used to turn the listed target firm into a wholly owned subsidiary of the takeover company. By excluding the minority shareholders of a subsidiary, the holding company can eliminate the duplication of operations among members of its group and consolidate the group's resources, as well as integrate research and development, manufacturing, sales, and other functions. Second, it promotes the use of M&As as a growth strategy. Since takeover firms can use their own stock to pay for takeovers, financially constrained but highly valued firms used stock swaps to acquire firms in emerging markets. For example, Livedoor, led by Horie Takafumi (which includes the former Livin' on the Edge and other companies), conducted 30 takeovers valued at a total of ¥50.7 billion. Stock swaps were used in 12 cases.

On the other hand, the introduction of the company divestiture system under the revised Commercial Code that took effect in April 2001 lowered hurdles for companies trying to sell their division. The corporate divestiture system made it easier to dispose of and spin off business operations as separate companies. If the shareholders' meeting passed a special authorizing resolution, a company could transfer an internal division to another company and be compensated with the stock of the acquiring company. Under this new type of business transfer, acquiring companies could be freed from needing to raise funds for the purchase.

Furthermore, the previous stipulations requiring an audit performed by a court-appointed auditor in cases of investment in-kind deals, and the need to acquire the consent of creditors were relaxed under the new system. Both of these changes made it easier to sell off businesses. The new system made it possible (1) for a division of a company to ally or merge with divisions of other companies engaged in the same line of business; (2) to pursue strategic management by casting off main lines of business or turning them into subsidiaries to be managed by a holding company; and (3) to pursue a strategic business restructuring by spinning off certain operations so that they can be sold to other companies within the same group (source: Recof data). In the five years since this system was introduced, there have been 208 cases in which corporate realignment was used to promote alliances and integration of operations engaged in the same line of business but under different companies (Table 8.1).

Building an M&A infrastructure

The Industry Revitalization Law of 1999 (Kigyo Katsudo Kassei-ka Ho) is an additional piece of legislation that further promoted M&A activity. This law provided tax and legal support measures for revitalization projects certified by the minister with authority over the project, such as a reduction or exemption from the registration and licensing taxes on investment, as well as investments and loans from the Development Bank of Japan. The law allowed firms (1) an exemption from inspection by an auditor for investment in-kind and post hoc incorporation, and (2) the ability to restructure without convening a shareholders' meeting (streamlined restructuring).[9] Furthermore, the certified company was (3) given more flexibility in paying for the merger[10] and (4) would receive accelerated screening under the Anti-Monopoly Law. It is believed that these measures provided room to maneuver and smoothed the way for M&As.

In contrast, Rossi and Volpin (2004) stress the protection of minority shareholder rights and accounting practices as key institutional factors that determine the frequency of M&A activity across countries. While there were no major changes to the legal framework protecting minority shareholders' rights in the late 1990s, there were substantial changes in accounting standards. The level of disclosure required under Japan's accounting standards had been considerably lower than that required under the U.S. Generally Accepted Accounting Principles and the European International Accounting Standards. Therefore, if a domestic or foreign firm was considering a merger or acquisition, there was the risk that the target firm's financial statements would not accurately reflect the firm's actual financial condition. Beginning in 1999, firms were required to disclose quasi-guarantee acts (which occur when the parent extends a guarantee to the creditor holding the debt of its subsidiary), and beginning in 2000, consolidated firms were required to adhere to an "actual control" standard. The disclosure of financial information was revised from a non-consolidated to a consolidated basis. Firms were required to use tax-effective accounting and disclose their consolidated cashflow. Market-value accounting was introduced for pension liabilities in 2001 and for holding companies in 2002. These reforms made it easier to grasp the financial condition of a target firm from publicly disclosed information prior to a merger or acquisition (Hattori, 2004, chapter 2).

Finally, the increase in M&As encouraged domestic and foreign investment banks to enter the M&A market. The creation of an infrastructure for M&A intermediation, due diligence, valuation, and other services played an important role. From the late 1990s, foreign financial institutions entered the M&A intermediation business. Japanese banks and securities houses followed suit by expanding their M&A departments. In a parallel development, big law firms began to treat M&A advising as one of their important services. The M&A infrastructure became irreversible, and accordingly the costs associated with M&A activity, including the search for potential acquisition targets, were reduced.

These institutional changes were not completely exogenous to the increase in M&As. Firms that sought to reorganize and achieve growth through M&As pursued legal reforms, which in turn promoted M&As. But if that were indeed the case, why did firms seek legal changes that promoted M&As during this time? Because all Japanese firms benefited from institutional changes, the changes alone do not sufficiently explain why M&A activity surged during this particular period and in certain industries. The next section notes that the M&A wave in the late 1990s was clustered in particular industries. Apart from institutional factors, the analysis that follows in the rest of this chapter is also necessary to explain what happened.

M&A clustering in specific industries: a feature of the M&A boom in the 1990s

Along with the M&A deals executed by foreign firms, M&A deals conducted between domestic firms rapidly surged from the late 1990s to the early 2000s. In the first half of the 2000s, there were an average of 1,497 deals annually, up more than sixfold from an average of 232 deals annually in the late 1980s. In the late 1980s, deals between domestic firms accounted for 44.6 percent of all deals. This number grew to 76.3 percent of all deals in the new millennium. One could say that since 1999, Japanese firms have been actively participating in an M&A boom targeting other domestic firms.

Moreover, M&As in the late 1990s were concentrated in just several industries. Table 8.2 provides a breakdown of the number of mergers between domestic listed firms, as well as the number of acquisitions valued at ¥200 million or more involving at least one listed firm. Between 1991 and 2004, there were a total of 1,605 deals (the subtotals are provided for 29 industry categories, which were compiled from Recof data's 33 categories). Mergers between listed firms were most common in the wholesale, retail, financial, construction, information and telecommunications, chemicals, machinery, and electric machinery sectors. Acquisitions were mainly concentrated in the information and telecommunications, wholesale, retail, and services sectors.

The above figures do not adjust for the distribution of listed corporations across industries. Therefore, we standardized the number of mergers and acquisitions by sector according to the number of listed corporations in each sector at the start of the period. We call this the M&A ratio. Traditional sectors, such as paper and pulp, glass and stone and clay, coal and oil, steel, and so on, with high numbers of deals had a higher M&A

Table 8.2 M&A ratio by industry (1991–2004)

Industry	*No. of M&A deals*	*Ratio*	*No. of merger deals*	*Ratio*	*M&A ratio*
Mining	10	0.005362	0	0	0.090476
Grocery	67	0.035925	5	0.028571	0.044903
Fabric	34	0.018231	3	0.017143	0.040207
Pulp and paper	19	0.010188	6	0.034286	0.089286
Rubber products	5	0.002681	2	0.011429	0.02577
Ceramic industry	25	0.013405	7	0.04	0.044857
Chemistry	76	0.040751	10	0.057143	0.034126
Medical drag	20	0.010724	3	0.017143	0.030812
Coal and oil	10	0.005362	3	0.017143	0.069048
Iron and steel	12	0.006434	4	0.022857	0.02937
Nonferrous metal	53	0.028418	6	0.034286	0.037753
Machinery	77	0.041287	11	0.062857	0.030441
Transport equipment	50	0.02681	7	0.04	0.044392
Electric equipment	82	0.043968	10	0.057143	0.023976
Precision mechanical equipment	18	0.009651	2	0.011429	0.021262
Other manufacture	65	0.034853	2	0.011429	0.069907
Electric power and gas	10	0.005362	0	0	0.027396
Real estate	30	0.016086	0	0	0.029503
Construction	76	0.040751	14	0.08	0.036772
Transportation and storage	36	0.019303	8	0.045714	0.029619
Information and communication	276	0.147989	13	0.074286	0.054649
Wholesale	220	0.117962	19	0.108571	0.069775
Retail	158	0.084718	7	0.04	0.051587
Banking	48	0.025737	15	0.085714	–
Insurance carriers	19	0.010188	5	0.028571	–
Security brokers and dealers	25	0.013405	6	0.034286	–
Other financial services	84	0.04504	1	0.005714	–
Service	260	0.13941	6	0.034286	0.10874
Manufacturing sector	623	0.334048	81	0.462857	–
Non-manufacturing sector	1,242	0.665952	94	0.537143	–
Total	1,865	1	175	1	0.04745

Note: The number of M&A deals is based on publicly disclosed information excluding unrealized deals. The numbers represent the number of mergers between domestic listed firms, and acquisitions valued at ¥200 million or more that involved at least one listed firm.

Source: Compiled by the authors using figures from Recof (2006).

ratio. In contrast, the electric and construction sectors had a relatively lower M&A ratio. The information and telecommunications, wholesale, retail and services sectors had a higher occurrence rate, even when seen through the relative M&A ratio. In contrast, electricity and gas, transportation and warehousing, real estate, and so on, had a lower M&A occurrence ratio.

In order to determine when particular sectors experienced an M&A boom, we followed Harford (2005) and present our results for each sector in Table 8.2. Our calculations were based on the 120 months from 1995 to 2004 for each industry. Randomly, with a probability of 1/120 per month, we calculated a value for 24 months with 1,000 simulations. Next, we compared actual totals for 24 months with the predicted value, and if the actual total exceeded the 95th percentile of the simulated figure, we coded it as an M&A boom. For example, of the 158 M&A deals in the retail sector, 65 deals occurred since February 2001. On the other hand, the maximum aggregate value for M&As exceeding the 95th percentile was 57. Therefore, we can conclude that the M&A boom in the retail sector began in February 2001. [11]

According to Table 8.3, the M&A boom occurred in 13 sectors in the late 1990s. More specifically, the M&A boom between domestic firms began in 1998 in the coal and oil sector, and continued in 1999 in the nonferrous metals, financial and insurance sectors. A surge in M&As began in the retail and electric machinery industries in 2001. Rapid technical innovation produced a similar spike in 2003 in the information and telecommunications sector. Given this activity, the question remains: what accounts for the clustering of M&As in these particular industries?

Why M&As have clustered

Hypotheses

Why did the surge in mergers and acquisitions concentrate in particular industries? The following factors have been cited by previous scholars as causes of rapid increases in M&A activity clustered in particular industries (followed by rapid declines).

The first argument emphasizes real shock. Mitchell and Mulherin (1996) and Andrade and Stafford (2004) emphasize the role of industry-level economic shocks on the allocation of economic resources. Documenting the M&A clustering, Harford (2005) suggests that merger waves happen because of industry-wide economic shocks, which trigger the reallocation of the economic resources thorough M&A activity. In this case, economic shocks can be both positive and negative.

Table 8.3 Identification of the M&A boom

	Total no. of M&A deals	*Maximum no. of M&A deals in 24 months*	*Estimated threshold with 95% confidence level*	*Starting point of M&A boom*	*1995*	*1996*	*1997*	*1998*	*1999*	*2000*	*2001*	*2002*	*2003*	*2004*
Agriculture	1	1	2	Dec 01										
Mining	10	8	10	Oct 01										
Grocery	67	24	30	Jan 01										
Fabric	34	17	18	Apr 02										
Pulp and paper	19	8	14	May 05										
Rubber products	5	3	5	Mar 01										
Ceramic industry	25	10	15	Mar 02										
Chemistry	76	31	31	Apr 02										
Medical drag	20	9	11	Apr 02										
Coal and oil	10	9	9	Mar 98										
Iron and steel	12	7	9	Sep 00										
Nonferrous metal	53	25	25	Jul 99										
Machinery	77	29	30	Jan 03										
Transport equipment	50	26	25	Aug 02										
Electric equipment	82	32	32	Nov 01										
Precision mechanical equipment	18	8	11	Jan 02										
Other manufacture	65	27	26	Apr 01										
Electric power and gas	10	8	9	Aug 01										

Real estate	30	17	19	May 02	
Construction	76	28	32	Dec 01	
Transportation and storage	36	13	19	Jan 03	
Information and communication	276	143	110	Jan 03	
Wholesale	220	84	76	Jul 02	
Retail	158	65	57	Feb 01	
Banking	48	27	25	Aug 99	
Insurance carriers	19	17	14	Sep 99	
Security brokers and dealers	25	14	14	Aug 02	
Other financial services	84	40	34	Jan 03	
Service	260	110	89	Dec 02	

Notes: The numbers represent the number of mergers between domestic listed firms, and acquisitions valued at ¥200 million or more that involved at least one listed firm.

[light shaded box] represents the M&A boom. We identified the M&A boom when the actual number of M&A deals in a 24-month period exceeded 95 percent of the number estimated by simulation for the estimation period (1995–2004).

[dark shaded box] represents the period with the largest number of M&A deals in 24 months in the industry.

Source: Compiled by the authors using figures from Recof (2006).

Positive shocks include technological innovations that enable firms to reap economies of scale and scope, and deregulatory measures that make it easier for firms to enter sectors with high profitability. For example, technical innovations that primarily magnify economies of scale encourage horizontal M&As, while technological innovations that yield economies of scope bring about non-horizontal M&A including the fusion of telecommunications and finance.

On the other hand, some studies emphasize the role of adverse shocks. Jensen (1993, p. 839), stresses that after the oil crisis, American corporations faced a serious excess capacity problem due to the plunge in demand, rapid expansion of scale, and technical innovations that made much of the existing capital obsolete. "Takeover activities were addressing an important set of problems in corporate America, and doing it before the companies faced serious trouble in the product market."

Second, Harford (2005) explains that for M&As to occur in an economy as a whole, the financial constraints on parties to M&As need to be minimal. In other words, an increase in liquidity at the macro level eases financial constraints on M&A activity and consequently leads to an overall increase in the number of M&As.

Third, a stylized fact of M&A activity in the U.S. is an increase in the number of M&A transactions occurring during stock market booms. For example, Golbe and White (1988) report that there is a positive correlation between stock prices and M&A activity. When a stock market boom promotes an M&A boom, there are dual welfare effects. On one hand, assuming that the stock market is efficient and accurately assesses the high growth opportunity of a particular industry, the stock market boom reflects improvements in fundamentals, and resource allocation should be efficient.

On the other hand, if the stock market overprices an industry above its fundamental value for some reason, there will be a major difference between the stock market boom's welfare effect on the M&A boom. This perspective is called the market-driven hypothesis, and assumes that the stock market is characterized by inefficiency. While the 1980s M&A boom in the U.S. was characterized by leveraged buyouts and other deals that used cash as a means of payment, the M&A boom of the 1900s was characterized by an increase in the number of deals that were financed with stock. Focusing on this feature, Shleifer and Vishny (2003) advanced a theory that when managers possess information that the market's valuation is higher than a firm's fundamental value, they have an incentive to reap profits through M&A deals that involve the swap of their own company stock. Myopic managers of target firms will ignore the expected long-term profits and have an incentive to sell their own firm in response to a favorable offer from the acquiring firm.[12] In that case, the acquisition will generate losses for the stockholders of the target firm. Next, we investigate these different explanations about M&A activity in industry-level using the industry-level data.

Data

Following the hypotheses discussed above, we begin to analyze the determinants of Japanese M&A in the 1990s using industry-level data.

The database originates from Recof's M&A database of Japanese companies. We exclude the financial sector from our sample because this sector faces different regulations. Our measure of the frequency of M&A activity in each sector is the M&A ratio. The ratio is calculated based on the M&A deals by firms listed on the Tokyo Stock Exchange (TSE) first section (large companies) or second section (medium-size companies) with a transaction value of at least ¥200 million from 1991 to 2004.[13] Consequently, we exclude deals by the firms listed on Mothers, JASDAQ, Hercules, and those by non-listed firms. Furthermore, we exclude the deals within the same group firm and the deals that result in the shareholdings of the acquirer being less than 50 percent. We assign bidders and target firms to one of the industry sectors based on the industry code of the TSE.[14]

The independent variables are constructed based on the following process using financial data from AMSUS, NEEDS and Toyokeizai Financial Database.

First, to examine the effect of fundamental factors on M&A, we control for the industry's growth opportunities and profitability. As a proxy for growth opportunities, we use Tobin's q. Under the neoclassical hypothesis, the number of M&A deals will increase in a particular industry when the productivity of that industry as a whole increases (or decreases) because of technological innovation, demand expansion (reduction), or a dramatic change in competitiveness due to deregulations.

Second, as a proxy for profitability, we use the return on assets (ROA) and the first principal component (PROF) where four variables (the ratio of cashflow to sales, the ratio of sales to total assets, employee growth, sales growth) are applied. We predict that the probability of M&A is higher when these variables are larger (or lower).

Following Mitchell and Mulherin (1996) and Andrade and Stafford (2004), we also include the lagged sales growth and the deviation of sales growth from its five-year mean (Econshock) to capture industry shocks. The industry shock is one of the determinants of the merger wave if the M&A ratio is negatively related with this shock. Since the

Econshock only captures shocks on the demand side, we also add the standard deviation of the median three-year stock return (σ(ER)) to capture the much broader shocks to the industry. We assume that more highly volatile stock returns reflect negative shocks that the industry faced over the previous three years.

To control the effect of capital liquidity, we add the one-year change of the base money in money supply.[15] We expect a positive relationship between the percentage change of base money and the probability of M&A in the case where higher capital liquidity in the macroeconomy makes financial constraints less severe.

Finally, to examine the validity of the effect of overvaluation in the stock market on M&As, we follow Harford (2005) and add the average three-year stock return (ER). We expect a positive relationship between ER and the probability of M&A if the overvaluation encourages M&A activity. The value of all the independent variables that we use in the following analysis represent industry medians.[16]

Descriptive statistics

Table 8.4 lists the descriptive statistics for the average M&A ratio, growth opportunity, profitability, ratio of physical investment to total assets, percentage changes of total factor productivity (TFP), level and percentage changes of regulation index, and correlation between the M&A ratio and other variables. Here, the regulation index shows the extent to which each industry faced regulation. A high number implies greater regulation. This variable serves as a proxy for industry shocks like TFP.[17]

Table 8.4 does not suggest a clear relationship between the M&A ratio and the growth opportunity or profitability. While q is larger in the sectors with higher M&A ratios, like IT, service, and retail, it is also above average for the sectors with lower M&A ratios, like medical, machinery, electronics. We find a similar tendency for ROA. In fact, the correlation between the M&A ratio, Tobin's q, and ROA is relatively low.

Second, we find a negative relationship between the M&A ratio and the investment ratio. This suggests that these variables are substitutes, a result that is consistent with Jovanovic and Rousseau (2002).

Finally, the correlation coefficient on the bottom indicates a negative relationship between the percentage change in regulation and the M&A ratio. In contrast, the percentage change in TFP is positively related to M&A. These observations are consistent with the neoclassical view that fundamental economic shocks drive merger waves.

Table 8.5 lists the descriptive statistics and correlation matrix for each variable we use in a later regression. Note that each variable lagged one

Table 8.4 M&A ratio and performance variables

Industry	*M&A ratio*	*Tobin's q*	*ROA growth*	*Sales*	*Capital expenditure / total asset*	*Regulation index*	*Percentage changes of regulation index*	*Percentage changes of TFP*
Agriculture, Forestry and Fisheries	1.19%	1.397	1.34%	–0.28%	2.3%	0.635	–0.069	–0.158
Mining	9.05%	1.122	1.32%	1.60%	2.9%	0.558	–0.055	–0.005
Groceries	4.49%	1.181	1.84%	0.84%	3.7%	0.733	–0.041	0.002
Fabric	4.02%	1.082	0.97%	-2.67%	2.1%	0.001	–0.004	–0.015
Pulp and paper	8.93%	1.076	0.97%	–0.98%	3.9%	0.000	0.000	–0.006
Rubber products	2.58%	1.162	1.97%	–0.48%	4.4%	0.623	0.034	–0.003
Ceramic industry	4.49%	1.111	0.98%	–0.77%	3.0%	0.065	0.020	0.001
Chemistry	3.41%	1.121	1.50%	–0.31%	3.6%	0.154	0.009	–0.004
Medical drag	3.08%	1.410	2.84%	1.70%	2.5%	1.000	0.000	0.025
Coal and oil	6.90%	1.167	1.07%	0.45%	2.7%	0.438	–0.094	0.002
Iron and steel	2.94%	1.052	0.62%	-1.32%	3.5%	0.000	0.000	0.007
Nonferrous metal	3.78%	1.093	1.20%	-1.14%	2.8%	0.054	–0.001	–0.010
Machinery	3.04%	1.184	1.34%	0.02%	2.1%	0.093	–0.028	–0.019
Transport equipment	4.44%	1.080	1.35%	0.18%	4.9%	0.282	0.015	0.006
Electrical equipment	2.40%	1.240	1.31%	0.23%	2.6%	0.299	–0.038	0.025
Precision mechanical equipment	2.13%	1.216	1.45%	0.21%	2.5%	0.577	0.077	–0.015
Other manufacture	6.99%	1.136	1.94%	0.42%	2.6%	0.156	–0.014	0.005
Electricity and gas	2.74%	1.107	1.31%	1.35%	10.2%	1.000	0.000	–0.002
Real estate	2.95%	1.093	1.65%	2.55%	2.2%	0.286	0.057	–0.006
Construction	3.68%	1.045	1.05%	–0.61%	1.1%	0.537	0.088	–0.012
Transportation and storage	2.96%	1.202	1.10%	0.92%	4.9%	0.942	0.013	–0.007
Information and communication	5.46%	1.598	2.27%	1.06%	2.3%	0.047	–0.026	0.023
Wholesale	6.98%	1.053	1.30%	0.35%	0.8%	0.000	0.000	0.023
Retail	5.16%	1.208	2.27%	3.90%	5.3%	0.000	0.000	0.006
Service	10.87%	1.327	2.45%	2.95%	3.1%	0.526	0.009	–0.009
All industries	4.74%	1.166	1.45%	0.50%	3.2%	0.360	–0.002	–0.006
Correlation with M&A ratio	–	0.065	0.152	0.260	–0.162	–0.234	–0.236	0.276

Notes: The sample consists of companies listed on the first and second sections of the TSE from 1991 to 2004.We use the RIETI JIP 2006 index for constructing TFP and the regulation index. Since the JIP 2006 index is available up to 2002, we assume the index is the same from 2002 to 2004. Changes in regulation and TFP represent the mean yearly change during the sample period.

Source: Compiled by the authors using figures from Recof (2006).

year to the M&A ratio. The correlation between Tobin's q and ER is smaller than expected at 0.20, while the correlation between Tobin's q and ROA is 0.48. The correlation between base money as a proxy for capital liquidity and Tobin's q is –0.177. This result suggests that M&A activity does not increase with a higher Tobin's q during periods with larger capital liquidity.

Table 8.5 Descriptive statistics and correlation matrix

A: mean

	No.	*Mean*	*Std dev*
M&A ratio	351	0.032	0.100
Tobin's q	351	1.188	0.266
ER	351	0.064	0.951
σ(ER)	351	10.586	2.125
ROA	351	0.015	0.008
PROF	351	–0.162	0.962
Econshock	351	–0.025	0.049
Base money	352	0.081	0.076

B: correlation matrix

	M&A ratio	*Tobin's* q	*ER*	*σ(ER)*	*ROA*	*PROF*	*Econshock*	*Base money*
M&A ratio	1							
Tobin's q	0.275	1						
ER	–0.093	0.198	1					
σ(ER)	0.129	0.077	–0.072	1				
ROA	0.042	0.480	0.366	–0.033	1			
PROF	0.138	0.362	–0.112	–0.038	0.420	1		
Econshock	–0.103	0.119	0.410	–0.155	0.310	–0.076	1	
Base money	–0.177	–0.288	0.072	0.017	–0.209	–0.238	–0.219	1

Notes: The number of M&A deals is based on publicly disclosed information excluding unrealized deals. The numbers represent the number of mergers between domestic listed firms, and acquisitions valued at ¥200 million or more that involved at least one listed firm.
ER represents the 36-month average stock return.
σ(ER) represents the standard deviation of ER.
ROA represents the operating income on assets.
PROF represents the first principal component estimated by principal component analysis on ROA, the cashflow/sales ratio, the growth rate of the number of employees, and sales growth.
Econshock is the deviation of sales growth from its previous five-year average.
Base money is the yearly change in base money at money supply.

Source: Authors' calculations.

Industry-level analysis

In this section, we examine the determinants of M&A ratio and focus on positive and negative fundamental shocks, as well as stock price returns.[18] Since the dependent variable is censored, we mode the M&A ratio using a Tobit specification.

As in shown in Table 8.6, model 1, the coefficient on Tobin's q as a proxy for growth opportunity is significantly positive at the 1 percent level. This evidence suggests that M&As occur in industries with relatively higher growth opportunities.

Table 8.6 Estimating the frequency of M&A deals by industry

Model	*1* *Tobit(PANEL)*		*2* *Tobit(PANEL)*		*3* *Tobit*		*4* *Tobit(PANEL)*	
q	0.190	***	0.203	***	0.176	***	0.263	***
	4.740		5.000		3.870		5.810	
ER	–0.023		–0.024	*	–0.022		–0.052	**
	–1.630		–1.690		–1.470		–2.880	
σ(ER)	0.015	***	0.015	**	0.011	*	0.020	***
	2.750		2.810		1.760		3.250	
ROA			–0.063					
			–0.040					
PROF	0.011				0.022		0.013	
	0.910				1.470		1.020	
Econshock	–0.501	**	–0.475	**	–0.495	**	–0.429	*
	–2.200		–2.050		–1.950		–1.740	
Base money	–0.032		–0.025		–0.067		0.063	
	–0.220		–0.170		–0.440		0.380	
Constant	–0.461	***	–0.479	***	–0.407	***	–0.628	***
	–5.710		–6.080		–3.510		–6.520	
Industry dummy	No		No		Yes		No	
Year dummy	No		No		Yes		No	
Log likelihood	–25.082		–25.498		–4.769		–31.074	
No.	349		347		349		303	

Notes: The sample consists of companies listed on the first and second sections of the TSE, from 1991 to 2004. The sample is from 1991 to 2002 in model 4.
ER represents the 36-month average stock return.
σ(ER) represents the standard deviation of ER.
ROA represents the operating income on assets.
PROF represents the first principal component estimated by principal component analysis on ROA, the cashflow/sales ratio, the growth rate of the number of employees, and sales growth.
Econshock is the deviation of sales growth from its previous five-year average.
Base money is the yearly change in base money at money supply.
Coefficients and standard deviations are listed.
***, **, * denote significant differences from zero at the 1 percent, 5 percent, and 10 percent levels, respectively.

Source: Authors' calculations.

This result is consistent with the hypothesis that M&A activity is driven by the overvaluation of the bidding firm's stock price. In model 1, we include the three-year stock price return (ER) in the regression to test directly the market driven hypothesis following Harford (2005). Since the coefficient of ER is negative and less significant, we have no reason to think that the overvaluation of stock prices is the driver of M&A activity in that sector. Using pooled data instead of panel data (model 3) or adding a one-year lag of the M&A ratio (not shown) produces similar results.[19] These results imply that sectors with higher growth opportunities on average are likely to see more M&As, while we cannot find any clear evidence of an effect of stock price overvaluation. The proportion of stock swap deals to total M&A in Japan was very low (only 4 percent in 2006), and it was heavily used by firms listed on emerging markets like Mothers. Consequently, the market-driven hypothesis does not seem appropriate for explaining M&A activity among larger, established firms.

Next, we address the effect of profitability on industry-level M&As. As a proxy for profitability, we use PROF and ROA. The estimation results show that the coefficient on PROF is positive but insignificant (models 1, 3). When we use ROA instead of PROF, the coefficient is again negative and insignificant (model 2). Unlike the studies examining M&A in the U.S. in the 1990s, we cannot find a positive relationship between the M&A ratio and profitability in Japan. These results suggest that M&A activity in Japan occurs more heavily in sectors that had a positive industry shock in terms of growth opportunity.

The coefficient of Econshock, which is the deviation of current sales growth from the previous five-year average, is significantly negative at the 5 percent level (model 1). We find similar results when we use ROA instead of PROF (model 2), or change the estimation method from panel to pooled (model 3). The rapid increase of M&As in Japan from the late 1990s is motivated by the remarkable decline of sales.

Further, the coefficient on σ(ER), the proxy for exogenous shocks to each industry, is significantly negative. For example, based on model 1, an increase of one standard deviation in σ(ER), or 2.125, raises the M&A ratio about 3.2 percent, which is almost the same magnitude as the 3.2 percent of M&A ratio.

Considering that the Japanese economy gradually recovered from 2003, we estimate the regression using years up to 2002 (model 4). In this limited estimation period, we find the coefficient of Econshock and σ(ER) are highly significant. If stock price volatility reflects negative industry shocks, we can conclude that the merger boom in Japan was due to both positive and negative industry shocks.

Finally, the coefficient on base money, the proxy for capital liquidity, is always insignificant.[20] On average, capital liquidity as a whole is not a good proxy for explaining the M&A boom in the 1990s at the industry level.[21]

In summary, the above results suggest that the rapid increase of M&A activity is due to a change in growth opportunities and decreasing sales. These conclusions are consistent with Mitchell and Mulherin (1996), Andrade and Stafford (2004), and Harford (2005). After his case study of M&A in the U.S., Kaplan (2000) suggests that most of the M&As resulted from technological shocks, deregulation, a change in growth opportunities, and a change in profitability. The results of this section show that positive and negative changes to growth opportunities and the decreasing sales due to industrial shocks triggered the merger boom in Japan. Contrary to the U.S. case, however, stock price overvaluation for bidding firms and macro-level capital liquidity do not affect the M&A boom in Japan substantially. We cannot find any evidence that supports the market-driven hypothesis among large listed firms.

A firm-level investigation of M&As

Hypothesis

In this section, we investigate the relative characteristics of acquiring and target firms at the firm-level. We focus on whether M&A activity of acquiring and target firms is explained by their growth opportunity, even though other factors like size or competition level are likely to matter. Jovanovic and Rousseau (2002) show that M&A decisions can be explained by q theory, as in the case of internal investments.[22] That is, firms with a higher Tobin's q are likely to be the acquiring firms. Since M&As are regarded as an effective tool for corporate restructuring, firms with a lower q are likely to be targets of M&As. M&As between high-q acquiring firms and low-q target firms are likely to create value.

For the financial aspects, Shleifer and Vishny (1992) suggest the following theory concerning the relationship between a firm's financial constraint and M&As. Suppose a firm's cashflow increases mainly because of an improvement in the fundamentals factor. This increase relaxes financing constraints for the bidding firm, which tends to offer the target firm a price that more closely resembles its fundamental value. Testing this reasoning, we examine whether the firms with less severe financial constraint are likely to engage in M&A activity or not.

For target firms, we test whether more highly leveraged firms tend to be targets of M&A as the result of the manager's fear of defaulting as Jensen (1993) emphasized. We also investigate the effect of cross-shareholdings on M&As. Opposite to the predicted direction of the effect of leverage, managers of firms with higher cross-shareholdings might face less pressure for the restructuring, and therefore be more likely to avoid accepting an offer for acquisition.

Data

We begin by examining differences in characteristics between acquiring firms, target firms, and non-M&A firms. All the M&A deals are related to firms listed on the TSE first or second sections. That is, M&As are composed of (1) mergers between listed firms, and (2) acquisitions where either the bidder or the target is a listed firm. We include acquiring firms in deals valued at ¥200 million or more in the analysis. On the other hand, we include all targeted firms that are listed. Note that listed firms are more likely to be acquiring firms than targeted firms. The sample period is 1995–2004 for the analysis of bidding firms and 2000–04 for the analysis of target firms. Firms are classified as engaging in M&As in the year in which they carried out the M&As activity. In other years, the firm is classified as a non-M&A firm unless it undertook additional M&A activity.[23] When mergers occur, we identify the bidder and the target according to the definition in Recof. The financial characteristics of the sample firms are shown in Table 8.7.

Table 8.7 Comparison of M&A and non-M&A companies

	Non-M&A company	*Acquiring company*		*Target company*	
Total assets (¥ millions)	11.104	11.956	***	10.799	*
Tobin's q	1.219	1.395	***	1.303	
INV (capital spending/total assets)	11.715	0.045		–0.072	***
DA (debt/total assets)	0.552	0.509	***	0.598	
Sales growth (%)	0.036	0.051	***	–0.038	**
Net debt (¥ millions)	–0.373	–0.367		–0.353	
ROA	0.007	0.020	***	–0.001	
Risk	11.730	11.532		13.779	***

Notes: *Net debt* is defined as [total cash equivalent – debt]/total asset.
Risk represents the standard deviation of a 36-month average stock return.
We employ the Wilcoxon test for comparing M&A and non-M&A firms.
***, **, * denote significant differences from zero at the 1 percent, 5 percent, and 10 percent levels, respectively.

Source: Authors' calculations.

Table 8.7 shows that the size of acquiring firms is larger than that of non-M&A firms. The size of target firms is significantly small. Tobin's *q* is higher for acquiring firms than target firms. This is consistent with the result in the former section that higher growth opportunity triggers M&A activity. Similarly, the ROA of acquiring firms is significantly higher than that of targeted and non-M&A firms. Leverage for acquiring firms is significantly lower than that of target firms. Risk, as measured by the 36-month volatility of stock returns, is significantly higher for target firms. This is consistent with the view that higher risk firms are more likely to be the target in M&A. Finally, we do not find any significant differences for net debt, which is the ratio of liquidity assets minus debt to total assets.

Firm-level analysis I: acquisitions

In this section, we model the choice to acquire a firm by using a Logit specification. The dependent variable takes the value 1 if a firm engages in M&A activity as an acquiring firm, and 0 otherwise. Under this definition, 4 percent of all cases are M&As.[24]

The independent variables are similar to those in the previous section of this chapter, except that they vary at the firm level rather than the industry level. We use Tobin's *q* as a proxy for growth opportunity again. We expect a positive relationship between M&A activity and growth opportunity.[25] To investigate the relationship between growth opportunity and M&As more clearly, we also include two dummy variables as additional proxies for growth opportunity. The first is H*q*, which equals one if a firm's Tobin's *q* is in the top quintile. The second is L*q*, which equals one if the firm's Tobin's *q* is in the bottom quintile of the total distribution. We also include real sales growth for the same purpose.

To examine the effect of financial constraints, we include the net debt (Net debt), which is defined as the ratio of total cash equivalents minus debt to total assets. Because business portfolio diversification is a motivation for buying other firms, we include the three-year standard deviation of stock returns (Risk) as a proxy for risk.[26] Further, to control for the degree of substitutability between firm or asset purchases and internal investment, we use investment (Investment). Finally, we add industrial level and year fixed effects.

Table 8.8 reveals that size is clearly an important determinant of acquisitions. The coefficient of *q* is insignificant and the sign is unstable.

Specifications (2), (3), and (4) include the H*q* dummy and the L*q* dummy. The coefficient on H*q* is significantly positive while the coefficient on L*q*

Table 8.8 Estimation results for acquiring firms

Model	*1*		*2*		*3*		*4*	
q	0.000		–0.001		–0.001		–0.001	
	0.001		0.001		0.001		0.001	
L*q*					–0.005	**	–0.004	
					0.002		0.002	
H*q*			0.007	**			0.006	*
			0.003				0.003	
Sales growth	0.001		–0.001		0.000		–0.001	
	0.006		0.006		0.006		0.006	
Net debt	0.008	**	0.007	*	0.009	***	0.008	**
	0.004		0.004		0.004		0.001	
Size	0.008	***	0.008	***	0.008	***	0.008	***
	0.001		0.001		0.001		0.004	
Risk	0.000		0.000		0.000		0.000	
	0.000		0.000		0.000		0.000	
Investment	–0.001		–0.001		–0.001		–0.001	
	0.003		0.003		0.003		0.003	
1996	–0.003		–0.004		–0.001		–0.003	
	0.005		0.005		0.006		0.005	
1997	0.013		0.010		0.014		0.011	
	0.008		0.008		0.009		0.008	
1998	0.010		0.007		0.011		0.008	
	0.008		0.007		0.008		0.007	
1999	0.024	**	0.019	**	0.026	**	0.021	**
	0.011		0.010		0.011		0.010	
2000	0.015	*	0.012		0.017	*	0.014	
	0.009		0.008		0.009		0.009	
2001	0.033	**	0.028	**	0.036	**	0.030	**
	0.013		0.012		0.014		0.013	
2002	0.039	**	0.032	**	0.042	***	0.034	**
	0.015		0.014		0.016		0.015	
2003	0.044	***	0.036	**	0.046	***	0.039	
	0.017		0.015		0.018		0.016	
2004	0.086	***	0.077	***	0.091	***	0.082	***
	0.026		0.024		0.027		0.026	
Industry dummy	Yes		Yes		Yes		Yes	
R^2	0.131		0.133		0.132		0.134	
Log likelihood	-1232.129		-1228.817		-1230.075		-1227.745	
Positive observation	491		491		491		491	
No.	11,589		11,589		11,589		11,589	

Notes: The sample consists of companies listed on the first and second sections of the TSE. The sample period covers 1995 to 2004.
Lq is a dummy variable that equals 1 if Tobin's *q* of the sample firm is in the bottom quintile of the total distribution.
Hq is a dummy variable that equals 1 if Tobin's *q* of the sample firm is in the top quintile.
Net debt is defined as [total cash equivalent – debt] / total assets.
Size is the log of total asset. *Risk* is the three-year standard deviation of stock return.
Investment is the ratio of physical investment to fixed assets.
Marginal effects and standard deviations are listed.
***, **, * denote significant differences from zero at the 1 percent, 5 percent, and 10 percent levels, respectively.
We use a Logit model for the estimation specification.

Source: Authors' calculations.

is negative and significant in some specifications. This shows that firms with a higher q are more likely to attempt takeover bids. We can conclude that the probability of making a takeover bid for a firm is higher for firms with larger growth opportunities.

Net debt is positive and significant at the 1 percent level. The magnitude of the coefficient is almost similar to that of Hq and size. This suggests that the firms with larger internal funds are more likely to engage in the M&A activity as a bidder.[27]

Firm-level analysis II: targeting

We now turn to an examination of the behavior of target firms. The dependent variable is an indicator that equals one if a firm is the target of an M&A deal and zero otherwise.[28] The independent variables are similar to those in the previous section.

To proxy for restructuring incentives, we use the ratio of debt to total assets (DA). We also add the ratio of cross-shareholding to total issued shares as a proxy for weak corporate governance because cross-shareholdings may reduce shareholder pressure to restructure (Cross). As in the case of acquiring firms, we add the log of assets to control for firm size (Size), and the three-year standard deviation of the stock return to control for risk (Risk). Year and industry-level fixed effects are also included.

Table 8.9 illustrates that the coefficient on Lq is significantly positive, suggesting that the firms with a lower Tobin's q are more likely to be targeted for M&A. The growth rate of sales is negative and significant in (1). This indicates that firms facing stagnating sales are also likely to be targeted for M&As. The fact that both mature firms and ones with slower sales growth are more likely to be targeted suggests that M&As are used as a means of corporate restructuring.

Although Risk is not significant, the coefficient on the ratio of debt to total assets, DA, is significantly positive. The more highly leveraged firm stands a greater risk of being targeted for M&As. This result is consistent with the standard understanding that higher leverage is a driver of M&A targeting because of the higher default risk.[29] Finally, we cannot find any evidence that cross-shareholdings have a substantial effect on the M&A decision.

Conclusion

In this chapter, we have examined the causes of the merger boom that has occurred in Japan since the late 1990s. We have found that M&As

Table 8.9 Estimation results for target firms

Model	*1*		*2*		*3*		*4*	
q	0.001		0.001		0.001		0.001	
	0.001		0.001		0.001		0.001	
L*q*			0.004	*	0.004	*	0.004	*
			0.002		0.002		0.002	
H*q*	–0.001				0.000		0.000	
	0.002				0.002		0.002	
Sales growth	–0.008	*	–0.007		–0.007		–0.007	
	0.005		0.005		0.005		0.005	
DA	0.009	***	0.010	***	0.010	***	0.010	***
	0.003		0.003		0.003		0.003	
Size	0.000		0.000		0.000		0.000	
	0.001		0.001		0.001		0.001	
Risk	0.000		0.000		0.000		0.000	
	0.000		0.000		0.000		0.000	
Cross							0.000	
							0.000	
2001	–0.001		–0.001		–0.001		–0.001	
	0.003		0.003		0.003		0.003	
2002	0.004		0.005		0.005		0.005	
	0.004		0.004		0.004		0.004	
2003	0.012	*	0.013	**	0.013	**	0.013	**
	0.006		0.006		0.006		0.006	
2004	0.010	*	0.011	*	0.011	*	0.011	*
	0.006		0.006		0.006		0.006	
Industry Dummy	Yes		Yes		Yes		Yes	
R^2	0.0769		0.083		0.083		0.0822	
Log likelihood	–355.47		–353.322		–353.320		–353.184	
Positive observation	88		88		88		88	
No.	7760		7760		7760		7726	

Notes: The sample consists of companies listed on the first and second sections of the TSE. The estimation period covers 2000 to 2004.
Lq is a dummy variable that equals 1 if Tobin's *q* of the sample firm is in the bottom quintile of total distribution.
Hq is a dummy variable that equals 1 if Tobin's *q* of the sample firm is in the top quintile.
Sales growth is the percentage change in sales from previous year.
DA is the debt–asset ratio.
Size is the log of total assets.
Risk is the three-year standard deviation of stock returns.
Cross is the percentage share of cross-shareholdings.
Marginal effects and standard deviations are listed.
***, **, * denote significant differences from zero at the 1 percent, 5 percent, and 10 percent levels, respectively.
We use a Logit model for the estimation specification.

Source: Authors' calculations.

are mainly driven by economic shocks. While industries with higher growth opportunity are likely to engage in more M&A activity, the same is also true for industries facing negative fundamental shocks like sales declines. These results imply that the neoclassical model can explain the recent merger wave in Japan.

While these results are consistent with findings based on U.S. data by Mitchell and Mulherin (1996), Andrade and Stafford (2004), and Harford (2005), it is remarkable that the merger boom is driven by both positive and negative shocks in Japan. In the U.S., the merger wave in the 1980s was mainly driven by negative economic shocks. In contrast, the wave in the 1990s was mainly driven by positive economic shocks like technological innovation. Capital liquidity at the macro level, as well as the stock market boom, have not had positive effects on merger activity in Japan, as they have in the U.S. and other countries (Jackson and Miyajima, 2007). Overall, the view supported here is that the merger activity that resulted from economic shocks was itself driven by the need to reallocate assets among industries.

At the firm level, we have found that bidders are generally growing firms and targeted firms tend to be more mature. This suggests that Japanese firms improved their efficiency through merger activity in the 1990s. Furthermore, we find that internal funds for acquiring firms play a very important role in bidding activity. This suggests that it is much easier for a firm with less severe financial constraints to succeed in M&As. This is consistent with the fact that M&A activity increased rapidly during the beginning of the twenty-first century, a time when large Japanese firms started large-scale reductions in their leverage. Finally, we concluded that firms with more leverage are more likely to be targeted for M&A because the increased default risk applies pressure on the manager to entertain M&A offers.

Notes

1. This work is the result of joint work with Kee Hong Bae and Yishay Yafeh on M&A in Japan. We thank them for allowing us to use some of the results and ideas from our joint work. We also thank Naoto Yoshioka, Yusuke Omi and Michael Cutler for excellent research assistance on this project. We are grateful for research support from the Research Institute of Economy, Trade and Industry (RIETI), and the Open Research Center Program of the Ministry of Education, Culture, Sports, Science, and Technology.
2. The figures for total volume of transactions are from Recof data, and the figures for the total value of the transactions are from Jackson and Miyajima (2007). Current data is from Thomson Financial.

3. A predominant view of the causes of such waves has yet to take root. Brealey et al. (2006) cite M&A waves as one of the ten puzzles of finance theory.
4. They are frequently the non-core enterprises of diversified corporations.
5. The case that is frequently cited is America Online (AOL)'s purchase of Time-Warner. AOL's stock price plunged from US$73.75 prior to announcement of the purchase to US$27.28.
6. Andrade and Stafford (2004) also stress that M&As are substitutes for investment.
7. This section draws on Hattori (2004).
8. The *tasukigake* approach to personnel management requires that the top two posts of the new firm (chairman and chief executive officer) be occupied by an official from each of the merger parties.
9. Under the new law, restructuring was possible without sanctioning a shareholders' meeting and simply by a vote of the board of directors if the target company was only one-fifth the size of the bidder, or if the certified company held two-thirds or more of the voting rights of the subsidiary.
10. During reorganization, a company would be permitted to refrain from issuing stock in its own company, instead offering "cash" or stock in another company. With this approach, the target company in the reorganization could be turned into a wholly owned subsidiary.
11. We wish to extend our gratitude to Kee Hong Bae for his cooperation in this estimation.
12. Furthermore, Rhodes-Kropf and Viswanathan (2004) theoretically demonstrate that firms whose stock prices are overvalued by the market have an incentive to carry out M&As through stock swaps. Their model assumes that the managers of the buying firm have complete information regarding the value of their own firm, while the managers of the target firm cannot accurately calculate the future synergies to be reaped from M&As. When the stock market is booming, managers of a target firm who do not have complete information based on excessive expectations of future synergies, will accept offers for a buyout paid for with the overpriced stock of the buying firm.
13. ¥20 million is the first quartile of the amount of money for deals.
14. We corrected some codes based on the TSE industry code.
15. Harford (2005) uses the spread, which is the difference between the loan rate and a risk-free asset, as the proxy for the macroeconomic liquidity. Considering that the BoJ took the zero-interest rate policy from the end of 1990s, we use the base money instead of using the spread.
16. Healy et al. (1992) use the median of each profitability index.
17. TFP and the regulation index are based on the Japan Industry Productivity Database (JIP database 2006). While the original JIP database has 108 industries, we reorganized them into 29 industries weighted by sales volume. Because of data aggregation, these numbers will not be as precise as other variables.
18. We could not find any significant result for TFP and the index of regulations.
19. The coefficient on the one-year lag of the M&A ratio is positive, while the coefficient on the one-year stock return is positive but insignificant.
20. We also include the spread, the average bank loan interest minus JGB yield, following Harford (2005). The spread is also insignificant.

21. We investigate the effect of financial constraints on M&A activity at the firm level later.
22. Andrade and Stafford (2004) emphasize the degree of substitutability between M&As and physical investments.
23. The M&A indicator takes the value of 1 for firms that undertake multiple M&As in one year.
24. The number of sample firms in which the dummy variable equals one is 491.
25. Since we could not find any evidence in support of the market-driven hypothesis in the previous section, q serves as a proxy for growth opportunity only.
26. M&As that are driven by the desire to diversify business portfolios tend to decrease shareholder value.
27. This result does not contradict the conclusion that mature firms are more likely to engage in M&As. Blanchard et al. (1994) showed that the performance of M&As by firms with excess internal funds tends to be lower.
28. Most of the deals we use in the sample are between listed bidding firms and non-listed target firms. The analysis of target firms is relatively limited as a result. In fact, the dependent variable takes the value one only 1 percent of the time (88 cases).
29. The Japanese banking sector accelerate the bad-loan cleanup in this period, and this might influence this result.

References

Andrade, G., and Stafford, E. (2004) "Investigating the Economic Role of Mergers," *Journal of Corporate Finance*, 10, 1–36.

Blanchard, O. J., Lopez-de-Silanes, F., and Shleifer, A. (1994) "What do Firms do with Cash Windfalls," *Journal of Financial Economics*, 36, 337–60.

Brealey, R., Myers, S., and Allen, F. (2006) *Principles of Corporate Finance*, 8th edition (New York: McGraw-Hill).

Clark, R., and Ioannidis, C. (1996) "On the Relation between Aggregate Merger Activity and the Stock Market: Some Further Empirical Evidence," *Economics Letters*, 53, 349–56.

Golbe, D., and White, L. J. (1988) "A Time-Series Analysis of Mergers and Acquisitions in the U.S. Economy," in A. J. Auerbach (ed.), *Corporate Takeovers: Cause and Consequences* (Chicago: University of Chicago Press).

Harford, J. (2005) "What Drives Merger Waves?" *Journal of Financial Economics*, 77, 529–60.

Hattori, H. (2004) *Jissen M&A Manaeigement* [*The Practice of M&A Management*] (in Japanese), (Tokyo: Toyo keizai sinposya).

Healy, P., Palepu, K. and Ruback, R. (1992) "Does Corporate Performance Improve After Mergers?" *Journal of Financial Economics*, 31, 135–75.

Jackson, G., and Miyajima, H. (2007) "Varieties of Takeover Markets: Comparing Merger and Acquisitions in Japan with Europe and the USA," RIETI Discussion Paper.

Jensen, M. C. (1993) "The Modern Industrial Revolution, Exit, and the Failure of Internal Control Systems," *Journal of Finance*, 48, 831–80.

Jovanovic, B., and Rousseau, P. L. (2002) "The Q-Theory of Mergers," *American Economic Review*, 92, 198–204.
Kaplan, S. (2000) "Introduction," in S. Kaplan (ed.), *Mergers and Productivity* (Chicago: University of Chicago Press).
Mitchell, M. L., and Mulherin, J. H. (1996) "The Impact of Industrial Shocks on Takeover and Restructuring Activity," *Journal of Financial Economics*, 41, 193–229.
Recof (2006) MARR M&A database and documentation (in Japanese) (Tokyo: Recof).
Rhodes-Kropf, M., and Viswanathan, S. (2004) "Market Valuation and Merger Waves," *Journal of Finance*, 59, 2685–718.
Rossi, S., and Volpin, P. (2004) "Cross-country Determinants of Mergers and Acquisitions," *Journal of Financial Economics*, 74(2), 277–304.
Shleifer, A., and Vishny, R. W. (1992) "Liquidation Values and Debt Capacity," *Journal of Finance*, 47, 1243–366.
Shleifer, A., and Vishny, R. W. (2003) "Stock Market Driven Acquisitions," *Journal of Financial Economics*, 70, 295–489.

Part II

Evolving Corporate Governance Practices: Selective Adaptations

9
The Strange Role of Independent Directors in a Two-Tier Board Structure in China's Listed Companies

Jiangyu Wang

Introduction

Corporate laws around the world, when they were first enacted, were very similar,[1] largely because of the inherent nature of commerce and capitalism that originated in Western Europe and later spread to North America. The transplantation of corporate law from the leading countries of origin (Holland, then England, France, Germany, the United States, and other civil and common law countries) to other countries led to tremendous similarities in the basic legal framework of corporations across the globe. However, as the corporate world grew, divergence began to emerge between the origin countries as they sought to provide legal and institutional solutions to problems occurring in national settings with sometimes very different legal and sociocultural traditions. As a result, in terms of corporate law, the origin countries differ "in how they responded to the challenges of the rapid growth of the enterprise and financial sectors and to the booms and busts of financial markets that accompanied it."[2] In spite of the differences, the corporate laws in the origin countries have been, in various degrees, successful. Time is to be credited for this: the development of capitalism and the credit culture in Western Europe and North America has lasted for over two centuries, a timespan wide enough for those countries to adjust and rationalize their regulatory and market institutions of corporations through a process of trial and error.

In the successful origin countries, a central task of corporate governance is to control the "controller," which is normally the corporations' management. But countries differ in their systems of corporate governance, and "[m]ost important are differences, particularly between the common law and civil law families, in the allocation of control rights."[3] With few exceptions, the board of directors is the primary governance organ in Western corporations. Over the years, two types of board structures had evolved, namely the unitary board and the two-tier board. The unitary system, adopted in Anglo-American countries, allows for only one board, or the board of directors, which "directs" and oversees the company, including providing strategic guidance for the company, and appointing the executives and monitoring their performance. In the Anglo-American system, the board is mainly comprised of independent directors, to ensure its independence. In the two-tier board structure, most notably adopted by Germany, the governing body of the corporation is comprised of two separate boards: the management board (also called the board of directors), and the supervisory board. In most cases, the supervisory board chooses the directors of the management board and monitors their performance.

In the area of corporate law, the legal systems of developing and transitional countries have been transplanted from one or two of the origin countries mentioned above. Pistor (2003) has surveyed the transplant effect of six representative countries that adopted foreign law[4] and concludes that

> [C]ountries that adopt foreign law are frequently unprepared for it or the changes it brings. It is therefore not surprising that the new law does not become well incorporated into the institutional landscape or contributes to an ongoing process or institutional change.[5]

This conclusion's overgeneralization is apparent.[6] After all, companies in quite a number of countries that have transplanted legal systems from abroad are running well: even the legal system of the U.S. has its origins in English law. Further, a country's adoption of foreign corporate institutions might be prompted by internal pressure to rationalize its enterprise sectors. Despite this weakness, the survey correctly suggests that "legal transplantation is not an easy (and certainly not a short-term) solution for countries with less developed legal systems."[7]

China is also a country whose corporate law has been transplanted from other countries. As its Company Law (or Corporation Law, as some translate it) represents, China has imported the organizational structures of Western capitalist business into its own enterprise sectors.[8] However, as some commentators observe,

> Differences from Western models bracket this general similarity at both the broad level, in ideology and over objective, and the technical level, in details and specific rules. The melding of Western forms with the goal of promoting a "socialist market economy" has produced a Corporation Law with distinctly Chinese characteristics.[9]

Further, although China's corporate law framework, as embodied in the Company Law and other regulations, embraces a significant amount of institutions imported from foreign sources, it is difficult to identify the single most significant "origin" country. Broadly speaking, the Chinese system is a hybrid one, containing institutions borrowed from both the common law family, mainly the U.S., and the continental civil law family, notably Germany. This is most obvious in the board structure of China's listed companies. In brief, a listed company in China is mandated to have both a supervisory board and independent directors on the management board. But even with these two "safety nets" in place, corporate governance in China's listed companies is still very unsatisfactory.[10] In fact, both empirical studies and analysis of the legal framework show that the supervisory board and the independent directors, the "strange partners" in China's listed companies, have not achieved any significant improvements to the overall corporate governance of those companies.

This chapter examines the role and effectiveness of independent directors in China's listed companies. In the following sections, we analyze the legal framework of the independent directors, and discuss their relationship with the supervisory board. We then evaluate the effectiveness of the independent directors' system from a mainly legal perspective. The legal evaluation is of course conducted in the light of the historical evolution of and empirical studies on the practices and effects of the supervisory board and independent directors. The chapter concludes that, compared with the supervisory board, which can be fairly regarded as a complete failure, the independent directors' system has made a certain, albeit limited, contribution to the improvement of corporate governance in China's listed companies. However, given the inherent defects in the overall corporate governance environment in China, it is not easy to be optimistic about how much more progress can be made via the independent directors' system. The chapter suggests that the authorities in China take measures to tackle the problems which affect the independence of independent directors as well as their access to corporate information and other governance facilities.

The two-tier board structure in China's listed companies

China's first national Company Law (hereafter referred to as the PRC Company Law) was promulgated in 1993, and significantly amended – with, to some extent, revolutionary changes – in 2005.[11] The PRC Company Law adopts a two-tier board structure for joint stock companies (also known as "companies limited by shares") which is the prerequisite form for corporations aiming to be listed on a stock exchange both in China and overseas. Every joint stock company must have a board of directors (BoD) as well as a supervisory board (SB). In China's transition from a planned economy to a market economy, the autonomy of enterprises has been expanded enormously, and as a result, the "Chinese Communist Party no longer dominates the management decisions of the factory directors."[12] The BoDs of Chinese companies enjoy a range of managerial powers comparable to their Western counterparts.[13] The BoD is comprised of 5–19 directors who elect, by a simple majority, the chairman of the board.[14] The BoD may also elect any of its directors – in most cases the chairman – to serve as the "manager" of the company, known as the chief executive officer (CEO) in other jurisdictions.[15] As will be discussed below, listed companies in China are also required to have independent directors on their board.

The SB was intended to be the sole internal watchdog of the company's management, and it oversees the board of directors and managers to insure that they comply with state laws and company policies. Specifically, PRC Company Law 1993, before it was amended in 2005, granted the SB the following powers: (1) examining the financial records and statements of the company; (2) demanding that directors and senior managers correct their wrongdoings that harm corporate interest; and (3) proposing the convening of an extraordinary shareholders' meeting.[16] The 2005 revisions to the Company Law add the following substantial powers to the arsenal of the SB: (1) proposing, to the shareholders' meeting, the removal of directors or senior managers who have violated any laws, articles of association, or resolutions of the shareholders' meetings; (2) convening and presiding over the shareholders' meeting as required by the law if the BoD refuse to fulfill their legal obligation to convene the meeting; (3) putting forward proposals to the shareholders' meeting; and (4) bringing lawsuits against directors and senior managers for professional misconduct.[17] In addition, at least one-third of the members of the supervisory board shall be shareholders' representatives and an appropriate percentage of employee representatives.[18]

The ineffectiveness of the supervisory board

China hence has a hybrid system of board structure, featuring both independent directors and a supervisory board. The system of a supervisory board was seemingly inspired by the German style of corporate governance. However, it is important to note that the SBs in China are fundamentally different from those in Germany and other EU countries which have adopted the two-tier model, in terms of both the legal powers and the supervisory practice. According to the German Stock Corporation Act,[19]

> The supervisory board is responsible for appointing and dismissing members of the management board (§ 84(1)) and representing the corporation in its dealings with such board (§ 90), including entering into employment agreements with its members (§ 112). The management board reports to the supervisory board, though the latter is independently entitled to inspect the books, records and properties of the corporation (§ 111(2)). The supervisory board must consent to certain business decisions of the management board if required by the articles or the supervisory board's rules. The supervisory board may not, however, encumber the management board's ability to manage the corporation with excessive consent requirements. If the supervisory board withholds consent, the management board may nevertheless act if it can obtain a three quarters majority of votes cast at the shareholders' meeting (§ 111(4)).[20]

Clearly, compared with their counterparts in China, the German SB has a much broader power base, although it must refrain from excessive interference with the management board, which is empowered to manage the day-to-day operations of the business. In essence, the BoD in a German stock corporation is responsible to the SB to a great extent as the members of the BoD must (a) be appointed and removed by the latter, and (b) seek consent from the SB regarding important business decisions. China's SBs apparently do not possess such a wide range of powers. The powers granted them by law do not include any authority to control the appointments to or business decision making of the management board. Hence, as a matter of law, it is impossible for the SB to act "as supervisory organ in the sense of checks and balances, which appoints, controls, advises – and where necessary also dismisses – the Management Board,"[21] as prescribed in the German corporate governance structure.

In practice, the effectiveness of a typical SB is undermined, first of all, by its composition. The membership of the SB typically consists of "political officers," leaders of a non-functional trade union,[22] or close friends and allies of the senior managers.[23] According to a survey of the Shanghai Stock Exchange Research Center on the educational background of members of the SBs and members of the boards of directors of corporations listed on the Shanghai Stock Exchange, overall, the professional qualifications of supervisors are inferior to those of the members of the board of directors.[24] Further, supervisors, appointed by the executives who also determine the supervisors' compensation, have virtually no independence from the management.[25] In addition, the SB has limited access to corporation information, rendering it impossible to make informed business decisions. Last but not least, because of the highly concentrated leadership (in the hands of either the state or other controlling shareholders), many SBs are at best a "censored watchdog," not permitted to speak out against a management controlled by the majority shareholder.[26]

In short, it is widely recognized that the supervisory board system in China is a failure in terms of improving corporate governance. This has been publicly admitted by one senior official of the China Securities Regulatory Commission (CSRC), China's chief watchdog of the capital markets:

> It is sometimes argued that more authority should then be given to the supervisory boards, which sit on top of the boards of our listed companies. However, experience has shown that this system of supervision is not effective as it is often unclear whose interest is being represented by the supervisory board. In many cases, the supervisory board duplicates the authority of the board itself but without corresponding responsibilities. In fact, the presence of the supervisory board may give the illusion of certain checks and balance in the listed company when none existed.[27]

The legal framework of the independent directors system in China

Disappointed at the poor corporate governance of China's listed companies and the ineffectiveness of the supervisory boards, in August 2001 the CSRC issued its "Guidelines on the Introduction of the Independent

Directors System in Listed Companies."[28] Although it is not the CSRC's first mention of independent directors in its regulations,[29] the major difference is that, for the first time, the Guidelines mandate that "[a]ll domestically listed companies shall amend their articles of associations and ... appoint qualified persons to be independent directors."[30] Specifically, "By June 30th, 2002, at least two members of the board of directors shall be independent directors; and by June 30th, 2003, at least one third of [the] board shall be independent directors."[31] The installment of independent directors to the board of directors of listed companies was further required by the CSRC's "Code of Corporate Governance"[32] issued on 7 January 7, 2002, and the 2005-amended Company Law.[33]

Independence requirements

The Guidelines define an independent director as one "who holds no posts in the company other than the position of director, and who maintains no relations with the listed company and its major shareholder that might prevent him from making objective judgment independently."[34] This general (positive) definition is followed by the following negative qualifications which would designate a director as not independent:[35]

(1) An employee of the listed company or its affiliated enterprises, or his/her direct relatives [spouse, father, mother, and children, and so on] and major social relationships [brothers, sisters, father-in-law, mother-in-law, daughter-in-law, son-in-law, sister-in-law, brother-in-law, and so on];
(2) A shareholder who holds more than 1% of the outstanding shares of the listed company directly or indirectly;
(3) A natural person shareholder[36] who is one of the 10 largest shareholders of the listed company, or such person's direct relative;
(4) An employee of a unit which holds more than 5% of the outstanding shares of the listed company directly or indirectly, or of the unit which ranks as one of the 5 largest shareholders of the listed company, or such employee's direct relative;
(5) A person meeting any of the three above-mentioned conditions in the immediate proceeding year;
(6) A person providing financial, legal or consulting services to the listed company or its subsidiaries;
(7) A person stipulated as not qualified as an independent director in the articles of association;
(8) A person determined by the CSRC as not qualified.

In brief, independent directors are required to be independent of the company and its major shareholders and employees, as well as its major professional services providers. Obviously absent is an independence requirement in connection to major business relationships, namely companies with which the listed company has significant transactions. In contrast, the "Final NYSE Corporate Governance Rules" (2003) mandates that a director is not "independent" if he/she is "an executive officer or an employee, or whose immediate family member is an executive officer, of a company that makes payments to, or receives payments from, the listed company for property or services in an amount which, in any single fiscal year, exceeds the greater of $1 million, or 2% of such other company's consolidated gross revenues."[37] Singapore's Code of Corporate Governance 2005, issued by the Ministry of Finance of Singapore, has similar guidelines.[38] The UK Combined Code of Corporate Governance also deems a director not to be independent if he/she has a "material business relationship with the company."[39]

Nomination, election, and retirement of independent directors

An independent director is to be nominated by the board of directors, the supervisory board, or a shareholder or shareholders who independently or jointly have more than a 1% stake in the company. The nominee, before the election in the shareholders' meeting, shall issue a public statement that he/she has no relationship with the listed company that may affect his/her independent objective judgment. The CSRC intervenes before the election, as it requires listed companies to submit the nomination for examination and approval by the CSRC. A nominee who is not approved by the CSRC can stand as a candidate for an ordinary directorship, but not for an independent directorship. If elected, an independent director is not to occupy the position for more than six years. He/she may be removed by the shareholders' meeting, upon the request of the board of directors, if he/she fails to attend the board meeting in person three consecutive times. The Guidelines also state that an independent director may resign before the term expires, but the notice of resignation is to take effect only "after the subsequently appointed independent director fills the vacancy," which implies compulsory board membership and attendance until the replacement director takes up his/her seat.[40]

The powers of independent directors

The Guidelines grant a variety of powers to independent directors. A proposed related-party transaction (defined as a transaction concluded between the listed company and related parties which is in excess of

RMB 3 million or 5% percent of the company's net assets) should be approved by the independent directors before it is submitted to the board of directors for discussion. The independent directors may also appoint outside auditors and consultants and solicit proxy votes before the shareholders' meeting. They can also propose to the board of directors the calling of an extraordinary shareholders' meeting or a meeting of the board of directors, as well as hire or dismiss the company's accounting firm.[41] In addition, the independent directors may issue "independent opinions" with regard to matters relating to the appointment and replacement of directors and senior managers, remuneration for directors and senior managers, and any significant existing or new loans or fund transfers between the listed company and its shareholders, *de facto* controllers, and affiliated enterprises, as well as any other issues or events that the independent directors consider detrimental to the interests of the minority shareholders.[42]

Evaluating the Chinese system of independent directors

By the end of 2004, almost all of China's more than 1,300 listed companies had installed independent directors on the board. On average, each company has three such directors.[43] Has the system proved to be effective, or at least more effective than the supervisory board?

It is important to observe, from a global perspective, there is a lack of empirical evidence on the efficacy of the independent directors in relation to improved corporate governance and firm performance.[44] Bhagat and Black have surveyed the literature on independent directors and concluded that "[t]here remains no convincing evidence that the composition of the board of directors affects overall firm performance."[45] As Tan observes,

> There is a tendency to think that simply having independent directors improves corporate governance. The reality is sometimes the opposite. Unless there are independent directors who are truly independent, and have the strength and ability to perform an effective monitoring function, the presence of independent directors acts as a smokescreen and a snare for the unwary investor who may pay a higher price for the equity on the basis of a supposedly better corporate governance structure.[46]

However, in spite of the debate on the link between board composition and corporate performance, countries undergoing institutional transition still compete to appoint independent directors to the corporate board.[47]Since the independent directors system was implemented in 2002, China has accumulated only four years' experience in this area. It is hence too early to evaluate the effectiveness of the system in that country. However, China, a leading emerging economy, provides an interesting "research laboratory" for corporate governance theorists.[48] There are few signs that independent directors have played a more effective role than the supervisory board in providing checks and balances in relation to management. For example, one CSRC official expressed optimistic views about the role of independent directors in the 2005 OECD Policy Dialogue on Corporate Governance in China, emphasizing in particular that:

> as the Chinese independent directors system has not been established too long and experienced independent directors are badly in need, we must wait longer to witness the obvious significant effects of independent directors on corporate governance; however, we are deeply convinced that the establishment of the independent directors system has already enabled the Chinese people and companies take a big step towards a better understanding of the idea of corporate governance.[49]

However, the purpose of the independent directors system cannot be confined merely to educating the "Chinese people and companies" on corporate governance; the system itself should be part of a purported good corporate governance structure. In this section, we examine the effectiveness of the Chinese independent directors system from a mainly legal perspective, with, fortunately, the assistance of several timely recent empirical studies on the correlations between outside independent directors and firms' performance.

Empirical studies on the effectiveness of independent directors

A joint survey by the Association of Board Secretaries of Listed Companies of Shanghai and Shanghai Jinxin Institute of Securities Research conducted in 2003, two years after China's formal launch of the independent directors system, demonstrated that independent directors had helped to improve corporate governance, especially in terms of bringing professional expertise to the board and protecting the interests of minority shareholders.[50] Empirical research by the Research Center of the Corporate Governance Center of Nankai University shows that the level of competence of independent directors has an obviously positive relationship with the profitability, market value, and financial security of listed companies. It has a negative relationship with the scale of illegal activities of companies.[51] Although the data are still limited and rudimentary, it is increasingly recognized that independent directors can make a difference in firms' governance and performance in China.

Explaining the (limited) efficacy of independent directors in Chinese companies

Compared with the total failure of the supervisory board, the independent directors system has been regarded – albeit with limited empirical evidence – as conducive to good corporate governance. At least in theory, this limited success can be explained from the following perspectives.

First of all, any meaningful – no matter how limited – checks and balances imposed on the management of China's listed companies is supposed to have a positive effect on corporate governance, as poor governance practice in those companies is rampant. According to an "incomplete" survey by the *Beijing Modern Business Daily* in 2004,[52] ten senior managers of several of China's listed companies "disappeared" with corporate funds taken through collusion with related parties and other corporate officers under their direct control, resulting in the loss of over RMB 10 billion (around US$ 1.2 billion) to those corporations. In the first month of 2005, 14 senior managers of listed companies either disappeared or were arrested by the police, causing enormous damage to the companies.[53]

In the state-owned companies, the state is, after all, only an abstract owner. It is common in China that the agents appointed by the state to manage the companies, who were usually civil servants and government officials before their appointment, do not always align their own interests with that of the state. Thus, the agency problems in China's listed SOEs are characterized by the "absence of effective ultimate principal."[54] This has led to the development of one model of insider control, namely the so-called "*guanxiren kongzhi*" [key-person control].[55] The "key person" is usually the CEO, the chairman of the board of directors, or a senior executive manager of the company. In appointing them, the government often loses control over their activities. As a result, the key person usually becomes the *de facto* sole controller of the company. Being the ultimate decision making body in corporate affairs, he/she is in fact endowed with all the powers of control, execution, and supervision.[56] In other cases – whether the company is an SOE or a private enterprise – if the key-person is appointed and controlled by the parent company, he/she acts solely as the representative of the controlling shareholder, having little or no regard for the proprietary rights of minority shareholders.[57] Therefore, the board of directors, comprised of insiders selected by the key person on behalf of the state or the controlling shareholder, can hardly monitor the activities of the key person.

It is reasoned that, at least from a theoretical point of view, the independent directors, not working in the company on a full-time basis and hence less subject to the control of the key person, would impose constraints on the key-person's exercise of power. As noted above, the empirical surveys also reveal that, so far, the installment of independent directors on the board has a positive correlation with the performance of the listed companies.

Limits on the effectiveness of independent directors

Although the independent directors system is, overall, more effective than the supervisory board, the surveys mentioned above all revealed that there was a tremendous gap between the current performance of independent directors and the expectations of the public.[58] This is hardly surprising. Indeed, given the significant limits on the functions of independent directors, as discussed below, it is not easy to sustain optimism on the effectiveness of this system.

Independence

The biggest problem is still how independence is to be maintained. Although independent directors are outsiders, their independence is somehow constrained by their nomination. The CSRC Guidelines for Independent Directors prescribe that they should be nominated by the board of directors, the supervisory board, or a shareholder or shareholders who separately or jointly own more than a 1 percent stake in the outstanding shares of the company, and should be elected by the shareholders' meeting. However, it is difficult to believe that the CSRC is unaware of both the high concentration of ownership among shareholders (that is, a small number of shareholders owning most of the company's outstanding shares) as well as the dysfunction of supervisory boards in China's listed companies. A survey by the *China Securities Daily* has shown that 67.5 percent of independent directors have been nominated by the board of directors, while 27.5 percent have been directly nominated by the controlling shareholders.[59] Further, 52.5 percent of independent directors surveyed said that their remuneration was determined by the company's "senior managers," while 37.5 percent revealed that it was the "controlling shareholders" who decided their remuneration.[60] Clearly, for a significant proportion of independent directors, their constituency is the controlling shareholders.

Will this constituency base affect the independence of the outside directors? Although those directors appear to be more independent than the inside directors, in reality they are far from being as "independent" as one would expect from an outsider who is really free from the insider influence of the company. One independent director pointed out that, in many listed companies, the controlling shareholders wished independent directors to be satisfied with serving as "ornaments" on the corporate Christmas tree, "raising just their hands."[61] Not surprisingly, 65 percent of the independent directors surveyed by the *China Securities Daily* indicated that they had never said "no" to proposals put forward in the meetings of the board of directors, with 100 percent indicating that they had, at least "occasionally," voted "yes" when they should have voted "no" based on the merits of the proposal.[62]

The legal framework designed by the CSRC has created the problems which undermine the effectiveness of independent directors. The CSRC is certainly aware of the extensively reported problems of high-ownership concentration and key-person control in China's listed companies. Nevertheless, it still imposes no restrictions on the power of the controlling shareholders to nominate independent directors, and grants no special privilege to minority shareholders who are the major victims of the agency problems associated with the key-person control model.

The independence of independent directors is further undermined by the "*guanxi*"-based cultural environment which is still prevalent in contemporary Chinese society. *Guanxi* requires one to show respect for the feelings of – or "give face" to – others, especially to one's friends. As one commentator observes,

> In Chinese culture, with its history of several thousand years, the concept of "saving face" or "giving no cold face" to friends is so persistent that it has a huge impact on every personal interaction. Affected by this special cultural environment, it is inevitable that an independent director would be very reluctant to offend his friend, namely the chairman or CEO of the company, even though the chairman or CEO has done something which is detrimental to the interests of the company and its shareholders.[63]

Access to corporate information and other facilities

It is not only the independent directors' independence that is limited; their access to corporate information is also largely controlled by the company's management. A survey conducted in 2004 revealed that about 90 percent of independent directors relied primarily on the company's management for obtaining information, either through the company's annual reports and other materials or through briefings by senior managers of the company.[64] That is to say, very few independent directors had actually employed the tools granted them by the law, such as proxy voting contests, the right to hire external independent auditors, or direct communication with the company's employees or other stakeholders, to supervise the management.

Regarding independent directors' access to information, the legal regime does not offer much help. The CSRC Guidelines for Independent Directors mandate that the listed companies shall provide the independent directors with adequate access to corporate information. It is further required that, "when the independent director performs his/her duties, the relevant persons concerned in the listed company shall cooperate actively and shall not turn down the independent director's proper request, nor shall they hinder the independent director's work or conceal the information."[65] In addition, "the company shall make the necessary working facilities available to the independent directors for them to perform their duties."[66]

The key question here is whether these requirements could be enforced. As noted above, an overwhelming majority of the independent directors depend mainly on the senior corporate officers for information, and are hence influenced or even controlled by the company's management in terms of access to information. When management are determined to withhold negative information from conscientious independent directors who have doubts about the disclosure of corporate information, those directors normally have no other choice than to offer their resignation. They cannot resort to China's corporate law regime, including the CSRC Guidelines for Independent Directors, as the system provides no legal solution if the listed company refuses to provide information. Clearly, when the requirements are not associated with enforcement measures, their legal effects are essentially minimized.

Similarly, although the Guidelines require the company to provide the necessary facilities for independent directors to perform their duties, they do not specify the consequences of violation by the company. For instance, though the Guidelines provide that independent directors can appoint outside auditing or consulting institutions to review the financial affairs of the company, this provision is unlikely to be implemented if the management of the company does not cooperate by bearing the necessary auditing or consulting costs. In a high-profile case in 2004, which is also believed to be the first case in which independent directors challenged the management of the company, the four independent directors of Lianhua

Gourmet Power Co., a company listed on the Shanghai Stock Exchange, requested the management to retain independent outside auditors to review the illegal occupation of the funds of the listed company by its largest shareholder to the amount of RMB 949 million. The request was simply ignored by both the management and the controlling shareholder, resulting in a situation referred to as "*buliao liaozhi*" in Chinese, meaning "settling a matter by leaving it unsettled."[67]

Liability of independent directors

Independent directors are assigned a number of rights and duties by the Guidelines. From a legal perspective, rights and duties must necessarily be associated with liability. In other words, the directors should face legal consequences if they fail to perform their duties. With regard to duties, the Guidelines require that

> The independent directors shall bear the duties of good faith and due diligence and care towards the listed company and all the shareholders. They shall earnestly perform their duties in accordance with laws, regulations and the company's articles of association, shall protect the overall interests of the company, and shall be especially concerned with protecting the interests of minority shareholders from being infringed. Independent directors shall carry out their duties independently and shall not subject themselves to the influence of the company's major shareholders, actual controllers, or other entities or persons who are interested parties of the listed company.[68]

But what are the legal consequences if the independent directors fail to fulfill their duties? Again, the Guidelines do not specify the consequences of violation, except that an independent director shall be removed if he or she fails to attend a board meeting in person three times in a row.[69] Of course, an independent director is also subject to the legal liabilities imposed by the Company Law on any director who violates his/her duty of good faith and loyalty.[70]

A judicial case decided in 2002 revealed that if an independent director fails to perform his/her legal duties, he/she may be subject to the disciplinary actions of the CSRC. Lu Jiahao, a former independent director of the listed company Zhengbaiwen, was fined RMB 100,000 by the CSRC because he failed to take remedial action when the company made false disclosures to the public. Lu then took the CSRC to the Beijing Number One Intermediate Court to appeal, but his appeal was rejected on the grounds of procedural error. The case has served as an alarm call to independent directors, reminding them of the high risks involved in their role within the company.[71]

However, the current issue for China's independent directors is not how harsh the punishment should be. If such strict liability is not counterbalanced with the proper institutions to support the independent directors in the performance of their duties (for example, ensuring that administrative and judicial remedies are available to the independent directors or shareholders if the company's management refuses to grant the independent directors access to corporate information and facilities), it can only prevent more able persons from joining the pool of independent directors, which badly needs more members. In fact, there was a race to resign among independent directors in 2002 in the wake of the Lu Jiahao case.[72]

Concluding remarks

The creation of independent directors in China's listed companies was a direct response of the CSRC to the virtually complete failure of the supervisory board system. Empirical studies, rudimentary as they are, suggest that independent directors have contributed to the improvement of corporate governance, but one has to attribute this to the extremely poor quality of corporate governance in China's listed companies prior to the establishment of the independent directors system in 2001. However, independent directors are able to exercise some checks and balances on the powers of the manager or the representative of the controlling shareholder.

As the independent directors system has been in place in China for only four years, it is still too early to assess the effectiveness of this institution. Note also that it was imported into China from its origin countries (mainly the U.S. and the U.K.) which have a very different legal and cultural environment from that of the transplant country. Although the institution has achieved limited success, it is not easy for observers to be very optimistic about the role of independent directors in corporate governance in China, unless certain fundamental problems, which are deeply rooted in the economic, political, and legal environment surrounding China's enterprise sectors, are remedied. Those problems include, most notably, the lack of true independence of the independent directors and the weak enforcement measures in relation to violation of the legal rules giving powers and privileges to independent directors.

Notes

1. Pistor et al. (2003, p. 89) (noting: "[w]hen the first corporate statutes were enacted, there were remarkably few differences among countries and legal families").
2. Ibid., p. 94.
3. Ibid.
4. The countries in this survey have transplanted corporate law as follows: Chile, Colombia and Spain – from French law; Israel and Malaysia – from English common law; and Japan – from German and U.S. law).
5. Pistor et al. (2003, p. 98).
6. The authors of this survey admit this by saying "the small size of the sample cautions us against overgeneralization" (see ibid., p. 109).
7. Ibid.
8. Art and Gu (1995, p. 275).
9. Ibid.
10. Wang (2004, pp. 40–2, discussing the poor corporate governance of China's listed companies). See also Yang and Fan (2004).
11. Zhonghua Renmin Gongheguo Gongsifa (The Company Law of the People's Republic of China) was promulgated on December 23, 1993, with 230 Articles. In 2005, the National People's Congress of China brought amendments to almost all Articles of the law, making it almost a new Company Law, with 219 Articles.
12. Art and Gu (1995, p. 295).
13. Company Law (2005 Rev.), Articles 109 and 47. See also Art and Gu (1995, p. 295).
14. Company Law (2005 Rev.), Article 110.
15. Company Law (2005 Rev.), Article 115.
16. Company Law (1993), Article 54.
17. Company Law (2005 Rev.), Articles 119 and 54.
18. Company Law (2005 Rev.), Article 118.
19. Schneider and Heidenhain (1996).
20. Ibid., p. 10.
21. Berlin Initiative Group (2006, Part I:6).
22. A non-functional trade union may be one that is dormant due to workers shifting to another union, or a union set up solely as a framework to accommodate Chinese Communist party members, and so on.
23. Tenev and Zhang (2002, p. 100), Dahya (2003, pp. 313–16), SSE (2004, p. 44).
24. SSE (2003, p. 160).
25. SSE (2004, p. 44).
26. Dahya et al. (2003, p. 315). See also SSE (2004, p. 44).
27. Cha (2001).
28. *Zhongguo Zhengquan Jiandu Guanli Weiyuanhui Guanyu Fabu <Guanyu Zai Shangshi Gongsi Jianli Duli Dongshi Zhidu De Zhidao Yijian> De Tongzhi* [The China Securities Regulatory Commission Notice on Issuing the Guidelines for Introducing Independent Directors Listed Companies], Zhengjianfa [2001] No. 102, August 16, 2001, English text available at: http://www.csrc.gov.cn/

en/jsp/detail.jsp?infoid=1061947864100&type=CMS.STD (accessed February 12, 2006).

29. The CSRC indicated in its "Guidelines on Articles of Associations of Companies" issued in 1997 that "companies may set independent directors according to their needs."
30. CSRC Guidelines on Independent Directors, Article I:3.
31. Ibid.
32. *Zhongguo Zhengquan Jiandu Guanli Weiyuanhui Shangshi Gongsi Zhili Zhunze* [CSRC Code of Corporate Governance for China's Listed Companies], January 7, 2002, Zhengjianfa [2002] No. 1, available at: http://www.csrc.gov.cn/en/jsp/detail.jsp?infoid=1061968722100&type=CMS.STD.
33. Company Law (2005 Rev.), Article 123.
34. CSRC Guidelines on Independent Directors, Article I:1.
35. CSRC Guidelines on Independent Directors, Article III.
36. A "natural person shareholder" refers to a real person, whereas a "legal person shareholder" refers to an economic entity such as a company or some form of social or economic organization.
37. New York Stock Exchange, "Final NYSE Corporate Governance Rules" (2003), available at: http://www.nyse.com/pdfs/finalcorpgovrules.pdf (accessed February 15, 2005).
38. See Code of Corporate Governance 2005, Article 2.1(d), at: http://www.ccdg.gov.sg/news/pdf/AnnexE_Code_of_Corporate_Governance_2005.pdf (accessed February 14, 2006).
39. See UK Combined Code on Corporate Governance (2003), Article 3.1, available at: http://www.fsa.gov.uk/pubs/ukla/lr_comcode2003.pdf (accessed February 14, 2006).
40. CSRC Guidelines on Independent Directors, Article IV.
41. CSRC Guidelines on Independent Directors, Article V.
42. CSRC Guidelines on Independent Directors, Article VI.
43. Yang (2005, p. 2).
44. Tan (2003), Baysinger and Butler (1984).
45. Bhagat and Black (1998, pp. 299–300).
46. Tan (2003, p. 378).
47. Peng (2004, p. 453).
48. Ibid.
49. Yang (2005, p. 2).
50. *Securities Daily* (2003). The survey shows that, over 90 percent of the secretaries of the board of directors viewed that the independent directors can play a "certain" role in preventing listed companies from making misrepresentations and fabricating documents, and in improving corporate governance structure, enhancing disclosure and transparency, and protecting the interests of minority shareholders.
51. Li et al. (2004).
52. See *Beijing Modern Business Daily* (2004).
53. Chen (2005).
54. Clarke (2003, p. 499).
55. Tan and Wang (2007).
56. Ibid.
57. Ibid.

58. *China Securities Daily* (2005), *Shanghai Securities News* (2004a).
59. *China Securities Daily* (2005).
60. Ibid.
61. *Shanghai Securities News* (2004b) (comment by Prof. Dong Ansheng relating to his career as an independent director in several listed companies).
62. *China Securities Daily* (2005).
63. Xie (2004, p. 320).
64. *China Securities Daily* (2005).
65. CSRC Guidelines for Independent Directors, Article VII:3.
66. CSRC Guidelines for Independent Directors, Article VII:2.
67. *China Securities Daily* (2005).
68. CSRC Guidelines for Independent Directors, Article I:2.
69. CSRC Guidelines for Independent Directors, Article IV:5.
70. Company Law (2005 Rev.), Articles 147–53.
71. Gu (2003, pp. 70–1).
72. Ibid., p. 71.

References

Art, Robert C., and Minkang Gu (1995) "China Incorporated: The First Corporation Law of the People's Republic of China," *Yale Journal of International Law*, 20, 273–308.

Baysinger, Barry D., and Butler, Henry N. (1984)."Revolution Versus Evolution in Corporation Law: The ALI's Project and the Independent Director," *George Washington Law Review*, 52, 560–81.

Beijing Modern Business Daily [*Beijing Xiandai Shangbao*] (2004) "10 Billion Yuan Embezzlement out [of China's] Listed Companies. The Signs before the Impending Escape of Senior Managers from the Companies" ["Yinian Ban 10 Ren Juanzou Shangshi Gongsi Baiyi. Gaoguan Waitao Qian Zhengzhao"], June 23, available at: http://news.xinhuanet.com/stock/2004-06/23/content_1541441.htm.

Berlin Initiative Group (2006) "German Code of Corporate Governance," Berlin, June 2, Part I:6, available at: http://www.gccg.de/eng_German-Code-of-Corporate-Governance.pdf.

Bhagat, S. and Black, B. (1998) "The Relationship between Board Composition and Firm Performance," in K. J. Hopt and S. Prigge (eds.), *Comparative Corporate Governance: The State of the Art and Emerging Research* (Oxford: Clarendon Press).

Cha, Laura M. (2001) "The Future of China's Capital Markets and the Role of Corporate Governance." Speech at China Business Summit by the Vice Chairman of the China Securities Regulatory Commission, April 18, 2001, available at: http://www.csrc.gov.cn/en/jsp/detail.jsp?infoid=1061948105100&type=CMS.STD.

Chen, Hua (2005) "The Fall of 12 Senior Managers in One Month. Insider Supervision of Listed Companies is Worrisome" ["1 Ge Yue 12 Wei Gaoguan Luoma. Shangshi Gongsi Neibu Jianguan LIngren Danyou"], *Caijing Daily* [*Caijing Shibao*], February 5, available at: http://finance.sina.com.cn/stock/stocktalk/20050205/10191351494.shtml.

China Securities Daily [*Zhongguo Zhengquan Bao*] (2005) ["Survey on China's Independent Directors and Reflections on the Institutions" ["Zhongguo Dudong Diaocha Ji Zhidu Fansi"], July 28, available at: http://www.cs.com.cn/sylm/04/t20050728_723933.htm.

Clarke, Donald C. (2003) "Corporate Governance in China: An Overview," *China Economic Review*, 14, 494–507.

Dahya, Jay, et al. (2003) "The Usefulness of the Supervisory Board Report in China," *Corporate Governance*, 11(4), 308–21.

Gu, Minkang (2003) "Will an Independent Director Perform Better than a Supervisory?" *Journal of Chinese and Comparative Law*, 6, 59–76.

Li, Weian, et al. (2004) "Nankai Pandian Sannian Dudong Zhidu De Gongsi Zhili Jiazhi," 9 *Zhongwai Guanli* [*Sino-Foreign Management*], 9, available at: http://www.zwgl.com.cn/doc/Article/2004831183336-1.shtml (in Chinese).

Peng, Mike W. (2004) "Outside Directors and Firm Performance during Institutional Transitions," *Strategic Management Journal*, 25, 453–71.

Pistor, Katharina, et al. (2003) "Evolution of Corporate Law and the Transplant Effect: Lessons from Six Countries," *World Bank Research Observer*, 18(1), 89–112.

Schneider, Hannes, and Heidenhain, Martin (1996) *The German Stock Corporation Act* (The Hague: Kluwer Law International).

Securities Daily [*Zhengquan Shibao*] (2003) "A Survey of the Current Situation: What Happens to Independent Directors?" ["Xianzhuang Diaocha: Duli Dongshi Zenmeyang Le?"], August 7, available at: http://business.sohu.com/37/91/news211889137.shtml.

Shanghai Securities News [*Shanghai Zhengquan Bao*] (2004a) "Survey of China's Independent Directors: The State of Living of China's Independent Directors" ["Zhongguo Dudong Diaocha: Zhongguo Dudong Shengcun Xianzhuang Diaochao"], May 27, available at: http://paper.cnstock.com/ssnews/2004-5-27/liuban/t20040527_571548.htm.

Shanghai Securities News (2004b) "Survey of China's Independent Directors: My Career as an Independent Director" ["Zhongguo Dudong Diaocha: Wo De Dudong Shengya"], May 27, available at: http://paper.cnstock.com/ssnews/2004-5-27/qiban/t20040527_571546.htm.

SSE (Shanghai Stock Exchange Research Center) (2003) *China Corporate Governance Report 2003* [*Zhongguo Gongsi Zhili Baogao (2003 nian)*] (Shanghai: Fudan University Press).

SSE (2004) *China Corporate Governance Report 2004* [*Zhongguo Gongsi Zhili Baogao (2004 nian)*] (Shanghai: Fudan University Press).

Tan, Cheng Han (2003) "Corporate Governance and Independent Directors," *Singapore Academy of Law Review*, 15, 355–91.

Tan, Lay-Hong, and Wang, Jiangyu (2007) "Modeling an Effective Corporate Governance System for China's Listed State-owned Enterprises: Issues and Challenges in a Transition Economy," *Journal of Corporate Law Studies*, 7(1).

Tenev, Stoyan, and Zhang, Chunlin (with Loup Brefort) (2002) *Corporate Governance and Enterprise Reform in China: Building the Institutions of Modern Markets* (Washington D.C.: World Bank and the International Finance Corporation).

Xie, Chaobin (2004) *A Study of the Independent Director System* [*Duli Dongshi Falv Zhidu Yanjiu*] (Beijing: Law Press China [Falv Chubanshe]) (in Chinese).

Yang, Chao, and Fan, Qinghua (2004) "Independent Directors: The Vase was Broken," *Zhongwai Guanli* [*Sino-Foreign Management*], 9, available at: http://www.zwgl.com.cn/doc/Article/2004831183336-1.shtml (in Chinese).

Yang, Hua (2005) "Overview of Governance of State-owned Listed Companies in China," OECD Proceedings of the Second Policy Dialogue on Corporate Governance in China, Beijing, May 19, available at: http://www.oecd.org/dataoecd/14/6/34974067.pdf (conference materials website: http://www.oecd.org/document/45/0,2340,en_2649_201185_34965229_1_1_1_1,00.html).

Wang, Jiangyu (2004) "Dancing with Wolves: Regulation and Deregulation of Foreign Investment in China's Stock Market," *Asian-Pacific Law and Policy Journal*, 5, 1–61.

10
Low Structure, High Ambiguity: Selective Adaptation of International Norms of Corporate Governance Mechanisms in China

S. H. Goo and Anne Carver

The theme of this volume is the selective adaptation of international standards in dispute resolution. In the area of corporate governance, it is difficult to talk in terms of selective adaptation of international standards as there is not a single set of international standards in corporate governance which can be adopted or adapted by any country but a variety of models of laws, regulations and practices around the world.[1] Even the OECD Principles of Corporate Governance are no more than a mere statement of principles and aspiration, not detailed workable rules or standards which can be adopted or adapted. However, there are clearly certain corporate governance practices and mechanisms, mostly from the European and Anglo-American models, that are adopted and adapted in other parts of the world. In this chapter, we focus on the issue of selective adaptation of those Western models of corporate governance in China.

Western models of corporate governance and company law are tending to converge into what could be termed a global corporatism. For the international and institutional Western investors the model is epitomized by the OECD's[2] notions of what is "fair" with a strong emphasis on the protection of shareholders through transparency and disclosure mechanisms. These are said to be the preconditions for good corporate governance that create a strong capital market for which the investor is said to be willing to pay a premium in order to minimize risk and maximize potential gain. Arguably, therefore, corporate governance systems can be said to represent a microcosm of the legal expectations of shareholders who look to a system of checks and balances to protect their interests. If we accept this argument, then we must also accept that each corporate governance system has within it social, economic, and cultural variations that play a greater or lesser role in how flexible and accommodating those investors will be towards those who act as their economic agents.

With their shared common heritage and cultural traditions, the differences between the common law and civil law Western traditions are differences of form over substance. Nevertheless, it is the Anglo-American model with some civil law characteristics that has assumed central position on the world's stock markets, with civil law characteristics particularly the adoption of stakeholder theory as a value system. The more interesting issue is whether China's social, cultural, and legal traditions will continue to influence the continuing developments in Chinese company law, or whether the evolution of China's corporate governance system must inevitably follow the Anglo-American system if it is to succeed on the terms of the international investor. China's Company Law and the corporate governance system currently in place owe more to the longstanding and deeply held Chinese values upholding the importance of flexibility, resulting in tolerance for degrees of freedom in decision making depending upon the context. This has been described[3] as a system of "low structure, high ambiguity" in which the ambiguity itself allows for the context itself to determine what is fair. Chinese Company Law remains ambiguous and, on many important issues, fails to deal with the "who, what, where and how" of legislative drafting that we expect from the common and civil law systems. For the Western investor, therefore, the whole system appears to be legally 'deficient' when compared with the detailed drafting techniques of, for example, the Hong Kong Companies Ordinance.[4] The problem is further complicated since there is no body of case law to supplement the gaps and no doctrine of precedent with which to predict outcomes and to comfort the investor with a sense of deeply held traditions of law, structure, and stability.

This chapter explores the value system captured by the current corporate governance mechanisms in place and the problem of "ambiguity" in China's Company Law. We see China's Company Law as highly flexible and intentionally leaving space for agreement or discretion depending upon the context of the particular situation. The model is, therefore, in direct contrast to Western ideas of corporate governance in which the context of the law is intended to be neutral. The Chinese system assumes the merits of flexibility and discretion. In contrast, the Western model assumes predictability with explicit remedies, stated exceptions to the rule and a reliance on detail to fill in the gaps supplemented by case law developed by judges on a case by case basis, all of which may have value as precedents. This, we suggest, highlights the difference between the legal cultures and is an important factor in identifying how the two systems can achieve consensus in what serves as the appropriate model for a modern Chinese corporate governance system. However, we see that China's Company Law and corporate governance system are beginning to show signs of convergence in the China Securities Regulatory Commission's (CSRC's) Guidelines of 2001 and the 2005 amendments to the Company Law to the Anglo-American model of certainty and predictability, albeit at a slower pace.

However, the success of the convergence will depend not only on learning from the West and designing laws, rules, and regulations that are suitable to the Chinese social and economic developments and legal culture, but also on the supporting legal infrastructure such as the quality of judges and the independence and efficiency of the judiciary,[5] the doctrine of judicial precedents, and the appropriate mix of government regulation and self-regulation, as well as effective enforcement and remedies.[6] Pitman Potter argues that China is engaging in selective adaptation of international norms and the success of that exercise depends also on institutional capacity building.[7]

The background of the current system of corporate governance in China

Western values of independence and the separation of interests

When China's Company Law established the joint stock company and the limited liability company as separate independent legal entities in 1993, there was particular emphasis on transforming the state-owned enterprise into an independent entity. The intention was to use the legal machinery processes and procedures of Western company law models to separate the interests and powers of owners and managers in the supervisory, executive, and managerial roles allocated to them. However, the history of China's corporate governance and company law reforms since 1993 has been a story of the mismatch between the twin concepts of "independence" and the separation of interest and powers enshrined in the ideal of the Western model and the Chinese equivalent. In Western corporate governance parlance, the question is always "Who controls the company?" In Chinese corporate governance terms, the concepts of "independence" and "the separation of powers" do not play the same pivotal role, thus creating much of the difficulty that China has experienced with the imposition of the Western company law model on Chinese-style company law.

The gap between expectation and reality might be more successfully negotiated if the international investors, whom China wishes to impress, recognize the strengths and weaknesses in both systems. Clearly, the way a society functions its goals and its priorities expresses that society's cultural values and, in corporate governance terms, the problems are the same worldwide, but the solutions are different, depending upon the different values that are placed upon individual rights and the interests of the group or wider community. We begin, therefore, with a perspective on what corporate governance means as a value system in China, and where the priorities are fixed and where they are flexible.

The value system of the enterprise as "family" – the stakeholder and the supervisory board

Inventing a legal tradition is never easy. The paradoxes inherent in Western systems of company law and the Western corporate governance "traditions" have proved particularly complex for Chinese company law jurisprudence. In 1994 China recognized the importance of corporate governance as the regulators sought to impose internationally accepted corporate governance provisions onto "Chinese" company law. After studying the various available Western models, they chose the German model of a two-tier board system because the ideal of co-determination between capital and labor would seem to enhance internal unity and company performance.[8] However, it was not a complete adoption of the German two-tier board as the supervisory board in the German joint stock companies (the AG) has equal numbers of shareholders and employee representatives, whereas the employee representatives in a Chinese joint stock company must not be fewer than one-third of the supervisory board. Furthermore, the supervisory board in the German model is more powerful than the Chinese supervisory board even after the 2005 amendment to the Company Law.

At the same time as the regulators and company law reformers sought to measure the success of China's stock markets according to international benchmarks, they superimposed the longstanding rules that we take for granted in the West on China's company law and stock markets. Thus, they "transformed" the corporate legal system by reconstructing and restructuring state-owned enterprises into state-owned companies by establishing modern enterprises with well-defined ownership rights, and separated the role of government administration from that of the business enterprise and the role of management.

The difference between a state-owned enterprise and a state-owned company could not be more fundamental in terms of private property rights and the public/private law divide. Thus, the Company Law changed "state enterprises" into a form of modern corporation. Under the central planning system the state/government had, owned, used, controlled, and disposed of state assets in the state-owned enterprise through its administrative hierarchies, and enterprise managers were regarded as government officials, owing their duty to government.

Western models of corporate law and corporate governance systems (even including the German model) do not regard these economic actors as "one big family." Any analysis of China's corporate governance system must therefore question whether the economic, social, and cultural variations influencing the structure and evolution of China's company law continue to be important in the development of its own corporate governance model. If we accept that these traditions continue to influence the corporate governance structures and the choices that China makes for developing its corporate and regulatory structure then we must also accept that there are two profoundly important Chinese characteristics influencing the current model. The first is a firm belief in the principle of the corporation's responsibility to society and stakeholder relationships as a necessity to hold the society together, a product from the era of planned economy. The second is the belief in the importance of the two-tier board structure as a way of avoiding conflicts and promoting the interests of all the stakeholders. These traditions owe as much to Chinese beliefs and principles as they do to any Western notion of the communitarian model or stakeholder theory.

The characteristics of the Chinese corporate governance system

The board of directors is identified as the head of the company. The managers are responsible for running the company and the supervisory board supervises the acts of the directors and managers. But the supreme body of power is the shareholders. This is essentially the German two-tier board model.

Article 37 of the Company Law provides that the shareholders' meeting is the company's organ of authority and that the shareholders' meeting consists of all the shareholders of the company. Article 38 sets out the full powers of the shareholders' meeting, and in corporate governance terms the most important are:

1. To set out the company's operational guidelines
2. To elect and replace directors and to consider directors' reports
3. To elect and replace supervisors and to consider supervisors' reports.

However, as the largest shareholder in many SOEs, the government did not usually exercise its powers as shareholders to monitor the performance of the board of directors and managers. This leads to the Berle-Means type of "agency problem" seen in many of the large corporations with dispersed shareholders in the West. Thus, effective monitoring mechanisms are needed to prevent abuses by the directors and managers. Unfortunately, the weak Chinese supervisory board failed to perform its supervisory function. As a result, this German model has been modified in the context of Chinese listed companies, with the American influence seen in the CSRC's August 2001 "Guiding Opinion Concerning the Introduction of Independent Directors to Chinese Listed Companies," making the adoption of the "independent director" a compulsory feature of Chinese listed companies. Thus, the Chinese model now has the formal Anglo-American characteristics of independence but continues to mandate the two-tier board system. As discussed below, evidence suggests that the adoption of the Western idea of independent director on Chinese soil has also failed to perform the expected functions.

The selective adaptation of the German model and the Anglo-American model combined together has created a strange creature and confusion. Might it be the case that the two are working against each other despite the best intentions underpinning company law reform? The Chinese government appears determined to continue with this strange creature. In its latest attempt, the Chinese legislature has made it a formal requirement of the Company Law for listed companies to have independent directors and has increased the powers of the supervisory board.

The role of the state

Like company law in other parts of the world, Chinese Company Law establishes three separate levels for operational control: the shareholders' meeting, the board of directors (supervised by the board of supervisors), and management. Final authority rests with the shareholders' meeting which appoints the members of the board of directors and supervisors. The checks and balances are set out on paper, but the presence of government as a major shareholder in the state-owned enterprises (SOEs) has made it difficult to put effective corporate governance in place because of the vast concentration of shares and the role of the state, leading to ignoring minority views and failure to provide key information to the minority shareholders.

There is also the problem that the majority government shareholder will abuse its voting powers in the appointment of representatives to the boards and in the questions of executive pay. The issue of majority shareholders is not, of course, unique to China, and we have seen the problem of the family-controlled company raised in, for example, Hong Kong and identified as a corporate governance problem for institutional investors. What is unique to China, however, is the role of the state as a majority investor and the explicit blurring of the public/private law divide and legal duties in the public role and as investor. State shares are seen as a negative factor in corporate governance because of the close links to regulators and government departments who are unwilling to take action. This might either be because of the conflicts of personal interest, or because the wider interests of government may not be seen to be served by public disclosure and reprimand. There appears to be a reluctance to criticize other government officials publicly and the additional problem of the influence exerted by each government department on the company and what is or is not in the best interests of the company.

The Chinese government faced a dilemma in trying to modernize the corporate governance in SOEs, on the one hand, while maintaining controlling ownership in SOEs, on the other hand. As the government did not have the expertise and resources to exercise effective monitoring and control on directors and managers, it tried to improve the situation by reducing its controlling stake in the SOEs. As at 2005, the government's stake in the stock market amounted to two-thirds of the Chinese stock market capitalization. The government suggested for the second time since 2001 that it should sell off most or all of the state-owned shares and create a truly independent system of supply and demand. After an initial period of delay in mid 2005 amidst concerns about flooding China's market, the government has slowly sold off some of the non-tradable state-owned shares in a range of mainland industries.

Another sign that the government is trying to leave the market to function is its amendments to the Company Law and Securities Law. On August 28, 2004, The Standing Committee of the 10th National People's Congress (NPC) amended Article 131(2) of China's Company Law and revised China's Securities Law to bring it into line with the Company Law amendment. The amendment deleted Article 131(2), the requirement that a company wishing to issue stock over book value had to obtain prior approval from the Securities Administration of State Council. The deletion recognizes the reduced role of government in setting prices, and that it is supply and demand and investor confidence that sets the stock price, not the result of a government order.[9] This 2004 revision to the Company Law is an important step towards the clearer separation of powers, ownership, and control, and separation of government administration from enterprise management that have not traditionally formed part of Chinese corporate legal culture.

We now turn to a brief discussion of the 2001 reforms to China's corporate governance system by way of background to the current developments.

The 2001 major corporate governance reforms to the system

In 2001 the CSRC issued the "Proposed Guideline Opinions on the Establishment of Independent Directors Within Listed Companies" and the "Code of Corporate Governance for Listed Companies in China." We shall begin with an analysis of the guidelines on independent directors which followed on from the December 1997 "Guidelines Concerning Articles of Association of Listed Companies." It is significant that the concept of an "independent" director is an Anglo-American corporate governance term designed for the unitary board system and does not appear in the German two-tier board system where members of the supervisory board fulfill the same functions. Problems arise in identifying the different roles, a possible duplication of roles or indeed a possible lack of cooperation or a lack of objectivity between members of the supervisory board and the independent director. Quite why the independent director was adopted as the gold standard of good corporate governance to give effect to the OECD's Principles[10] is not clear to us – whether it was an idea picked up by the CSRC or whether it was suggested by the international investing community. Whether it fits China's "low structure, high ambiguity" modality is another question, but the evidence so far suggests that it has not worked well.

Independent directors and the SOEs

The CSRC's 1997 Guidelines for the first time introduced the appointment of an independent director as optional for listed companies. Article 112 of the Guidelines provided that:

> A company may establish independent directorships when necessary. The following personnel shall not serve as independent directors:
> 1. Shareholders or staff form a shareholders' unit;
> 2. Personnel inside the company; and
> 3. Those who have a relationship of interest with a person related to the company or with management ...

On March 29, 1999, the State Economic and Trade Commission and the CSRC issued the "Proposals on Further Promoting Standard Operation of Listed Companies Outside China and Deepening Reform," mandating at least two independent directors on the board. In November 2000 the Shanghai Stock Exchange issued its "Guidelines for Governance of Listed Companies," suggesting that there should be at least two independent directors in place. By 2001, the CSRC had prepared its Guideline Opinions on the Establishment of Independent Directors Within Listed Companies, with detailed provisions on the "who, what, where, how and when" of independent directors.

Under the 2001 Guidelines, independent directors for Chinese listed companies were no longer an option. The intention was that by June 2002 there had to be at least two independent directors on the board, and by June 30, 2003, at least one-third of the board members would be independent directors.

The 2001 CSRC Proposed Guidelines Opinion on Independent Directors

On August 6, 2001, when the CSRC adopted the idea of independent director under its 2001 Guideline Opinions on the Establishment of Independent Directors Within Listed Companies as one of the major corporate governance reform measures, the intention was to control the biggest shareholders – that is, government – in the state-owned entities. The issue was seen as how to prevent abuse of shareholder power by the largest shareholder, the government, which holds the majority of the shares, given that the state has allocated to itself the majority of the shares in the transformation of the SOEs into state-owned entities.

Article 2 of the 2001 Guidelines also adopts the common law and equitable duties of a director in the Anglo-American model of corporate governance.

It provides that:

> The independent director shall bear the duties of good faith and due diligence and care towards the listed company and all shareholders. They shall earnestly perform their duties in accordance with law regulations and the company's articles of association, shall protect the overall interest of the company and shall be especially concerned with protecting the interests of minority shareholders from being infringed. Independent directors shall carry out their duties independently and shall not subject themselves to the influence of the company's major shareholders, actual controllers, or other entities or persons who are interested parties of the listed company. In principle, independent directors can only hold concurrently the post of independent directors

in five listed companies at maximum. They shall have enough time and energy to perform the duties of independent directors effectively.

Part VI of the Guidelines provides that the independent director shall express the independent opinion on the major events occurring in the listed companies. Furthermore, apart from carrying out the above-mentioned duties, the independent director shall provide the independent opinion on the following matters to the board of the directors or to the shareholders' meeting:

(a) Nomination or replacement of directors
(b) Appointment or dismissal of senior managers
(c) Remuneration for directors and senior managers
(d) Any existing or new loan borrowed from a listed company, or other funds transfer made by the company's shareholders, actual controllers or affiliated enterprises that exceeds RMB 3 million yuan or 5 percent of the company's net assets and audited recently; and whether the company has taken effective measures to collect the amount due
(e) Events that the independent director considers to be detrimental to the interests of minority shareholders
(f) Other matters stipulated by the articles of association.

The Code of Corporate Governance

To address the lack of specificity in the Company Law, the CSRC issued a Code of Corporate Governance on January 7, 2001. In the Code, we see a continuing focus on the duty of loyalty of company directors (Articles 33–9 Chapter 3): directors must diligently perform their duties, ensure adequate time and energy is spent in the performance of their duties, and attend board meetings in a diligent and responsible manner; they must familiarize themselves with relevant laws, master the relevant necessary knowledge and strictly fulfill the undertakings they made publicly. The duties of the board of directors are set out in Articles 40–3.

The formal structure and the problem of the supervisory board's decision making in Western corporate governance terms

In 1994 when the Chinese chose the two-tier board structure for the corporate governance of SOEs, they sought to fuse the interests of labor and capital along the lines of the German co-determination model. The two-tier board system separates the executor (that is, management) and administrative functions of the company from the monitoring functions of the company. In theory, therefore, the system avoids the personal conflicts of interest that arise in the unitary board structure of the Anglo-American model between the interests of the company and the interests of the individual director. Under the Company Law the supervisory board is made up of representatives of shareholders and an appropriate proportion of staff and workers (Articles 52, 124). This follows the German model which divides the supervisory board into representatives of the stockholders and representatives of the employees.

Under German company law, upon which the Chinese model is loosely based, there is a mandatory two-tier structure with the managing board of directors "the board" and a supervisory board. The supervisory board has a pre-eminent position. As the name suggests, it has supervisory powers over the business decisions of the board of directors. It is above the board of directors and above the control of directors and managers. It may also make its own business decisions in addition to those decisions made by the board of directors. It supervises the company's financial affairs and the members are appointed by the shareholders in general meeting. After appointment, the supervisory board elects the members of the board of directors who are under a duty to report to the supervisory board. Thus the supervisory board in the German model is both a supervisory and a decision making body with authority over the board of directors. Most characteristic of all is the co-determination principle and legal requirement that the supervisory board must appoint an equal number of employee and shareholder representatives to sit as members of the supervisory board. In contrast, Chinese Company Law does not require an equal number but an "appropriate number" of representatives of employees.

The German supervisory board's functions are set out in the Stock Corporations Act and, while not directly involved in management decisions, it may approve major decisions. The supervisory board fixes the directors' salaries and has the right to appoint and dismiss the directors. What it does not have is the power to order the board to act in a certain way. In contrast, even after the amendment to the Company Law in 2005, the supervisory board in China still does not have the wide powers that the German supervisory board enjoys. Article 52 of the 1994 Company Law provided that a limited liability company with a relatively large business "will create a supervisory board with a minimum of three members." Under Article 124, a joint stock company had to have a supervisory board that consisted of at least three members. The supervisory board's responsibilities were set out in Articles 54 and 126, respectively, as:

1. financial review
2. supervising the directors' and management's compliance with the law
3. requiring directors and managers to rectify their actions if they were in conflict with the company's objectives, that is, making the directors remedy the situation personally
4. convening interim board meetings when necessary
5. fulfilling any other duties that were stipulated in the articles of association.

There was some overlap with the model of the Japanese Commercial (Business) Code, but the powers set out in Articles 54 and 126 were too limited in comparison with those set out in the German Stock Corporations Act (22 powers) and the Japanese Commercial (Business) Act (14 powers).

The supervisory board was to consist of the shareholders' representatives and "an appropriate proportion of the staff and workers of the company." Once elected, the supervisor served for three years, and consecutive terms if re-elected (Articles 53 and 125). In addition to complying with the articles of association, a supervisor had to work in "the best interests of the company" and not abuse their position, functions, and powers in the company to seek personal gain (Articles 59 and 128).

The gap between reality and expectation of the law in the role and powers of the supervisory board

The problem of the role of the supervisory board in China had been characterized as the inferior position in the corporate governance power structure. It was seen as a subordinate of directors and senior managers. In practice, despite its legal authority and powers to supervise the board's management and executive functions, the opposite occurred; as the board nominated members of the supervisory board, the supervisors did not always censure or criticize the board. The supervisory board in China did not have the right to sue on behalf of the company. Nor could it dismiss the directors.

The way forward

Chinese reformers have therefore made great attempts and continue to bring the corporate governance of SOEs and other non-SOEs in line with international norms and standards in the Company Law in 1994, the Securities Law, the CSRC's Code of Corporate Governance and Guidelines and now the 2005 Company Law. While the CSRC's Code of Corporate Governance and Guidelines on the establishment of an independent directors system were a big step forward, the success of the independent directors system had been called into question.

The problems

As we have seen, there were a number of problems[11] with the 1994 law which could be grouped under three headings:

1. Gaps in the law
   - lack of clear rules on directors' fiduciary duties
   - lack of rights of legal action by minority shareholders
2. Compliance problems
   - disseminating unrealistic or deliberately misleading information or overly optimistic forecasts to shareholders, or manufacturing false financial statements to cover up losses or to become listed,[12] or to secure loans[13]
   - companies obtaining land use with local government's approval illegally and violating environmental standards[14]
   - asset stripping[15]
   - directors running a parallel operation in competition with their companies[16]
   - "cooking" the books[17]
3. Enforcement problems
   - regulators do not have adequate resources to enforce the law
   - measures (for example, public censures) taken by regulators are not effective
   - lack of judicial independence in shareholder disputes
   - lack of legal rights by shareholders to sue for corporate wrongdoing.

Group (1) relates to problems encountered in selective adaptation, while (2) and (3) relate to institutional capacity building.

Explanations for the problems

There are a number of theories to explain the corporate governance problems in China. First, many problems were due to the fact that China's reformers did not pay enough attention to the Chinese characteristics in designing new Corporate Governance law.[18] They should identify the characteristics of Chinese SOEs and non-SOEs and design a system or systems that would deal with or play to the strength of these characteristics. The adoption of an independent directors system is an example of the lack of sensitivity to the Chinese characteristics, as Chinese business people do not traditionally trust outsiders and there are not enough qualified people to serve as independent directors. In Potter's framework of analysis, this means there is a problem of perception of the purpose, content, and effect of both foreign and local institutional arrangements, and the complementarity between the two.[19]

Second, the traditional kinship, which dominates the clan corporation, continues to affect and dominate contemporary Chinese society, even in Communist China.[20] In other words, the Chinese way of life continues to affect how business is run in China.[21] Business operations are traditionally run like a family (for example, within a clan corporation) in Chinese society and the younger and lower-ranking members of the family trust the older members of the family to look after them – a tradition of "high trust, low structure." This explains the lack of many laws, for example, the law on fiduciary duties, as such laws were not needed because of the high levels of trust. While in many cases this high trust is observed, there are many cases in modern times where this is not the case, and many instances of misconduct have occurred as a result (such as those mentioned above under the heading "compliance problems"). As pointed out, increased complexity in socioeconomic and political relations may require norms of formality and objectivity to replace informal and subjective relational norms associated with tradition.[22]

There are other possible explanations. There is the lack of clear understanding on the part of the Chinese legislature that Anglo-American law requires very clear rules as well as general principles, supplemented with case law and voluntary codes to make it a workable system. Even the 2005 Company Law continues to suffer from this problem. There is also a culture of not explicitly stating what is usually implicitly understood, thus giving the impression of "high ambiguity" to Western eyes. For example, Article 63 of the 1994 Company Law states that when directors, supervisors, and managers are in breach of law, administrative regulations, or articles of association in the execution of their responsibilities and cause loss or damage to the company, they should bear the responsibility to compensate, and it is probably understood that (1) they should compensate the company as it is the company that suffers the loss, and (2) shareholders can bring an action against the wrongdoing directors if the company does not bring an action, as otherwise the directors would not have to compensate. Again, a problem of perception and complementarity.

These points may very well explain the current problems in the system, but they do not justify the continued existence of these problems. We need to solve the problems that exist in the corporate governance system, but the question remains as to how to do so. Can we continue to rely on the Chinese ways of doing things, or must we adopt the Western style? The above explanations offer some support to the argument that adoption or transplantation of a foreign system without the necessary supporting preconditions and infrastructure would not yield the intended results. Selective adaptation with sufficient institutional capacity building, however, appears to offer a workable alternative, and is happening in China.

The right approach to the problems

We think that both Chinese reformers and the international investors should realize that there is not a single superior Western model of corporate governance. We are all in search of solutions that would work in different places to achieve the corporate goals we want to achieve within our ideologies, be it shareholder value or stakeholder interests. Because the West has a long history of corporate law and is, on the whole, reasonably successful with its corporate governance system, we want to see if there is anything we can learn from it. But the West has not got all the answers yet and is still searching for solutions to some of its corporate governance problems, as recent corporate scandals in the U.S. and Australia demonstrate. Chinese reformers, while learning from the successes and mistakes of the West, must also pay due regard to the circumstances of China and be confident enough to discuss, debate, and devise their own solutions which would work in China.

On the other hand, China needs to take into consideration the needs and concerns of the international investors as it becomes a member of the global community, particularly after its accession to the World Trade Organization (WTO), while the West needs to allow different solutions to be found for the problems in China. How to strike a balance is a very difficult task, depending on the nature of the problems and the peculiarity of conditions and circumstances in which the problems are found in China and the degree of tolerance the West is willing to show regarding the adoption of different solutions. But the ultimate mission is to find mechanisms that work.

For example, foreigners want to have clear and detailed provisions which spell out the fiduciary duties and the shareholders' rights of legal action. Should the Company Law be amended to contain such provisions (to have high structure and low ambiguity to suit the Western style), or be left as it is (to have low structure and high ambiguity) to suit the Chinese style? Given that a high degree of ambiguity can invite disputes even among Chinese people, let alone between Chinese people and the foreign investors, it makes sense to adopt the Western approach on this specific matter. In this regard, although it is pleasing to see that the Company Law 2005 contains provisions on directors' fiduciary duties and provisions for direct shareholder action and derivative action, there is still room to provide further details in those provisions, as we will explain below.

On the other hand, it is also important to note that there is a debate even in the Anglo-American system, for example, in the U.K. and Hong Kong, as to whether directors' fiduciary duties and duties of care and skill should be stated in statute. In the U.K., directors' fiduciary duties and duty of care and skills have recently been codified in the Company Act 2006, while in Hong Kong, the government decided against codification but issued a statement of duties as non-legal guidelines. Thus, while China should have detailed provisions on directors' duties, whether these provisions should be stated in the Company Law or in another, less formal, form (such as the CSRC's Code of Corporate Governance) is something which is just as important. In Hong Kong, and in the U.K. until the 2006 Act, directors' fiduciary duties are developed by judges and judges can develop the case law as new situations arise to fill the gap. But this is not possible in China as there is no formal system of judicial precedent. This is another obstacle that is likely to affect the effectiveness of detailed provisions on directors' duties in China, even though there is now an increased use of the casebook in China in the study and practice of law.

Understanding the Chinese characteristics

What we thus need is to identify and understand the characteristics of Chinese society and culture and devise a system (whether by adoption or selective adaptation or home grown) that would deal effectively with the problems in China. So what are the Chinese characteristics? We do not know China enough to identify all the relevant Chinese characteristics, but a few obvious ones spring to mind:

1. Most companies are SOEs, but there is an increasing number of non-SOEs. They are two very different animals with different "corporate" objectives and ownership and/or management structures. At the moment, there can be state-owned limited liability companies or privately owned limited liability companies, both governed by Chapter 2 of the Company Law. Likewise, there can be state-owned

joint stock companies or privately owned joint stock companies, which are both governed by Chapter 4 of the Company Law.

When the Company Law was promulgated in 1993, the government was exploring the possibility of turning SOEs (including state-owned banks) into incorporated companies (the corporatization process and the commercialization of banks). Thus, the Company Law contains a large number of measures to reform the SOEs. Many provisions were specifically aimed at SOEs' reform and investment. Many experts now agree that these provisions are inappropriate for the non-SOE sector and that company law and SOE law should be separated.

The 2005 amendments to the Company Law seek to modify the Company Law to suit non-SOEs, but SOEs and non-SOEs are still governed by the same law which may cause confusion and inconsistencies. For example, Article 18 relating to the operation of a labor union, and Article 19 relating to the activity of the Chinese Communist Party within a company, are more appropriate in the SOEs than, say, a small company with one or very few employees.

2. SOEs tend to exist for the interests of the workers, so it is logical that the management board should partly consist of workers' representatives. However, there should be proper mechanisms to prevent abuses by workers or to prevent workers seeing corporatization as an opportunity for personal gain, for example, asset stripping by workers and managers of SOEs.
3. SOEs are often run in inefficient ways, so new management techniques, expertise, or external experts from the private sector should be brought in. This relates to management practice and is not something the law can do much about.
4. Non-SOEs are run by private entrepreneurs – there is no lack of incentive, but non-compliance with the formal requirements of Company Law, minority oppression, and fraudulent or irregular financial statements are common, so we need proper mechanisms for minority protection, and timely and accurate financial reporting and disclosure for minority shareholder and creditor protection.
5. Most of the listed companies are SOEs, and mostly controlled by the state. Directors and managers as well as supervisors are nominated and appointed by the controlling shareholder, the state. Yet the controlling shareholder does not care to monitor the performance of the company. There is therefore an internal control problem. The company needs to balance the interests of workers and investors. The state as the dominant shareholder need not be a problem, but as it does not exercise effective control over the managers and directors,

we need mechanisms to prevent abuse by the directors and managers – like the directors and managers in the U.S. Theoretically, increasing the percentage of tradable shares (that is, reducing the shareholding of the state) is one possible solution to improve corporate governance as the percentage of non-state shareholders increases, but only if non-state shareholders could play an active role, which may not be forthcoming. It is not the only solution, and has its own problems which must be handled with care.[23] The government experienced some initial difficulties a few years ago in several attempts to sell its shares in some of the SOEs, which caused the stock market to plunge further.[24] The situation is improving largely due to the satisfactory compensation offered by the government to minority shareholders before the sale of state-owned shares.

6. Chinese entrepreneurs do not trust outsiders.[25] Secrets of the business and success are often kept "in the family." This makes it difficult for independent directors to function effectively in China.
7. Chinese legislation tends to be more general and lacking in fine details. There is no system of judicial precedents in China to allow judges to develop case law to fill in the legislative gaps. This makes legislation difficult to work in practice.

The interim measures

As mentioned earlier, the CSRC issued the Guidelines on the establishment of an independent directors system in 2000 and the Code of Corporate Governance for listed companies in January 2002. The Code contains provisions on directors' duties of loyalty, care, diligence, and fiduciary duties which attempt to fill the gap in the existing Company Law. The Code also introduced the concept of independent directors. This is further supplemented by the CSRC's Guidelines on the Establishment of Independent Directors, which, among other things, require that at least one-third of the board of directors should be independent directors. The use of independent directors does not however, take account of Chinese characteristics:

(a) Chinese businesses do not trust outsiders
(b) China does not have enough people who can act effectively as independent directors at this stage in its economic development
(c) independent directors are not paid adequately to do a proper job
(d) independent directors do not understand their role well enough, often treating the appointment simply as an honor.

The 2005 amendments

The 1994 Company Law was enacted on December 29, 1993, and came into effect on July 1, 1994. It received minor amendments in December 1999 and August 2004. But with the deepening of the economic reform in China, the 1994 Company Law could no longer meet the demands of the economic developments and there were calls for major changes to the law. A bill to amend the Company Law was introduced to the Standing Committee of the NPC on February 25, 2005. It proposed to add 44 new Articles, delete 13 existing Articles, and amend 91 Articles. The bill was passed on October 27, 2005, and came into force on January 1, 2006.

Changes were made in six major areas:

1. Relaxing the requirements for incorporation, thereby encouraging and facilitating the formation of companies. It is now possible to have a single shareholder limited liability company (Part 3, Chapter 2), and the capital requirement for a limited liability company is reduced from RMB 100,000 to RMB 30,000 (Article 26). It will no longer be necessary to obtain the approval of the State Council or the Provincial Government to establish a joint stock/share stock company (Chapter 4).
2. Improving the corporate governance structure, and clarifying the rights and obligations of shareholders' meetings, the board of directors, the board of supervisors, and management.
3. Improving the protection of minority shareholders, company creditors, other interested parties, and the interests of the community.
4. Changing the conditions and requirements relating to the issuance, transfer, and floating of shares.
5. Regulating the corporate governance of listed companies – the Corporate Governance Guidelines issued by the CSRC are put on a statutory footing (Part V, Chapter 4).
6. Clarifying the duties and fiduciary obligations of the company directors, supervisors, and managers (Articles 148–50) and the rights of shareholders and supervisors to sue directors and managers (Articles 151–3).

The guiding principles behind the changes are:

(a) maintaining the order of the market economy
(b) reducing transaction risks
(c) meeting the needs of the economy and social development.

According to Cao Kang Tai, the Chief of the Legislative Affairs Office at the State Council, the 2005 bill adopted a very "constructive but cautious" approach – attempting to realign the scope of the reform, the speed of the country's development, and the acceptability of reform to the society. There were more mandatory provisions in the 1994 Company Law, but under the 2005 law there are more voluntary and enabling provisions.

We now turn to three main areas of reform in corporate governance terms.

Protection of minority shareholders

The 2005 law now adopts the Western approach in having clear provisions on shareholders' right to sue. Under Article 153, "if company directors or senior managers are in breach of law, administrative regulations or company articles damaging the interest of shareholders, shareholders can sue them in the People's Courts." This allows shareholders to sue for breach of directors' duties which cause loss to shareholders personally, similar to the shareholders' action in Australia and class action in the U.S. It is more advanced than in Hong Kong, where such action is not possible.

The 1994 law only prescribed certain duties on directors and managers, for example, not to benefit from corporate opportunity, but did not state who could sue if directors and/or managers were in breach of their duties. This is now remedied under the new law which gives shareholders a right to bring derivative action (Article 152). The shareholders can request the board of supervisors or board of directors or executive director to bring an action. If such a request is turned down, or no action is brought by directors or supervisors within 30 days of the request, or, in an urgent situation, if an action is not taken the company will suffer irreparable damage, a shareholder can bring an action in his own name directly to protect the interests of the company (this is similar to a derivative action in the Anglo-American system). However, the new law does not state whether the action has to be in the interests of the company. Again, judicial interpretation may be needed. Also, definition of directors' duties is needed to help shareholders to frame their action for breach of such duties.

The new law also allows cumulative voting in joint stock companies for the appointment of directors and supervisors at the shareholders' meeting (Article 106), and expands shareholders' rights to know (Articles 34, 98).

These changes will hopefully encourage minority shareholders to play an active role.[26]

Improving the corporate governance mechanism

This is a major area of reform under the bill. The independent directors system in listed companies, first introduced in the Code of Corporate Governance, was put on a firm statutory footing (clauses 154–5). It proposed the adoption of the CSRC Guidelines that require at least one-third of the board to be independent directors. It also stipulated that apart from exercising the powers of a normal director, an independent director could investigate and express opinions on connected or related party transactions, the appointment and dismissal of company auditors, and other important matters. These matters require the approval of a simple majority by the independent directors before they are put to the board for deliberation.

While the use of independent directors is something familiar to the Anglo-American world, and is seemingly in line with international practices, its effectiveness in China continues to be highly doubtful. It is an example of "lost in translation" according to Donald Clarke's analysis.[27] Due to the criticism of the independent directors system in China, the provisions in the bill regarding the arrangement for the appointment of independent directors were dropped. The 2005 Company Law simply states that the detailed requirements relating to the establishment of independent directors are to be provided by the State Council (Article 123).

China has both supervisory boards and independent directors. U.S. companies have independent directors but no supervisory board. In Japan, companies have flexibility in choosing to use boards of directors including independent directors. Many experts, including Wang Bao Shu of Tsinghua University, are in favor of giving the company a choice because the company knows which system better suits its situation. Alternatively, perhaps independent directors could be required to report directly to the supervisory board, thereby assisting and complementing the work of the supervisory board rather than being in competition with it.

The 2005 Company Law also strengthens the role of the supervisory board, empowers the supervisory board to make recommendations to the shareholders' meeting for the removal of directors or managers and to raise questions or make proposals in relation to board resolutions (Articles 54, 55, 119), or to initiate actions against directors at the request of the shareholders (Article 152).

The 2005 law also contains provisions stipulating directors' duties of loyalty, care and diligence, and fiduciary duties, as well as their duty not to receive bribes or illegal income or misappropriate the company's property

(Article 148). Article 149 provides a list of prohibited conduct by directors, including misappropriating the company's business opportunities or other conduct amounting to breach of duty of loyalty and fiduciary duties. However, one problem with Article 148 is that the duty of loyalty and fiduciary duties and duty of care and skills are not defined in the Company Law. While the same duties were also not defined in the U.K. until recently, and are still not defined in Hong Kong, there is case law in the U.K. and Hong Kong to give meaning to these duties. There is no binding case law in China to provide assistance.

Related party transactions

The new law prohibits directors from entering into any contracts or transactions with the company in breach of the company's articles of association, or without the approval of the shareholders' meeting (Article 149). Article 123 further provides that directors who are connected to a transaction to be sanctioned by the board of directors must not vote on the resolution. Such a resolution can only be passed by the majority votes of unconnected directors. Where there are fewer than three unconnected directors present at the meeting, the matter must be handed over to the shareholders' meeting for resolution. These provisions are aimed at preventing directors from engaging in tunneling or propping,[28] and will complement CSRC rules requiring reporting within two working days of connected transactions of value greater than RMB 1 million or 0.5 percent of net assets, whichever is greater.

Remaining areas of concern

While China has made great efforts to improve the corporate governance by selectively adapting international norms and good practices, there are a number of areas that need further improvements in order for the system to work.

First, many SOEs are still struggling with outdated management systems and practices that are the legacy of the planned economy, and are desperately in need of more modern ones. They are also overburdened with liability and staff pensions. Furthermore, Western ideas of a good corporate governance system are still a very new concept for most enterprises in China. It takes time for all concerned to understand what it means and how it works.

Second, the quality of the judiciary has improved tremendously over the last decade or so, but judicial independence and expertise needs to be further enhanced. A system of binding judicial precedents would also help to enable judges to develop principles of law in a predictable way to fill any legislative gaps.

Third, the problem of lack of enforcement or selective enforcement needs to be tackled. For example, despite the rules prohibiting connected transactions, they are still occurring regularly. Evidence shows that the market reacts negatively towards connected transactions if the company is financially sound, as tunneling is likely to have occurred. On the other hand, the market reacts positively towards connected transactions if the company is financially not sound, as propping is likely to occur.[29]

Fourth, management appears to be underpaid. Executive compensation and independent directors' pay remain low. Evidence shows that the annual cash compensation (salary and bonus) for top executives is linked to shareholder value and sales growth, but the link is weakened in state-owned listed companies.[30]

Fifth, China still has not adopted international accounting standards. This, coupled with the common problems of fraud and false accounting, makes it hard for investors to be confident about the financial health of the companies. There is an increasing number of mainland companies listed or seeking listing in Hong Kong (H-shares companies), and such companies have to comply with the international accounting standards that Hong Kong has subscribed to and other higher standards of corporate governance (for example, the H-share mandatory provision of the Director Model Code, and the Code of Internal Controls, and so on). But to enforce these standards, Hong Kong Exchanges and Clearance (HKEx) and the Securities and Futures Commission (SFC) would need to work closely with the CSRC, which in turn needs cooperation which may not be forthcoming from local government or authorities in some cases; where, for example, the culpable directors are not present in Hong Kong.

Selective adaptation of corporate governance mechanisms in banks

It was well known that Chinese banks were burdened with the serious problem of non-performing loans (NPLs). There were multiple levels of command chains which led to severe agency problems (insufficient information and poor measures of managerial performance). There was state intervention in the loan decision making process. As China entered the WTO with its commitment to open up the banking sector to global competition five years after its accession, there was urgent pressure to reform the state-owned banking sector.

The solutions adopted were first to dispose of the non-performing loans and then to improve the quality of these banks by improving their corporate governance system. Thus, the Corporate Governance

Guidelines for State-owned Commercial Banks (effective April 24, 2006) were issued. These Guidelines contain many features of the Western good corporate governance practices. For example, shareholders' meetings, board, board committees, supervisory committee, and management all owe a duty of loyalty and diligence to the bank. A policy on connected transactions must be established based on fairness and openness, and connected transactions must be approved by the regulator.

There is also shareholder restructuring to introduce strategic investors of not less than 5 percent of the issued capital and holding shares for not less than three years. This will hopefully bring in modern management skills, practices, and strategies. There is also reform on the management structure by establishing an effective credit, market, and operational risk management structure; and an internal control, internal audit, and compliance structure. There is the adoption of performance and other indicators such as asset quality ratio, prudential ratio, and so on.

There is also reform on the governance structure. Shareholders' meetings must approve dividends; at least one-third of the board members must be independent non-executive directors, and three non-executive directors must be appointed from the strategic investors. Banks must establish an audit committee, a risk management policy committee, a connected transactions committee, a strategic committee, a remuneration committee, and a nomination committee. The first three of these committees must be chaired by independent non-executive directors. There is also to be a supervisory committee to be nominated by majority shareholders.

It is too early to say whether these measures adapted from the international norms will work well. However, the largest state-owned banks have been successfully listed in Hong Kong in the last few years and their share prices have done well since listing. Indeed, if the January 2007 stock market results in Hong Kong on Chinese company listings can be used as a benchmark for China's corporate governance success, it may be that the reforms should be seen as a triumph.

Concluding remarks

Reformers in China, like many reformers in other parts of the world, have in recent years tended to chase the international trend in corporate governance reform. This is inevitable as China needs to be seen to be implementing "international standards" to reassure and attract more investors to its equity markets and to improve the competitiveness of its SOEs as China opens up for global competition in the wake of its accession to the WTO. However, even international organizations such as the OECD and the World Bank recognize the importance of regional differences in the corporate governance measures to suit the local circumstances. Thus, reformers in China should feel confident about devising their own measures to enhance the corporate governance standards in China. Standards and measures are two different things. Standards refer to the quality of companies we like to see. Measures, on the other hand, are ways to achieve such standards.

We should all work towards the same high standards of corporate governance, but we do not all have to have the same measures or solutions. What works well in one country or society may not work well in another. There are signs of Chinese reformers devising their own measures or selectively adapting international norms in the new law, but more could be done – particularly in the area of institutional capacity building. When learning from the West in finding appropriate measures, care needs to be taken to understand the background and reasoning to the measures adopted in the West and whether such measures are likely to work in China. Simply copying from the West without effective implementation and compliance of the standards to appease the international investors is unlikely to work in the long run. So far, laws and regulations appear to be generally in place for listed companies and state-owned banks, though certain provisions in the Company Law still need further refinement. More difficult is the task of creating an international culture of good corporate governance practices. This may be a problem of both culture and institutional capacity building and it remains to be seen if it can be left to company law to create cultural changes when legal ambiguity may be preferable to legal detail.

Notes

1. For example, the German model of two boards, the French model of a presidential system, the U.S., Canadian, and U.K. unitary board (but with varying degree of differences in other aspects of their corporate governance mechanisms), and the Japanese cross-shareholding and main bank system within a keiretsu. For a quick summary of the various systems around the world, see S. H. Goo and A. Carver, *Corporate Governance: The Hong Kong Debate* (December 2003) (Sweet & Maxwell Asia), chapter 5.
2. See the OECD Principles of Corporate Governance (1999), preamble available at http://www.oecd.org/data. The five OECD Principles relate to: (1) the protection of the rights of shareholders; (2) the equitable treatment of shareholders; (3) the role of the stakeholders as part of successful teamwork with a more long-term view; (4) disclosure and transparency; (5) the responsibilities of the board of directors.
3. The authors thank Dr. Glenn Shive of the Hong Kong America Centre, The Chinese University of Hong Kong, for this insight into the different cultural

tolerances to ambiguity and structure in the Western and Chinese legal systems. Dr. Shive suggests that the Western model relies heavily on the "high structure" of specificity with elaborate rules, prescribed mechanisms, and detailed outcomes. Such detail and structure is, by definition, antithetical to the Chinese preference for flexibility and discretion according to context. See, for example, D. Bodde, *Essays on Chinese Civilization* (Princeton: Princeton University Press, 1981), p. 171. See also Y. Noda's perceptive comment explaining the concept and role of harmony in Chinese society in "The Far Eastern Conception of Law", *International Encyclopedia of Comparative Law*, Vol. 2 (Paris: Mouton, 1975), p. 126: "For [the Chinese], social peace is not attained by harmonizing the subjective rights of each member of society. For them, society as Westerners think, is not constructed by the efforts of individuals, each with his own interests to defend; it has existed since the beginning, without any intervention of the individuals composing it, and is always at peace – unless one of them disturbs it."

4. The Hong Kong Companies' Ordinance is modeled closely on the English Companies' Act of 1948 with modern variations, with the articles of association giving shareholders' contractual rights and, ultimately, control over the board of directors, but with recognition of the importance of directorial autonomy in commercial decision making.
5. Despite many improvements in the judicial system since 1978, concerns over judicial independence from state influence and the parties involved, and inefficiency, still remain. See "Trust Eludes an Improving Legal System," *South China Morning Post*, March 27, 2004, p. B4; Josephine Ma, "Corrupt Courts Seen as Biggest Threat," *South China Morning Post*, March 10, 2005, p. 8; Kristine Kwok, "Concern over Lawyers Colluding with Judges," *South China Morning Post*, March 10, 2005, p. 8. A new code of conduct for the judges and lawyers has been issued to curb conflicts of interest and bribery: Irene Wang, "New Code of Conduct on Judicial Corruption," *South China Morning Post*, March 20, 2004, p. 8. Extensive amendments to the law have been proposed by Professors He Weifang of Beijing University and Zhang Zhiming of the National Procurators Institute, and reviewed by the Supreme People's Court: Alice Yan, "Professors Propose Broad Judicial Reforms," *South China Morning Post*, 8 December 8, 2004, p. 8. However, foreign models of judicial independence are unlikely to be followed: Alice Yan, "Speculation on Court Reforms Quashed," *South China Morning Post*, December 8, 2004, p. 8.
6. Shichang, "How to Avoid Gangster Capitalism," *South China Morning Post*, March 22, 2004, p. 13.
7. Pitman Potter, "Legal Reform in China – Institutions, Culture, and Selective Adaptation, " *Law & Social Inquiry* 2(4) (2004), 465–95.
8. German company law is rigid and highly formalized and the provisions of the German Stock Corporation Act that correspond to the publicly held U.S. corporation, for example, are more tightly controlled than the U.S. or U.K. equivalents. The German Aktiengesellschaften (AG) is governed by three bodies: the management board (Aufsichstrat), equivalent to the Anglo-American Board of Directors; the supervisory board, and the shareholders' meeting (Hauptversammlung).The Co-Determination Act requires the supervisory boards of AGs with more than 2,000 employees to have equal

numbers of shareholders and employee representatives, and employees elect representatives by secret ballot. As a result of criticism of the excessively strict corporate governance rules of the "closed insider" system of German company law, a new German Corporate Governance Code was introduced in 2001 and now bears much closer resemblance to the Anglo-American model, although the core value remains the protection of the investor. This would seem to be the core value for both the civil and common law systems that are converging, but we question whether it is so clearly the dominant value in the Chinese system.

9. At the same time, Articles 28 and 50 of the Securities Law were amended. Article 28 was amended to comply with the new revision of the Company Law, removing the requirement to obtain government approval, and Article 50 was amended to bring China's securities law in line with international benchmarks. Now a company applying to be listed must gain approval from the stock exchange where the shares are held. Previously, the company had to obtain approval from the Securities Authority of the State Council.
10. The OECD Principles state that the board should be able to make objective judgments independent of management and that independent directors must make major contributions to board decisions with objective judgments on both the management's and the board's performance. The board should consider appointing enough independent directors to be able to make judgments in cases of conflicts of interest when the board assumes overall responsibility for financial reports, executive pay, and nominations, to provide extra protection for market participants.
11. See Anyuan Yuan, "Foreign Direct Investments in China – Practical Problems of Complying with China's Company Law and Laws for Foreign-Invested Enterprises," *Northwestern School of Law Journal of International Law & Business* (20(3) (2002), 475–508; Yongxin Song, "Some Special Features of the Organs of Governance of Chinese Business Corporations," *Capital University Law Review*, 24 (1995), 207.
12. Foo Choy Peng, "Mainland Six Apologize for Profit Shortfalls," *South China Morning Post*, June 19, 1997, p. B22 (since 1996, the CSRC requires that listed companies whose net profits are 10–20 percent below forecast must publicly apologize to their shareholders); Winston Yau, "TCL Corp Unit Prepares to go Private before Listing of Group," *South China Morning Post*, October 1, 2003, p. B1.
13. Bill Savadove, "Crackdown on Steel Plant Sets Example," *South China Morning Post*, April 30, 2004, p. 6.
14. Ibid.
15. "Asset Stripping Censure Limited as Deterrent," *South China Morning Post*, November 28, 2001, p. 5 (leaders of state-owned Ningxia national Chemicals Group and directors of Ningxia Ninghe National Chemicals, a Shenzhen listed subsidiary of Ningxia, were censured for stripping the assets of the listed company); Matthew Miller, "Official Defends Asset-Stripping," *South China Morning Post*, March 21, 2001, p. B3 (failed construction materials conglomerate Monkey King Group stripped assets of RMB 524 million from eleven companies just before its bankruptcy in February 2001); "Real Monkey Business," *South China Morning Post*, March 29, 2001, p. B14; Matthew Miller, "Entrenched Ideas Impede Asset Disposals at Bankrupt State Firms," *South*

China Morning Post, September 22, 1998, p. B4 ("asset-stripping ... often involves factory managers siphoning off the most productive parts of failed enterprises to related firms, or selling property on the cheap to friends and relatives"); Mark O'Neill, "Dismal Story of Hua Lu's Asset-Stripping Finally Revealed," *SCMP*, April 16, 2001, p. B3 (managers of Dalian Hua Lu, one of the biggest state firms in the northeast, stripped its assets for their own profit and drove it into bankruptcy, throwing 3,000 workers onto the street); Mark O'Neill, "Bosses Strip the National Grid," *South China Morning Post*, September 30, 2004, p. B2 (when the State Council dismantled the State Power Corporation (SPC) in December 2002 to end state monopoly, but without proper regulatory safeguards against malfeasance and graft, workers and managers of many provincial power stations set up private companies to take over valuable generation and distribution assets at steep discounts, turning a state monopoly into a private one); Mark O'Neill, "Mainland Tries to Rein in Blatant Asset Stripping," *South China Morning Post*, December 29, 2003, p. B2 (the State Council issued tough regulations from the asset administration commission to standardize the privatization process). Asset-stripping is also a serious problem in China's financial system: Laurence Brahm, "Solution now Part of the Problem," *South China Morning Post*, March 22, 2005, p. 13 (the China Banking Regulatory Commission recently found that the four asset-management companies set up to dispose of non-performing loans in the key state commercial banks, colluded with banks in massive asset-stripping).

16. Mathew Brooker, "Tannery Stink Spoils Theory," *South China Morning Post*, August 27, 2002, p. 2.
17. Eric Ng and Elaine Chan, "State Firms Ordered to Hire Accountants to Audit Books," *South China Morning Post*, September 13, 2004, B2 (since August 30, 2004, SOEs (whether listed or not) must hire accounting firms to audit their books, according to a recent circular "Provisional Rules on the Preservation of State-owned Enterprises' Asset Value" released by the State-owned Assets Supervision and Administration Commission (SASAC). Top SOE management and chief accountants are responsible for the veracity and completeness of their companies' financial data, and auditing firms and their registered accountants are also responsible for checking the data and the supporting evidence's authenticity and legality. SOEs must also report annually changes in their total asset value, non-performing assets, return on assets, net profit growth, debt–asset ratios and net cashflow–net profit ratios. Senior management's compensation will be partly linked to these performance parameters).
18. Donald Clarke, "Lost in Translation? Corporate Legal Transplants in China," GWU Law School Public Law Research Paper No. 213, July 3, 2006.
19. Potter, "Legal Reform in China," p. 478.
20. Teemu Ruskola, "Conceptualizing Corporations and Kinship: Comparative Law and Development Theory in a Chinese Perspective," *Stanford Law Review*, 52(6) (2000), 1599–729.
21. "Ultimately, there is the issue of market culture and the general murkiness of the China business environment. Can we really expect former government workers (as red-chip employees are) to embrace a culture of shareholder value, or are they more likely to view corporatisation as an opportunity for personal enrichment?" said a commentator. Brooker, "Tannery Stink Spoils Theory," p. 2.

22. Potter, "Legal Reform in China," p. 476, citing S. N. Eisenstadt and L. Roniger, *Patrons, Clients and Friends: Interpersonal Relations and the Structure of Trust in Society* (New York: Cambridge University Press, 1984) and R. K. Merton, *Social Theory and Social Structure* (New York: Free Press, 1965).
23. Stephen Green, "Do Sell Government Shares, but First Agree on How," *South China Morning Post*, January 5, 2004, p. 15.
24. Mark O'Neill, "China Shareholder Backlash," *South China Morning Post*, June 17, 2005, p. B2; Mark O'Neill, "Baoshan Sweetens Compensation Plan," *South China Morning Post*, June 29, 2005, p. B1; Elaine Chan, "Quest for Magic Bullet a Failed Strategy," *South China Morning Post*, July 11, 2005, p. B4.
25. The three independent directors in Guangdong Kelon Electrical Holdings who resigned recently stated in a resignation letter: "We think the company does not support our duty to protect shareholder rights," alleging that the company did not listen to their advice or provide enough information when they looked into several "abnormal" transactions.
26. For a rare example of minority activism see the recent story relating to Guangdong Kelon Electrical Holdings which is controlled by its chairman Gu Chujun: Alice Yan, "Minorities Activist Presses Bid to Remove Kelon Chief," *South China Morning Post*, July 15, 2005, p. B1.
27. Clarke, "Lost in Translation?"
28. Directors of China's state-owned enterprises often try to tunnel out funds (profits) to purposes other than those of the companies of which they are directors. Generally, company profits must be used for that company's objectives. Many of these directors are often government-appointed. This kind of misuse of company funds outside the company frame is called "tunnelling." On the other hand, when their company's performance is poor, directors of that company must be replaced by better qualified persons. At such times the current directors may try to inject outside funds (that they have collected somewhere, somehow) into the poorly performing companies to prop up the company's performance, so that they may keep their directorships in that company. This is called "propping." For an analysis of tunneling and propping, see Winnie Peng et al., *Tunneling or Propping: Evidence from Connected Transactions in China* (Hong Kong University of Science and Technology, 2006).
29. Ibid.
30. Takao Kato and Cheryl X. Long, "Executive Compensation, Firm Performance, and Corporate Governance in China: Evidence from Firms Listed in the Shanghai and Shenzhen Stock Exchanges," IZA Discussion Paper No. 1767, September 2005. Available at SSRN: http://ssrn.com/abstract=555794 or DOI: 10.2139/ssrn.555794.

11
Selective Adaptation of Anglo-American Corporate Governance Practices in Japan[1]

Masao Nakamura

"We're worried that as the number of companies with takeover defenses increases (in Japan) it's going to lead to an entrenchment of management and loss of the healthy pressure from shareholders on management to focus on shareholder returns."

Marc Goldstein, representative director,
Institutional Shareholder Services

Introduction

Japan's reform in corporate governance: from the 1990s to the 2000s[2]

This chapter applies a selective adaptation framework[3] for analyzing institutional change and business practices in corporate governance in post-bubble Japan. With the economy facing near-collapse in the 1990s, Japan undertook massive corporate governance reform. The Japanese government promptly introduced new laws that put in place new institutional settings for Japan's corporate governance. New laws and revisions of existing laws related to corporate governance, securities market transactions, and laws governing transparency and information disclosure are among the many changes made in the reform process.

The fact that the Japanese government was able to pass so many laws in corporate governance reform in such a short period of time indicates that there has been substantial public support for this institutional change,[4] from the traditional (post-World War II) inward-looking bank-based corporate governance system to a more transparent and market-based U.S.-style system.[5] Public support and the corresponding government initiatives for corporate government reform were based on the conviction that the demonstrated inability of Japan's bank-based corporate governance system to govern was one of the major reasons for the formation of the massive financial bubble in the 1980s and also for the ensuing prolonged recession from 1990.

A U.S.-style corporate governance system was chosen as the target of Japan's reform because of the robust economic growth of the U.S. economy over many years. For these reasons, Japanese government's reform initiatives have involved creating legal settings that will help Japanese companies develop U.S.-style corporate governance practices.

Corporate governance practices and institutions in transition

In this chapter we analyze the changes that have taken place (and that are still taking place) in the institutional settings that are relevant for corporate governance practices in Japan. These changes took place mostly in the 1990s and the early 2000s, but some additional changes are expected to continue taking place through 2010 and even later. In studying these institutional changes, we also pay special attention to what has not changed.[6] These areas of non-change are the areas where the Japanese government (or the Japanese public in general) chose not to adopt the U.S. practices, but purposefully made no change. Japan is practicing selective adaptation in transplanting the U.S. corporate governance system, and it is of interest to study why Japan has chosen not to accept U.S.-style practices in some areas. It is also of interest to investigate why businesses chose not to adopt certain U.S.-type corporate governance practices despite new Japanese laws on corporate governance allowing Japanese businesses to do so.

In this regard we are also interested in addressing the question: does Japan's acceptance of certain U.S. practices and non-acceptance of others imply potentially dysfunctional, or undesirable, interaction effects on the performance of its corporate governance system?[7, 8]

For convenience, we regard Japan's corporate governance reform in the 1990s and early 2000s as a transition from Japan's traditional bank-based corporate governance system (Institution I) to a new U.S.-type corporate governance system (Institution II).

Notable issues that must be dealt with in the transition

In achieving this transition, a number of important issues must be dealt with by the government and also the affected organizations, including business corporations. These issues include the clarification of the meaning of a corporation as related to its owners' (shareholders') individual rights. Another issue is the treatment (protection) of minority shareholders' rights, relative to the rights of majority shareholders. It is well known that, in Japan's bank-based corporate governance system that was in place until the early 1990s, a company's management had to pay attention only to the interests of the company's majority shareholders (that is, banks and other financial institutions, and shareholders of the other industrial firms which belonged to the same keiretsu group), but could safely ignore the company's individual and minority shareholders.

We regard the U.S. practice of caring for minority shareholders' rights and protecting individual shareholders' rights (protection of the rights of owners of private property) as reflecting Western liberal norms.

Consistency with these U.S. practices is an important principle for corporate management to follow based on shareholder value maximization. (Shareholder value maximization is not consistent with the Japanese traditional corporate operating criterion based on stakeholders' value maximization.)

In pursuing shareholder value maximization, a general requirement is that the market for corporate control must exist and must function well. For example, mergers and acquisitions (M&As), especially including hostile M&As, must be freely allowed so that firms' management can focus on shareholder value maximization.

In what we will refer to as Japan's Institution I, none of these practices were present until the 1990s. How Japan's move from Institution I to Institution II while incorporating (at least partially) these and other U.S. practices, many of which reflect Western liberal norms, is of interest, and will be discussed below.[9, 10, 11]

Our approach

In order to focus on selective adaptation, we primarily consider Japan-specific factors as surrogates for Japanese norms. In empirical studies some of these factors are proxied by some other observable factors, while others are treated as unobservable fixed effects. Since these factors often explain a significant fraction of variation in the dependent variable of interest, it is worthwhile investigating the role they play in a situation of institutional change like the one Japan has been going through with its corporate governance system. It is also the case that some phenomena that are associated with certain Japan-specific factors are not easily explainable using economic theory.[12] It should be emphasized, however, that after controlling for Japan-specific factors, most Japanese firms' behavior in corporate governance is explainable in economic terms.

We can characterize institutional change in the following three steps (Teranishi, 2003, p. 567; see also Aoki, 2001; North, 1990a):

> (1) As a result of some exogenous shocks or evolution of state variables, financial transactions come to be perceived as costly by one or both parties to an exchange. If the costs become high enough relative to their stakes, they may find it worthwhile to devote resources to changing the rules. (2) Rules could be changed within the private sector, with these most often being informal rules such as the main bank relationship. (3) Formal rules or regulations are changed through the political process, which quite frequently involves significant political transaction costs arising from agency problems among politicians, government bureaucrats, voters, and various interest groups (North (1990b) and Dixit (1996)).

In our selective adaptation approach, which is qualitative in nature, economic agents' endogenous reactions to exogenous economic shocks of the types described by steps (1) and (2) are not explicitly controlled for nor identified. However, this may not bias our analysis seriously because our interest is primarily in those cases where no change takes place in firms' corporate governance practices. For such cases, exogenous economic shocks in the 1990s might not have been large enough, compared to the forces of Japan-specific factors. Step (3) above acknowledges possible political costs associated with institutional changes, such as the overhaul of Japan's corporate governance reform. To the extent that almost all laws associated with the reform passed through parliament without any problem, this seems to indicate that the political costs associated with this particular reform, at least with respect to its legal changes, were minimal. This is probably because Japan's traditional centers of powers (for example, banks and corporate management) were largely discredited (that is, most Japanese banks were in miserable shape, facing bankruptcy) and leaders of industrial firms were blamed for letting Japan lose ground to its competitors.

The organization of the rest of this chapter is as follows. In the next section we briefly discuss some of norms that are considered in the literature as characterizing Japanese life. We also discuss a few examples where Japanese policies were influenced by these and other norms. In the third section we define some state variables that describe various states of Japan's corporate governance practices before and after the corporate governance reform. Then we show how our selective adaptation framework can explain the possible changes in the state variables after the reform as a result of interactions with Japanese business norms. In the fourth section we discuss how Japan's selective adaptation behavior may result in dysfunctionalities in its corporate governance practices. The fifth section offers some concluding remarks.

Norms underlying the Japanese business behavior

Many studies in the literature have investigated various aspects of the normative nature of Japanese life. Even though there is no single unique and agreed upon set of norms and values underlying all aspects of Japanese life, many researchers seem to agree that the following norms distinguish the cultural characteristics of Japan from those of the United States.[13, 14] These norms span overlapping areas of Japanese business behavior and hence are not exclusive.

Often cited Japanese norms identified in Japanese business behavior

1. *Group behavior*. Reischauer (1988, p. 128) notes the "Japanese tendency to emphasize the group at the expense of the individual. Reishauer (ibid., pp. 133, 685) also notes that "associations of business enterprises, from groups of petty retailers by street or ward to nationwide associations of great banks or steel producers, are more widespread and more important a feature in Japan than in America." As we discuss below, this is consistent with the important role that many types of corporate groups (referred to as keiretsu below) continue to play in the Japanese business system.
2. *Consensus*. "Consensus is the goal ... To operate their group system successfully, the Japanese have found it advisable to avoid open confrontations" (ibid., p. 136).
3. *Long-term relationships*. Until the early 1990s, long-term employment was the norm for most regular workers in Japan.[15] This is still the case, but, after the massive restructuring that took place at almost all Japanese corporations from the 1990s through the early 2000s, the size of the workforce of regular employees who enjoy long-term employment has decreased in most companies.[16] Despite this, many public opinion polls continue to suggest that most of the Japanese public prefer long-term same-firm employment security.[17] These preferences are reflected in many company decisions.[18]
4. *Vertical keiretsu relationships among corporations*. Japanese auto-assemblers and suppliers in vertical production keiretsu groups have managed to "sustain hybrid relationships – close, dependent, long-

term alliances, absent majority ownership, or contingent contracts – because (partly for cultural reasons) of a generally low taste for opportunism: strong norms favoring trust, obligation, and reciprocity in relationships, backed up by such reputation-enforcing formal mechanisms as supplier associations" (Ahmadjian and Lincoln, 2001, p. 685; Sako, 1996). These keiretsu firms are vertically integrated for production purposes, but the assembly firm in the center (for example, Toyota) owns less than the majority of equity (say, 20–30%) in its keiretsu suppliers.[19] In Japan's assembly-based production set-ups, keiretsu relationships provide organic bonding among member firms and have important implications for their business relationships (Korkie and Nakamura, 1997; Nakamura, 2002). The social and economic infrastructure in which Japanese supply networks are embedded makes abrupt termination of stable partnerships difficult. Ties between assemblers and their key suppliers have, in many cases, been in place for 30 years or more (Japan Fair Trade Commission, 1993). For example, as Ahmadjian and Lincoln (2001) note, " 'Lifetime' employment and low levels (by Japanese norms) of job rotation within purchasing departments enable purchasing managers to develop strong personal bonds with their suppliers' representatives."[20]

5. *Importance of group-oriented values.* Many authors have noted that Japanese businesses emphasize group-oriented values in their decision making. For example, Bartlett and Ghoshal (1998) state:

   > In contrast to European family capitalism and American managerial capitalism, the Japanese cultural heritage has fostered a form of management Chandler called "group capitalism." As many observers have noted, the homogeneity of Japanese society, its isolationism during the Tokugawa period, and the influence of Eastern religions and philosophies have reinforced strong Japanese cultural norms that emphasize group behavior and value interpersonal harmony. Such values carry over into the country's commercial organizations and have helped shape distinctive management styles and organizational practices ... At a corporate level, the group-oriented values were reflected in the zaibatsu and other enterprise groups, which paternalistically watched over their affiliated companies (Morck and Nakamura, 2005). Within the organization, such values were evident in the widespread norm of lifetime employment commitments – by both employer and employee – and such managerial practices as nemawashi or ringi, which institutionalized information sharing and joint decision making.

Lincoln et al. (1986, p. 343) also conclude that, in general, there is wide agreement that Japanese decision making is group- and consensus-oriented and involves low delegation of formal authority to positions held by individuals (see also Shibata et al. 1991, p. 137).

6. *Trust and networks.* Lincoln (2006, p. 216) describes Japanese customer–supplier relationships as follows:

   > At a micro-level, the trust, reciprocity, and stability typical of customer-supplier dyads in Japanese industrial goods markets have facilitated keiretsu firms to enjoy cooperation, synergy, and knowledge-sharing in product and process development ... At a more macro-level, webs of cross-shareholdings, director transfers, and preferential trade and lending flows have functioned both as information systems and as governance structures to disseminate while conserving and protecting knowledge assets.

   (See also Lincoln and Gerlach, 2004; Williamson, 1996.) By the same token, the breaks and "holes" in the network (Burt, 1992) – for example, between direct competitors or rival groups – have at times presented formidable barriers to Japanese firms' collaboration and learning.[21]

7. *Organizational learning.* Many researchers have found that organization-wide learning and campaigns are distinct features of many Japanese firms (for example, Fruin, 1992, 1997; Fruin and Nakamura, 1997). Consistent with this, Shibata et al. (1991) also note:

   > Norms held by executives may reflect in part learning from experience and in part the output of organizational and general societal socialization processes. The findings of this study indicate that the prevalent normative systems of Japanese business management are eclectic in nature, reflecting the needs of an uncertain, turbulent national environment and intensely competitive markets. Organizational learning is encouraged, but demands for efficiency are respected. Co-ordination is required, but without the sacrifice of flexibility and adaptive abilities.

8. *Gender inequality in the workplace.* Reischauer (1988, pp. 175, 183–4) notes:

   > The laws now give women full legal equality. But Japan is still definitely a 'man's world,' with women confined to a secondary position. Many Westerners wonder indignantly why Japanese

> women do not agitate more aggressively against their unequal status. (Japanese men are blatantly male chauvinists and women seem shamefully exploited and suppressed.) Despite the great gains made by women in recent decades, social limitations on them and discrimination in employment remain severe.

This aspect of Japanese culture is probably why exceptionally few Japanese women are found in high-level managerial and other professional positions compared to countries in the West. Despite the massive transfer of U.S. managerial methods to Japan since the end of World War II, equal employment opportunity laws of the type implemented in the United States have not been fully transplanted nor enforced in Japan.[22] Despite Japan's general acceptance of Western liberal norms, female employment conditions are generally marginal in comparison with the conditions males enjoy.[23] Japan's decision not to accept to enforce U.S.-style equal employment laws fully seems consistent with the notion that Japan behaved according to selective adaptation in this regard.

Statistically identified norms

A number of researchers have statistically identified factors (dimensions) that measure various aspects of cultural distance between country cultures. For example, Hofstede (1980, 1983) finds that four dimensions of national culture are helpful in explaining differences in countries' cultures: power distance, uncertainty avoidance, individualism and masculinity.[24] Using these four dimensions, Hofstede finds that Japanese society's values reflect (1) more power distance, (2) more uncertainty avoidance, (3) more masculinity, and (4) more collectivism than U.S. society. Hofstede (1997) and House et al. (2004) further identified more dimensions to measure cultural distance between countries.[25] These statistically identified cultural dimensions are generally consistent with other researchers' findings about Japanese norms.

Examples of Japanese policy decisions associated with norms

Some researchers found empirical evidence that suggests that certain Japanese policy decisions have been influenced by norms. We discuss some of these below.

1. *Filial care.* Ogawa and Retherford's (1993) findings suggest that "norms of filial care for elderly parents in Japan were fairly constant from 1963 until 1986, when a major weakening of norms began." This seems to have been triggered by government efforts to shift some of

the burden of caring for the elderly back to families. "In contrast to norms of care for elderly parents, expectations of old-age support from children have declined steadily over time, adapting continuously to changes in underlying socioeconomic and demographic conditions." A policy implication Ogawa and Retherford draw is that government efforts to shift the burden of caring for the elderly back to families may not be very successful.[26]

2. *Foundations of Japan's postwar pacifism.* In explaining the foundations of Japan's postwar pacifism policies, Miyashita (2007) argues that the norms have shaped policies, but the norms are often inseparable from material and structural forces.
3. *Impacts of global norms regarding gender relations and human rights on Japan.* Chan-Tiberghien (2004a, 2004b) examines the impact of global human rights norms on Japan. In particular, she questions why women's and children's rights saw dramatic discursive, political, and legislative changes in Japan in the 1990s, while changes in minority rights remained minimal. Chan-Tiberghien argues that political and legal changes occur when new norms arise in the global community (such as at world conferences) and spread within a nation through public and private initiatives such as the publication of government reports, books, and journal articles, as well as the organization of symposiums and workshops. Subsequently, legal and policy changes follow when NGOs and activists ally with legislators. However, while the presence of all these factors explains the blossoming of women's and children's rights in new legislation and policy changes in Japan in the 1990s, the lack of these same factors, despite new norms in the global community in particular, explains the relative lack of changes in the area of minority rights in Japan.[27] Alternatively, one might argue that, given global human rights norms, Japan acted according to selective adaptation, consciously adopting relevant changes regarding women's and children's rights, while not acting on minority rights.[28] (As discussed above, another example of selective adaptation may be that Japanese women's rights have not been dealt with, as far as their employment is concerned.)

Comparing Japan's corporate governance practices before and after the corporate governance reform: Japan's selective adaptation

In the above discussions, we have considered certain circumstances in which Japan only partially accepted certain U.S. practices, which seems consistent with selective adaptation theory. These U.S. practices, which embody Western liberal norms, include equal employment opportunity laws and global human rights norms. In this section, we apply a selective adaptation framework to analyzing Japan's reactions towards U.S.-style corporate governance practices. For most practical purposes, it is reasonable to think that all legal and institutional settings required by Japanese corporations for adopting U.S.-type corporate governance practices have been laid out by Japanese government reform measures. Nevertheless, to what extent the proposed U.S. practices are implemented in the end by Japanese corporations depends on the selective adaptation behavior of Japan's businesses, government, courts and public, among others.

State variables for describing Japan's corporate governance

Problems in corporate governance are primarily concerned with the legal protection of shareholders' rights, particularly those of minority shareholders; issues associated with large shareholders (that is, concentrated ownership); and the agency costs (to all shareholders) that arise because firms' managers do not implement policies to maximize shareholder value.

We use the following state variables to measure the change in the functioning of various aspects of corporate governance mechanisms discussed above before and after the reform. These state variables are not necessarily mutually exclusive in that if some factors affect one state variable, it is possible that the same factors also affect others.[29] Nevertheless, we view these state variables as one way to capture the essential aspects of Japan's corporate governance mechanisms (Table 11.1).[30]

- (s1) *Degree to which shareholder value maximization is achieved.* Describes the degree to which the management is faithful to the shareholders' objective to maximize the value of their shares. Prior to the reform, Japanese firms' management were able to pursue their own objectives which were significantly at variance with shareholder value maximization. Agency costs of this sort were a significant source of economic inefficiency.
- (s2) *Degree of outside independent directors' involvement in boards of directors' decisions.* Measures the degree to which the board of directors functions as a governance body. If the board is controlled by insiders, which was the case before the reform, it might be difficult to reduce the agency costs of the sort given by (s1).
- (s3) *Degree of competition in the market for corporate control (that is, activities associated with M&As).* Measures how active the market for

Table 11.1 Japan's selective adoption of U.S.-style corporate governance practices: selective adaptation in institutional change

	Institution I *(Post-WWII bank-based CG system)*	***Transition period***	***Institution II*** *(U.S.-style CG system)*
Time period	***From the early 1950s to the early 1990s***	***From the early 1990s to the early 2000s***	***Beginning in around 2007***
Examples of representative business norms underlying the CG system	(N1) Corporate groups (keiretsu). Special organizational structures of Japan's assembly and supplier firms in vertical production keiretsu groups may generate economic efficiency gains. Economic efficiency gains have not been verified for horizontal keiretsu groups. Keiretsu groupings have proved to be highly potent poison pills and have functioned as such since the early 1950s. Other keiretsu groups include those based on main banks and their client firms as well as firms along distribution channels. Firms in keiretsu groupings typically own some equity in other member firms and are expected to act as friendly shareholders. (N2) Consensus as to the goal, and avoidance of open confrontations. This kind of value system might encourage out-of-court settlements and impede full acceptance of new laws by individual business firms and shareholders. (N3) Group-oriented stakeholder value maximization as the objective for corporate decision making. Until the end of the 1980s, up to 70% of most Japanese listed corporations' outstanding shares were held by banks and other financial institutions, as well as other industrial firms. This allowed company managers to ignore the rights of individual shareholders and pursue objectives other than shareholder value maximization. Group-oriented objectives Japanese corporations are thought to have pursued include firms' stakeholder value maximization and value-added maximization. These objective functions put considerable weight on the welfare of the employees of the firm and allied firms.	Selective adoption of U.S. practices and the associated U.S. norms.	Japanese norms, imported U.S. norms.

Table 11.1 continued

Time period	***Institution I*** *(Post-WWII bank-based CG system)* ***From the early 1950s to the early 1990s***	***Transition period*** ***From the early 1990s to the early 2000s***	***Institution II*** *(U.S.-style CG system)* ***Beginning in around 2007***
Factors that connect the norms from two different countries (Japan and the U.S.)		How do U.S. practices appeal to Japanese in terms of *perception* (how the Japanese perceive the U.S. practices), *legitimacy* (how much legitimacy the Japanese find in U.S. practices) and *complementarity* (how much the new U.S. practices complement existing Japanese practices) in the context of enhancing firms' economic efficiency. These three instruments can play either positive or negative roles in facilitating the transition of Japanese institutions.	
State variables that describe the state of corporate governance practices reflecting the underlying norms	(s1) Shareholder value maximization behavior (i.e. firm exclusively owned by its shareholders; minimizing the agency cost due to managers) (s2) Status of independent outside directors (i.e. overseeing exclusive ownership of firm by its shareholders; minimizing the agency cost due to managers) (s3) Competition in the market for corporate control (i.e. optimal reorganization of business units; minimizing managers' moral hazard) (s4) Transparency and information disclosure in accounting and other reporting to investors and the public (i.e. protection of investors; good compliance behavior) (s5) Protection of minority shareholders (i.e. protection of the individual rights of minority shareholders).	*Hypothesis*: As the Japanese economy moves from Institutions I to II, values of all state variables (s1)–(s5) will approach those observed for the U.S. corporate governance system.	If the hypothesis is incorrect, then what kinds of values will the state variables take in equilibrium, assuming that an equilibrium is reached under Institution II?

Legal settings of interest	(c1) Commercial Code (c2) Securities and Exchange Law (c3) Financial Futures Trading Law (c4) Tax Law (c5) Anti-Monopoly Law (c6) government administrative guidance and the interpretations of the above laws (c7) accounting rules (associated with (c1), (c2), (c4) and other relevant laws, and generally accepted accounting practices).	Parts of (c1), including those on joint stock companies plus other relevant laws, have been integrated and revised to become the New Company Law (d1); (c2) and (c3), as well as other related laws, have been integrated and revised to become (d2); (c4)–(c6) have been partially revised (for example, (c5) allows establishment of holding companies.); (c7) has been extensively revised.	(d1) New Company Law; (d2) New Financial Instruments and Exchange Law, also termed the Japanese version of the U.S. Sarbanes Oxley (SOX) Act; (c4) revised Tax Law; (c5) revised Anti-Monopoly Law; (c6) revised government administrative guidance and the interpretations of the above laws; (c7) revised accounting rules.
Notes on the background	After the burst of the financial bubble in 1990, the Japanese government, business community and public accepted the failure of the institutions underlying Japan's corporate governance practices that had been in place since the 1950s.	The robustness of U.S. economic growth convinced the Japanese that a new U.S.-style corporate governance system (based on Institution II) should be established in Japan.	

corporate control is. While Japanese banks played some role as a substitute for the market for corporate control before the reform, they were not able to replicate the benefits of a more competitive market (Morck and Nakamura, 1999). Inability to replace a firm's poorly performing management with a more competent one in a timely manner has been a major source of agency cost, of the sort given by (s1), and a source of significant economic inefficiency. We are interested in how the reform impacted the degree of competition in this market.

- (s4) *Degree of transparency and information disclosure in accounting, financial, and other reporting to investors.* Measures the fair and transparent availability of firm information that is relevant to all investors concerned. Information disclosure and transparency is the basic prerequisite for efficient functioning of the stock market, allowing investors to evaluate the shares they own. Efficient stock markets also give managers information about the cost of capital which is required for their investment decisions. Efficient stock markets are also essential for developing an active market for corporate control. Japanese bank-based corporate governance mechanisms were generally insider-oriented and lacked transparency in many respects.
- (s5) *Degree of protection of minority shareholders.* Describes the degree to which the individual rights of investors, and particularly those of minority investors, are protected. It is well known that under the old bank-based corporate governance system, up to 70 percent of most listed firms in Japan were owned by financial and other corporate shareholders who were sympathetic to the incumbent management. Hence firms' management generally paid little attention to individual and other minority shareholders.

Japanese business norms and instruments that affect the degree of acceptance of new U.S.-style institutional settings and practices in corporate governance

Japanese business norms

The norms and related issues that generally characterize Japanese behavior in Japan's business, and society in general, have been discussed above.[31] Some of the business norms are particularly important for shaping Japan's acceptance of new U.S.-style practices of corporate governance, and below we list these in concrete terms (Table 11.1).

- (N1) *Corporate groups*. Group-oriented behavior reflecting economic efficiency effects may underlie Japanese keiretsu behavior, especially including vertical production keiretsu. Economic efficiency gains have not been verified for horizontal keiretsu, but horizontal keiretsu groupings have proven to be highly potent poison pills and have functioned as such since the early 1950s.
- (N2) *Consensus*. Consensus as the goal, and avoidance of open confrontations is the kind of value system that might encourage out-of-court settlements and impede full acceptance of new laws by individual business firms and shareholders.
- (N3) *Group-oriented value maximization as the objective for corporate decision making*. Until the end of the 1980s, up to 70 percent of most Japanese listed corporations' outstanding shares were held by banks and other financial institutions, as well as other industrial firms. This allowed company managers to ignore the rights of individual shareholders while pursuing other objectives. For example, some authors suggest that Japanese corporations have pursued firms' stakeholder value maximization (see, for example, Aoki, 1988; Araki, 2005; Jacoby, 2005)[32] and value-added maximization.[33] These sorts of objective functions, for example, put much weight on the welfare of firms' employees as well as the welfare of suppliers, customers, and creditors.

One of the cornerstones of Japan's corporate governance reform is formal acknowledgment by the Japanese government of shareholder value maximization as a corporation's primary objective in its decision-making.[34] Japan's New Company Law and other related laws focus on this point. Legal terms for the protection of shareholders' rights have been clearly set out, as in the United States.

Instruments that facilitate adoption of new institutional settings and practices

If firms and investors see the immediate or potential benefits of new laws, those laws may be implemented promptly with full force. The reasons for such full acceptance are in most cases economic and in some cases humanitarian.[35] There may be little reason for businesses to reject new rules if they perceive the new rules to be obviously better suited for modern economic activity compared to the old rules, all other things being equal. Such an element of perception and legitimacy may be needed for the new rules to be accepted by economic agents.[36]

Another reason that may facilitate acceptance of new laws is when new rules complement the existing old rules in some way. In this case as well, the utility of implementing the new rules is obvious. If such legitimacy or complementarity in the new laws is not obviously present and yet the new laws are adopted by the government, investors and businesses alike may not seriously implement the new rules and may instead look for loopholes.

In circumstances where new laws and institutions proposing new corporate governance practices have elements of legitimacy and/or complementarity as discussed above, these new practices will likely be accepted. Their acceptance will further be facilitated if the practitioners concerned perceive that the new laws are consistent with their personal belief and perceptions.

We expect that those new corporate governance practices, implemented in the new reform laws, are more likely to be adopted seriously if Japanese practitioners have a favorable perception of their legitimacy and complementarity. (We regard these laws as being more consistent with Japanese norms.) Otherwise, companies may not implement the new laws in full. In the following discussion, the likely adoption of new practices may be predicted if the instruments that favor *a priori* acceptance of the new practices can be determined.

State variables before and after the reform

In applying a selective adaptation framework to Japan's corporate governance reform below, we consider how Japanese business norms (N1)–(N3) interact with Western liberal norms which drive to enhance each of the state variables (s1)–(s5). However, in our selective adaptation analysis we use the three instruments (perception, legitimacy, complementarity) instead of the Western liberal norms directly in calculating the relevant interactions. We proceed as follows. For each state variable and the associated U.S. corporate governance practices which are thought to enhance the value of the state variable, we consider interactions (correlations) between the instruments and the relevant Japanese norms. If the overall effects of the interactions are positive, we conclude that Japan (and the underlying Japanese norms, in particular) accepts the relevant U.S. practices by selective adaptation and hence the state variable will increase its value as a result of the reform. Table 11.2 shows the results of our tentative analysis along these lines.[37]

Shareholder value maximization (s1)

Because of the general perception among Japan's policy makers and the public in the 1990s that Japan's outdated bank-based corporate governance system was one of the main causes for the near-collapse

Table 11.2 Do Japanese business norms help local acceptance of U.S.-style corporate governance practices reflected in state variables (s1)–(s5) in terms of their perceptions, legitimacy and complementarity? Processes of selective adaptation

		Instruments of selective adaptation	
Japanese business norms	*Perception*	*Legitimacy*	*Complementarity*
	Panel 1 (s1) Shareholder value maximization		
(N1) Corporate groups (keiretsu).	– (Presence of affiliated firms with equity and business relationships may interfere with individual firms' shareholder value maximization.)	? (Where keiretsu group firms own pieces of each other, each firm's independent shareholder value maximization might not be well-defined.)	? (Where keiretsu group firms own pieces of each other, each firm's independent shareholder value maximization might not be well-defined.)
(N2) Consensus as the goal, and avoidance of open confrontations.	– (Shareholders' exclusive claim to the ownership of the firm does not generate consensus among the firm's other stakeholders.)	+ (shareholder value maximization may be acceptable to non-keiretsu firms as an easily understood governance principle.)	? (No specific prediction.)
(N3) Stakeholder value, value added and other group-oriented value maximization as the objective for corporate decision making.	– (Shareholders' exclusive claim to the ownership of the firm is not acceptable to the firm's other stakeholders.)	– (Shareholders' exclusive claim to the ownership of the firm is not acceptable to the firm's other stakeholders.)	? (Paying serious attention to traditionally ignored shareholders' rights to some degree may even improve corporate governance.)
Summary: Perception under (s1) may generally be at an unacceptable level, but it may subsequently become accepted (at least partially) where its legitimacy and complementarity are evident. Policy and court judgments may accelerate such local acceptance.			
	Panel 2 (s2) Strictly outside independent directors' involvement in boards		
(N1) Corporate groups (keiretsu).	– (Keiretsu member firms may regard outside directors to be unable to deal with the keiretsu's internal governance issues.)	? (Strictly outside directors may be able to provide leadership in governance of keiretsu firms in a more transparent manner than insiders.)	? (Strictly outside directors, if found, may be able to provide leadership in governance of keiretsu firms in a more transparent manner than insiders.)
(N2) Consensus as the goal, and avoidance of open confrontations.	? (No specific prediction.)	? (No specific prediction.)	? (No specific prediction.)

Table 11.2 continued

Japanese business norms	*Instruments of selective adaptation*		
	Perception	*Legitimacy*	*Complementarity*
(N3) Stakeholder value, value added and other group-oriented value maximization as the objective for corporate decision making	– (Strictly outside and knowledgeable directors are hard to find, given the many stakeholders of a firm that they must oversee.)	– (Strictly outside and knowledgeable directors are hard to find, given the many stakeholders of a firm that they must oversee.)	? (Strictly outside directors, if found, may be able to provide leadership in governance of the welfare of many stakeholders in a more transparent manner than insiders.)
Summary: The local perception, that strictly outside yet qualified directors are difficult to find, being true, non-keiretsu firms may appreciate a proper role for outside directors for transparency and leadership in governance.			
Panel 3 (s3) Competition in the market for corporate control			
(N1) Corporate groups (keiretsu).	+ (Freer friendly mergers are helpful for developing keiretsu groups.)	+ (Freer friendly mergers are helpful for developing keiretsu groups.)	+ (Freer friendly mergers are helpful for developing keiretsu groups.)
(N2) Consensus as the goal, and avoidance of open confrontations.	– (consensus may be hard to obtain for hostile takeovers.)	– (consensus may be hard to obtain for hostile takeovers.)	? (No specific prediction.)
(N3) Stakeholder value, value-added and other group-oriented value maximization as the objective for corporate decision making .	? (Stakeholders may have competing views about possible friendly and hostile takeover possibilities.)	? (Stakeholders may have competing views about possible friendly and hostile takeover possibilities.)	? (Stakeholders may have competing views about possible friendly and hostile takeover possibilities.)
Summary: Under (s3), more friendly mergers than hostile mergers will take place. Completion of hostile takeovers may be hard because of complex keiretsu and shareholders' interests. Policy and court judgments play a limited role.			
Panel 4 (s4) Transparency and information disclosure			
(N1) Corporate groups (keiretsu).	– (Related firms are unwilling to disclose their transactions to the public, unless required.)	? (Transparency and disclosure required for sound development of capital markets.)	? (Transparency and disclosure required for sound development of capital markets.)

(N2) Consensus as the goal, and avoidance of open confrontations.	– (Transparency and disclosure requirements may interfere with non-confrontational and insider-oriented practices.)	? (Voluntary information disclosure by firms prevents potentially costly law suits by investors.)	? (Voluntary information disclosure by firms prevents potentially costly lawsuits by investors.)
(N3) Stakeholder value, value-added and other group-oriented value maximization as the objective for corporate decision making.	? (Some stakeholders may demand more transparency than other stakeholders in group-oriented valued maximization.)	? (Some stakeholders may demand more transparency than other stakeholders in group-oriented valued maximization.)	? (Some stakeholders may demand more transparency than other stakeholders in group-oriented valued maximization.)
Summary: While local perception of (s4) may be negative, it may subsequently become accepted (at least partially) where its legitimacy and complementarity are evident. Policy and court judgments may accelerate such local acceptance.			
Panel 5 (s5) Protection of minority shareholders			
(N1) Corporate groups (keiretsu).	– (Keiretsu firms as dominant shareholders can dominate the rights of individual minority shareholders.)	? (No specific prediction.)	? (No specific prediction.)
(N2) Consensus as the goal, and avoidance of open confrontations.	– (The presence of minority shareholders increases the amount of effort needed to reach consensus.)	? (Established rules to deal with minority shareholders make it easier for the firm management in coping with consensus building.)	? (Established rules to deal with minority shareholders make it easier for the firm management in coping with consensus building.)
(N3) Stakeholder value, value-added and other group-oriented value maximization as the objective for corporate decision making.	– (Unless minority shareholders are part of the group, minority shareholders' rights are likely to contradict those of the dominant stakeholders.)	– (Protecting minority shareholders' rights may reduce the overall stakeholder value.)	? (Established rules to deal with minority shareholders and avoid abusing them make it easier for the firm management to maximize stakeholder value net of the costs associated with the minority shareholders.)
Summary: While local perception of (s5) may be negative, it may subsequently become accepted (at least partially) where its legitimacy and complementarity are evident. Policy and court judgments may accelerate such local acceptance.			

Notes: –, +, and ? mean, respectively, negative, positive and undetermined correlations between the respective norms and instruments.

of the Japanese economy, it did not appear difficult for the notion of shareholder value maximization to be accepted by both businesses and policy makers. There was general agreement that Japan's bank-based corporate governance system was too insider-oriented and that the U.S.-style market-based system, with the clear management objective of shareholder value maximization, needed to be implemented. In order to achieve this objective, many laws were revised. Japan's New Company Law, in particular, was set up to provide a new framework within which Japanese corporations can organize their business activities and corporate structures so they are consistent with their respective profit maximization. To secure investor confidence, Japan's new Financial Instruments and Exchange Law of June 2006 was enacted. This law updated and consolidated all existing exchange laws, including the Securities and Exchange Law. It introduced the notion of flexibility in its mandate on regulating financial instruments.

Interestingly enough, Japan's apparent acceptance of the notion of shareholder value maximization did not necessarily lead to straightforward acceptance of various business mechanisms or business strategies associated with the U.S.-style shareholder value maximization.

Most changes regarding shareholder value maximization (s1) have taken place in the interactions between corporations and their shareholders. The general decline in bank shareholding has been replaced by a substantial increase in shareholding by individuals and investment funds (see Nakamura, Chapter 7, this volume). These new shareholders clearly view shareholder value maximization as an important objective to be pursued by firms' management.

Initial reactions.[38] Many domestic and foreign individual shareholders as well as investment fund managers began taking advantage of the new opportunities, where they could question the managers and directors of the firms in which they owned shares. For example, many foreign institutional investors (such as investment funds and pension funds) from North America and Europe have raised serious objections to the corporate governance policies of the Japanese companies whose shares they own. They typically voted against the following management proposals if the proposals were unacceptable to them for the reasons cited:

- voted against the proposed auditor: the outside auditor's qualifications were not satisfactory

- voted against the proposed "golden handshake" for retiring directors: the basis for calculating the "golden handshake" was unclear
- voted against conferring stock options to directors and employees: the basis for calculating the amount of stock options to be conferred and the basis for evaluating the market value of the stock options were unclear
- voted against the issuances of general new stock shares and also new issues of shares to specific third parties: the objectives for issuing these new shares were unclear.

Many lawsuits have been brought against corporate managers and directors, the main thrust of which has been to question the validity of managers' and directors' actions in the light of shareholder value maximization and their mandated responsibility.

During the court proceedings for these shareholders' legal suits, the Japanese courts initially showed their acceptance of the notion that shareholder value maximization must serve as the essential guidance for managers and directors. Proposed poison pills at many firms were rejected by their shareholders in their general shareholders' meetings in June 2006, the first year in which Japan's New Company Law became operational.

These lawsuits have convinced many managers and board directors that they might face potential legal action against them from their companies' shareholders if their business decisions result in major losses to their companies and hence damage their market value. It is for these reasons that Japanese managers have begun to take time to listen to their investment fund shareholders who have suggestions to make regarding corporate activities.

Reactions at a later stage. After the initial transitional period, it became clear to many Japanese managers that Japanese corporations could not accept the U.S. style shareholder-driven corporate management. Stakeholder value maximization theory was often used by Japanese managers as a tool to rebut attempts by investment funds, both foreign and domestic, to acquire control of their firms. Firms' management began to devise new poison pills to fight off hostile takeovers. This move was helped by Japan's shareholding patterns, in which large fractions of Japanese corporations' outstanding shares are owned by keiretsu firms and other related corporations.[39] Poison pills based on keiretsu relationships and cross-shareholding began to emerge. (These are potent tools as poison pills, the effectiveness of which was proven during most of the post-World War II period; see, for example, Morck and Nakamura, 1999.)

As shown in Table 11.2 (panel 1), standard Japanese business norms provide little support in terms of the perception and, to a lesser extent, legitimacy of shareholder value maximization. Japan's new laws acknowledge shareholders' ownership of their firms. However, if the majority of outstanding shares of a corporation are owned by friendly keiretsu firms, for example, the new laws telling corporations to follow shareholder value maximization may not necessarily be useful for individual shareholders.[40] We expect that the Japanese courts will be asked to resolve disputes about shareholder value maximization.

Outside independent directors' involvement in the board's decisions (s2)

Under Japan's New Company Law, corporations now have the option to choose between the traditional Japanese-style corporate board system and the U.S.-style executive committee system. Outside directors play different roles depending on which system a company chooses to adopt.

In Table 11.2 (panel 2), we show that directors who are strictly outsiders to firms' operations are hard to find and also unlikely to be acceptable to the firms as members of their boards. Such outsiders are not likely to generate enough confidence in the company's management because few insiders think that outside directors can understand all the complex relationship-based business issues that are often important to a firm's operations and decision making.

It is for this reason that many firms appoint directors from their related firms as their firms' outside directors.[41] On this basis, selective adaptation theory predicts that keiretsu firms whose interfirm business relationships are particularly complex are less likely to choose to have the U.S.-style outside director-based boards.

Consistent with our observation, Table 11.3 shows that Japanese firms generally use relatively few outside directors, regardless of their origins.

Table 11.3 Fraction of outside directors at Japanese corporations

% outside directors	0%	1–20	21–40	41–60	61-80	81–100
% corporations	56.2	31.4	9.1	2.5	0.0	0.8

Source: Yoshikawa (2003).

New Japanese laws also provide considerable flexibility about how firms can use outside directors, whose corporate governance may be valued particularly by non-keiretsu, independent firms. A number of such Japanese firms have implemented the new U.S.-style committee system involving outside directors as part of their corporate governance mechanism.[42] A recent survey of Japanese listed firms shows that, statistically, the firms that had adopted the U.S.-style committee system lagged behind their peers who continued to use the traditional Japanese system in terms of firm performance (Table 11.4).

Table 11. 4 Comparison of firm performance by the type of corporate governance (outside directors), Tokyo Stock Exchange, first section firms

	June 28, 2002	*June 30, 2005*	*Growth in sales revenue, 2002–2004*	*Growth in ordinary profit, 2002–04*
New committee system (31 firms)	¥166.948 billion	¥162.256 billion (–2.8%)	7.1%	36.9%
Traditional system with auditors	¥2,689.191 billion	¥3,431.376 billion (+27.6%)	9.2%	51.7%

Source: Nikkei, August 16, 2005.

Competition in the market for corporate control (s3)

There is no question that Japan's M&A activities increased after the reform (see, for example, Arikawa and Miyajima, Chapter 8, this volume).[43] One of the fundamental issues raised about the Japanese business system was that, under the bank-based corporate governance system, it was difficult to cut out inefficient parts of the company in order to allow for growth in the more promising areas of business. An active market for corporate control allows firms to exchange component parts in order to form mutually more efficient corporations. With this process, more share value is generated.

Table 11.2 (panel 3) shows that selective adaptation theory predicts that Japan's acceptance of a competitive market for corporate control will be more prevalent for friendly takeovers and mergers. On the other hand, hostile takeovers are less likely to be acceptable to Japanese businesses and society in general.

Even if this prediction turns out to be the case, we should not underestimate the potential gains in economic efficiency from this new state for Japan's M&A markets. Until the 1980s, there were virtually no large-scale friendly mergers, let alone hostile mergers. The few large-scale mergers that took place generally were value-losing events. One main reason for such failures was the difficulty for different Japanese firms of integrating two highly firm-specific management systems, particularly with respect to personnel management.[44] Japan's New Company Law allows more prompt reorganization of merged business units.

A function of an active M&A market in the U.S. is that the threat of a hostile takeover is often effective in improving the quality of a firm's management, and, if needed, such a takeover would allow the incumbent management to be replaced by more competent management, which could improve economic efficiency, thereby creating more value in the process. While Japan's bank-based corporate governance system worked satisfactorily until the 1980s as a substitute for the market for corporate control (see, for example, Morck and Nakamura, 1999), it was not able to cope with the huge problems in the 1990s. This was particularly so because the lack of proper governance of the banks themselves led almost all Japanese banks to suffer from massive bad-loan problems; most of them, facing bankruptcy, had to be bailed out by the Japanese government.

Based on selective adaptation, we predict that Japan's reform will not bring many hostile mergers and, as a result, there may be less efficiency gain than would otherwise be associated with such mergers or the threats of them.

We conclude that selective adaptation theory implies that Japan's M&A markets after the reform, unlike those in the U.S., will not be well balanced, in that most active transactions will still be friendly M&As. Relatively few possibilities for hostile takeovers are expected. Nevertheless, hostile takeover attempts will undoubtedly occur, and disputes resulting from unsuccessful attempts at hostile takeovers of Japanese firms by domestic and foreign firms will resort to the new laws as well as the courts.

This is consistent with what we have observed so far for post-reform M&As: most domestic M&A activity occurs between affiliated firms and they are friendly mergers by definition.[45] However, a number of disputes over unsettled hostile takeover attempts have also been brought before the courts for resolution.

Transparency and information disclosure in accounting, financial, and other reporting to investors and the public (s4)

Transparency and information disclosure is essential for the protection of all investors. It is particularly important for minority shareholders who may not have legal access to company books and other sources of information. Japan's corporate governance reform resulted in significantly increased requirements for transparency and information disclosure for corporate activities and protection of investors. The primary laws that are relevant here are the New Company Law, the new Financial Instruments and Exchange Law and the revised Certified Public Accountants (CPA) Law. In addition, Tokyo and other stock exchanges impose their own disclosure rules on the listed firms.

Japan's New Company Law now requires corporations to use consolidated financial statements as their primary means of reporting. It also requires corporations to report annually the value of financial securities and unrealized losses and profits.[46] Since Japanese firms conduct large amounts of transactions with their affiliated keiretsu firms of all kinds, individual (typically minority) shareholders would have difficulty determining a corporation's overall soundness unless its consolidated statements were available. Japanese firms also own large amounts of securities, often including stocks of affiliated companies, to maintain their keiretsu relationships. New rules require corporations to report their financial positions for these securities annually. In the past, many firms have used their affiliated firms to manipulate their own financial positions. For example, parent firms always post significant amounts of profits while their unlisted subsidiaries post losses. Under the new rules on disclosure and reporting, these questionable reporting practices are expected to decline. This is a positive implication for public investors.

However, we point out that, given Japanese corporations' persistent reliance on transactions with their related firms, these new laws are not likely to eliminate fraudulent accounting practices involving affiliated firms. Third-party monitoring of these interfirm transactions between affiliated firms is difficult at best and firms are likely to continue conducting questionable or illegal transactions in these areas.[47]

Another implication of consolidated financial statement-based reporting is that detailed stand-alone financial statements for each of the business unit companies under a holding company are no longer required. Since public investors invest in listed holding companies, not in their individual business units, such stand-alone financial reporting for each business unit might not appear essential. Yet, these business units are often the objects of M&As, and in those cases, potential acquirers and their shareholders, as well as the shareholders of the potential target firms, may be concerned about the accuracy with which specific segment information related to the unit being transacted is being disclosed. Table 11.2 (panel 4) suggests that, while Japanese perception of transparency and information disclosure may be negative where keiretsu firms are involved, there is also room for Japanese acceptance of the legitimacy and complementarity of (s4). It is possible, then, that the new laws could be particularly effective for enforcing transparency and information disclosure, if they are properly implemented. Even keiretsu firms realize the importance of (s4), for example, for transparent transactions of M&As.[48]

Another factor that contributes to transparency is revision of Japan's Certified Public Accountants Law, which has gone through a number of revisions since the 1990s. All revisions were intended to strengthen the CPA's monitoring capacity and improve the quality of the accounts auditing of Japanese listed and unlisted corporations. A number of scandals triggered these revisions. The most recent revision of 2007 requires accountants more stringently to audit and report fraudulent bookkeeping by firms. It will also be accompanied by a strengthening of the penalties for accountants who violate the rules. The Japanese parliament passed the 2007 revision in December of that year, and it took effect in April 2008.

We also expect that the new Financial Instruments and Exchange Law and revised CPA Law will significantly improve corporations' reporting transparency and the protection of both investors and creditors.

Protection of minority shareholders (s5)

As shown in Table 11.2 (panel 5), selective adaptation combined with Japanese business norms implies that Japan may choose corporate governance practices which are not as effective as those in the U.S. system for protecting minority shareholders. Although Japan's new laws will allow minority shareholders a new voice in the general shareholders' meetings, and also in the courts to some extent, the rights of majority shareholders might still prevail in many cases.

In particular, if a firm's majority shareholders consist of keiretsu and other corporate and institutional investors who are management-friendly, minority shareholders' objections raised in the general shareholders' meeting may fall on deaf ears.

A number of recent events are consistent with this implication regarding selective adaptation behavior; we discuss these below. However, our analysis suggests that some room exists for certain policies and legal means promoting (s5) to generate complementarity with the Japanese practices.

Stable shareholding as a poison pill. Facing potential hostile takeover threats, many Japanese firms have resumed their efforts to establish their base of stable shareholders which deteriorated considerably after the burst of Japan's financial bubble in 1990 (see Nakamura, Chapter 7, this volume, Table 7.1). These stable shareholders typically consist of affiliated (or keiretsu) firms, banks and other financial institutions, and other corporations; some of which may also engage in cross-shareholding. They are friendly in the sense that they do not sell off their shares in an opportunistic manner. While some of this type of shareholding may enhance efficiency for the firms involved,[49] most probably lacks any compelling foundations in terms of shareholder gains.[50] The primary purpose of many recent incidents of stable shareholding appears to be to protect the incumbent management from hostile takeovers. Stable shareholding has proved to be highly effective as a poison pill.[51] If up to 70 percent of a firm's outstanding shares are owned in pieces by many friendly corporate shareholders, no outsiders can succeed in their hostile takeover bids (TOBs) (see Nakamura, Chapter 7, this volume, Table 7.1). As expected, most hostile takeovers or unsolicited TOB attempts have failed in Japan.[52]

Example: Steel Partners versus Bull-Dog Sauce. Until recently, poison pills were virtually unheard of in Japan. But a recent survey reports that, as of May 15, 2007, 14 percent of Japanese firms listed in the first section of the Tokyo, Osaka, and Nagoya Stock Exchanges, and 8 percent of all listed firms (316 firms), have already implemented or are planning to implement anti-takeover defense schemes.[53] This is despite the argument by Warren Lichtenstein, chairman and chief executive of Steel Partners (and many other investors from the U.S.) that "companies with poison pills in the United States typically have demonstrated poorer returns on invested capital, resulting in many of them being redeemed."[54]

Since the early 2000s, Steel Partners has been aggressively buying shares in Japanese companies for takeover purposes, such as Bull-Dog Sauce (a maker of condiments), Yushiro Chemical Industry (manufacturer of machinery lubricants), Myojo Foods (noodle maker) and Sapporo Holdings (brewer). However, Steel Partners failed in all its offers to take over the target companies – either because of the target company's anti-takeover measures, or because of friendly tenders by other companies.

Bull-Dog's defense began on June 24, 2007, with its shareholders' approval of the company-proposed measures to fend off Steel Partners' US$260 million takeover bid, including a warrants issue on terms that would dilute Steel Partners' stake. Steel Partners asked the Tokyo District Court for an injunction, but the Court rejected the request on June 28, 2007, arguing that the defensive plan was legal. Steel Partners appealed to the Tokyo High Court.

The Tokyo High Court rejected Steel's appeal on July 9, 2007. Steel Partner's final appeal to Japan's Supreme Court also failed on August 7, 2007.

Bull-Dog became the first Japanese company to have successfully avoided a hostile takeover using a poison pill. Bull-Dog's poison pill, which is one of the most popular ones being adopted by many Japanese companies, allows the company management to issue stock warrants to general shareholders so that the potential acquirer's stake will be diluted.

It is by no means obvious that Steel Partners' offer would have disadvantaged most of Bull-Dog's general individual shareholders. Nevertheless, Bull-Dog's management was successful in convincing them that Steel Partners, as company owner, would jeopardize the firm's ongoing business operations. More than 80 percent of shareholders voted for the management's proposals.[55]

The main argument used successfully by the management was that Steel Partners, being ignorant of Bull-Dog's business, would focus on maximizing the returns to shareholders at the expense of other stakeholders such as employees, customers, suppliers, banks, and the like.[56, 57] This argument is consistent with the stakeholder value maximization discussed above.[58] The potential problem with this is that it can be used to support incompetent management.

It is expected that, if Steel Partners decided to terminate its TOB and accept the management warrants issue plan, it would make about ¥5 million (about US$4.2 million). On the other hand, after paying all the costs related to its anti-takeover activities, Bull-Dog's financial conditions are expected to deteriorate significantly, registering significant losses throughout the 2007 fiscal year.[59]

Whether the Japanese court ruling on the Bull-Dog case will make it harder for investment funds as well as other potentially hostile acquirers to gain acceptance in Japan remains to be seen. This is particularly so given our analysis above that hostile takeovers might not be part of Japan's selective adaptation behavior. But it might be that, by passing over hostile takeover opportunities, Japanese shareholders may also be passing over significant economic gains.[60]

The New York-based Steel Partners has failed in all its takeover bids for Japanese companies, prompting Lichtenstein to say last month that the company was "misunderstood" in Japan. For example, commenting on their takeover attempt of another Japanese company, Tenryu Saw Mfg., Steel Partners said earlier that it did not plan to sell its Tenryu stake to a third party, and would keep the current management if its bid succeeded.

Example: Koito and T. Boone Pickens. In many respects, Steel Partners' experience in Japan is similar to that of T. Boone Pickens in the late

1980s and early 1990s. Both these U.S. investors found that stable share ownership by cross-holding in Japan is a potent barrier to takeovers. In 1990 the American takeover entrepreneur T. Boone Pickens owned 26.43 percent of the Japanese company Koito Manufacturing, and was its largest shareholder. Despite this, he could not force management to give him a seat on the board. Together, 19 Japanese firms owned the majority of Koito's stock, and all supported the management. Although the fortitude of cross-held ownership as a takeover barrier is clear, it is less widely known that, in many cases, ownership by cross-holding in Japan developed expressly as a barrier to takeovers (Morck and Nakamura, 1999, p. 320).

We should note also that, despite the real difficulties Japanese minority shareholders face, there have been some successful revolts in general shareholders' meetings, where important management proposals on corporate governance can be rejected if more than one-third of the firm's shareholders oppose.[61]

Management buyouts (leveraged buyouts). An increasing number of Japanese firms are considering management buyouts (MBOs) as a way to alleviate the pressure imposed by the stock market. In 2006, there were 80 known cases of MBOs by listed firms (67 cases in 2005) involving ¥701.7 billion (about US$6 billion), a 2.4-fold increase over the previous year (¥292.375 billion, about US$2.6 billion).[62] These firms include some well-known small- to medium-size corporations.

The companies which have chosen MBOs so far have all argued that MBOs were needed for them to focus on fundamental reform in the management of the companies without worrying about the short-term financial performance required by the stock market.

During the process of these MBOs, some issues were raised by both institutional and individual shareholders, mostly concerning the price at which the MBO-proposing firm was intending to buy the outstanding shares. Generally, minority shares suffer most from any injustice that might be done in MBOs. The following is an example of a recent MBO where these issues were explicitly discussed.

Rex Holdings Co. Ltd. is a holding company which owns Japan's largest barbecue beef restaurant chain (Gyu-Kaku), a large convenience store chain (am-pm), a restaurant chain (Red Lobster) and other franchise store chains. It started as a property management company in 1987, but entered the fast-food and other food-related retail business in 1996. After having transformed itself within six years into the owner of a number of successful restaurant chains, in 2005 the company reorganized itself as a holding company under its present name. Its annual sales revenues for 2006 were ¥161.8 billion (about US$1.41 billion) and it had 2,063 employees as of December 31, 2006.

With the stated objective to restructure its business in order to meet the challenge of growth in a highly competitive food business, the company announced its plans to turn itself into a private company, using an MBO, in a rather complex deal involving outside investment partners. Rex's management conducted a TOB with an asking price of ¥230,000 per share in November 2006 and acquired almost 92 percent of the company's outstanding shares. On April 29, 2007, Rex Holdings delisted itself from the DASDAQ exchange in Tokyo, where it was first listed six years before with an IPO (initial public offering) price of ¥570,000 per share.

A major issue raised in this process was the lack of transparency and information disclosure in the determination of the share price used in the TOB and also the general process of the MBO. There were also accusations of insider trading.

In January 2006, Rex's share price was ¥568,000, but it went down rapidly in August when the company revised its performance prediction downward. As its TOB price, Rex's management used the average share price calculated over one month prior to the TOB plus a 13.9 percent premium. This price was unusually low compared to other MOBs that took place in 2006. For example, MOBs conducted by Skylark Co., Toshiba Ceramics and Q'sai Co. all used TOB share prices which exceeded the highs observed for the 12 months prior to the dates of the TOBs. Furthermore, their TOB prices were set 30–40 percent higher than the average prices observed for the 12 months prior to the dates of the TOBs.

About 75 percent of Rex's shareholders accepted the TOB, but about 120 individual shareholders kept hold of their shares, arguing that the TOB price was too low. Meanwhile, Rex decided to buy up these still outstanding shares. In response to this, the remaining Rex shareholders decided to bring a lawsuit against Rex, based on the Company Law. The shareholders are asking the Tokyo District Court to determine a fair price with which Rex may purchase their shares. These individual shareholders argue that TOB prices usually use observed share prices averaged over time intervals starting at least six months prior to the date of the proposed TOB. Rex's management intentionally ignored the rights of (particularly minority) shareholders by setting the TOB price so low.

This case has revealed the types of problems that can occur in MOBs in Japan where no U.S.-style neutral MBO pricing mechanism has been instituted,[63] and these problems are rooted in the unpredictable interaction between Japan's New Company Law and the Financial Instruments and Exchange Law. It is possible that further issues and consequences peculiar to Japan will be generated in this regard.

In the case of Rex, there was no obvious violation of these laws. The TOB pricing was fair according to the Financial Instruments and Exchange Law (as the TOB price applied to all shareholders); it was also consistent with the Company Law since minority shareholders were given the same opportunity as others to sell their shares.

Nevertheless, many analysts, as well as many members of the public, felt that there was an obvious violation in the protection of the rights of Rex's minority shareholders.

New government regulation

In response to the problematic MBO process at Rex, the Financial Services Agency (formerly the Financial Supervisory Agency) introduced new administrative guidelines, such as mandating that a management team proposing an MBO must attach the calculation basis of their TOB price. But many consider these regulations to be highly inadequate.

In response to this, the Japanese government (METI, and others) began formulating rules about TOB price-setting and laws that would allow shareholders to oppose MBOs in cases where the loss of the company's market value would likely result if the MBO proceeded.

The lack of a legally mandated transparent mechanism by which TOB prices for MBOs are determined is still a major way in which minority shareholders' rights are not protected.

The Rex case also shows that managers can potentially exploit shareholders by first listing their company's shares at a high IPO price, then, after a failed management experience, they can allow the share price to go down, and finally buy back the company at a much reduced price from the shareholders. Because the managers are paying to buy back the company's outstanding shares from the shareholders, they prefer low TOB prices. This causes a serious moral hazard problem in the Japanese corporate governance system. This type of minority shareholders' experience and moral hazard problem are in part responsible for the continuing lack of strong support for Japan's stock exchanges, particularly those for emerging companies. Unless the problems of transparency, information disclosure and protection of minority shareholders are addressed, the current problems at Japan's stock exchanges may continue.

Dysfunctionality in Japanese acceptance of U.S.-style corporate governance practices: implications of selective adaptation

If Japan, using its traditional business norms, follows selective adaptation in shaping its new corporate governance practices, then consistent application of the liberal norms that underlie U.S. practices will be lost in Japan's corporate governance reform.[64] This can occur, for example, if the three instruments (perception, legitimacy and complementarity) that drive selective adaptation interact with Japanese business norms in different ways for practices associated with different state variables describing corporate governance (s1)–(s5), as is shown in Table 11.2. For example, legitimacy may negatively affect outside directors and protection of minority shareholders, but have a more ambiguous effect on shareholder value maximization, competition for the market for corporate control, and transparency and information disclosure.[65] This implies that even though Japan's reform has solidly established the legal settings required for U.S.-style corporate governance, the resulting specific corporate governance practices actually adopted by Japanese businesses may deviate from the originally intended practices in varying ways.[66]

Another case of inconsistency we discussed above is that competition in the market for corporate control after the reform would be facilitated for friendly mergers but not for hostile takeovers.[67] We know that both types of merger can potentially increase efficiency, but we also know that friendly mergers tend to increase managerial inefficiency while hostile takeovers or the threat of them could reduce managerial inefficiencies.[68] If hostile takeovers are ruled out by selective adaptation in Japan, as we have argued above, then this may cause some unexpected efficiency losses in the Japanese economy.

Another example is poison pills based on keiretsu shareholding. Historical evidence suggests they are potent and can function as a tool to protect incompetent management. But this clearly runs counter to the original intention of Japan's corporate governance reform to promote shareholder value maximization.[69, 70]

At this time it is not possible to predict the overall economic consequences of various dysfunctionalities as a result of Japan's selective adaptation. At least the above examples suggest possibly negative efficiency implications.

We conclude that, because Japanese business norms' interactions with the instruments of selective adaptation are not uniform and vary depending on the specific state variable of corporate governance in question, dysfunctionality of the sort discussed above will occur.

This is also likely to have potentially important practical implications for investment strategies by foreign investors. Evidence so far suggests that Japanese firms do not welcome hostile or unsolicited takeovers. However, they are willing to pay off greenmailers.[71]

Concluding remarks

We have applied a selective adaptation framework to analyzing Japan's corporate governance reform which began in the 1990s. The reform was undertaken with a conviction that Japan's discredited post-World War II bank-based corporate government system must be replaced by a U.S.-style corporate governance system. The U.S. corporate governance system was chosen as Japan's model because of the robust economic performance of the U.S. economy. Japan's reform has introduced new laws which emphasize: shareholders' rights and shareholder value maximization; minority shareholders' rights; competition in the market for corporate control; and transparency and information disclosure. With strong public support, the Japanese parliament promptly passed these new laws which reflect Western liberal norms.

We have shown that, despite the U.S.-style corporate governance laws that have come into effect for Japanese businesses, Japanese businesses' actual implementation of corporate governance practices so far have been quite selective and uneven. Our selective adaptation framework shows how (Western liberal norm-based) U.S.-style corporate governance practices interact with Japanese business norms, and shows why some practices are more likely to be adopted than others.

Notes

1. An earlier version of this chapter was presented at the Law and Society Association Annual Conference in Berlin ("Law and Society in the 21st Century"), July 25–28, 2007.
2. Details of various corporate governance practices in post-bubble Japan are discussed in Chapters 7 and 8 of this volume.
3. The term "selective adaptation" is used in many areas in different contexts (for example, linguistics (Kirby, 1998), policy studies (Millar, 1972), technology management (Zeitlin, 2000), economics (Corning, 1996; Freeman, 1991), law (Milhaupt, 2005), management (Cailluet, 1998) and vision research (Kremers et al., 2003; Harris and Nakayama, 2007). In these applications selective adaptation is hypothesized to give observational units a potential source of variation (or non-convergence) in some of their characteristics in

a cross-sectional sense. Cross-sectional contexts vary depending on specific applications. (In social sciences, the presence of selective adaptation often leads to rejection of the convergence hypothesis.) In this chapter, by selective adaptation we mean the specific analytical framework proposed by Potter (2003, 2004, 2007). We use this framework to study implications of Japan's selective adaptation behavior to U.S.-style corporate governance practices. A selective adaptation framework of this type has not previously been applied to cross-border transfers of corporate governance practices.

4. Japan clearly chose the U.S. system as a model for its new corporate governance system, based on the robust economic performance of U.S. corporations and the U.S. economy during the 1990s.
5. Compared to the significant differences that have existed in corporate governance practices between Japan and the U.S., those among Anglo-American countries (for example, the U.S., the U.K., Canada, Australia) are minor. For this reason, in order to simplify our notation in the rest of this chapter, we use the term "U.S. corporate governance system" to mean the Anglo-American corporate governance system. However, where specific country practices matter, we state this.
6. We define institutions here to include not just legal and political settings but also the basic framework that characterizes Japan's business and economic system.
7. For example, dysfunctional adoption of foreign legal practices may lead to unpredictable (or unpredicted) behavior in corporate governance by some Japanese firms.
8. Other researchers have also pointed out the problems caused by this kind of behavior in Japan. For example, Hoshi and Kashyap (2001) argue that Japan's piecemeal and dysfunctional adoption of market-based financial policies in its deregulation of Japanese financial markets was a primary cause of the subsequent bad loans problem in the 1990s, forcing many banks to face bankruptcy.
9. In our analysis, we will pay attention not only to recent changes in Japan's legal settings, with new requirements on corporations, but also to the changes in the economic incentives that these new institutions bring with them. Political reallocation of these economic incentives during the reform may have taken place. If so, how was selective adaptation affected by this? These issues are beyond the scope of this chapter and will not be fully discussed here.
10. We should note that Western liberal norms and the business practices associated with them (for example, individual rights, competition, transparency) are well accepted in Japan. In formulating specific business policies, however, these liberal norms are not uniformly and consistently applied. Selective adaptation explains this behavior as a consequence of Japanese compromise behavior, incorporating both Japanese and Western liberal norms.
11. Different authors give different predictions. Some predict that Japan will accept U.S.-style corporate governance practices. For example, Hoshi and Kashyap (2001) note that Japan's corporate governance system in the twenty-first century will become like the system found in the U.S.; also, in post-World War II Japan, where the role of the banks is much diminished, capital markets are driven by institutional investors, and corporate managers are disciplined by active markets for corporate control.

12. For example, Gilson and Milhaupt (2004) found that, as of March 2003, no firm which was a member of a bank-centered horizontal keiretsu group had adopted the executive committee system of governance. Explaining this in economic terms is difficult.
13. These items on the list are not exclusive nor exhaustive. In the following, we define cultural norms and the associated values broadly and consider norms in both the business and the non-business contexts.
14. Most of the discussions below hold in a comparative context for other countries in the West. We focus on Japan–U.S. comparisons because our interest is comparisons between Japan and the U.S. regarding corporate governance practices.
15. But, as noted above, regular workers in Japan tend to be (prime-age) male workers (see, for example, Nakamura, 1993).
16. Many Japanese corporations now use agency staff working side-by-side with the company employees at the worksites. Agency workers are formally employed by labor agencies and generally enjoy little employment security.
17. Kiyokawa and Yamane (2004) report that 65 percent of managers and 71 percent of workers in Japan believe lifetime employment is desirable for employees.
18. For example, consider vertical production keiretsu groups in which large assembly firms (such as Toyota) buy auto parts from their keiretsu suppliers. Customers and suppliers are bound by common norms of expected behavior, for example, a conviction on both sides that a customer simply does not let a supplier go without cause (Lincoln and Nakata, 1997). Even when grounds for switching exist, there is wide agreement that suppliers deserve ample warning, and even assistance in locating other business (ibid.). Ahmadjian and Lincoln (2001, p. 695) also note: "Besides fears that an infraction of the norms governing the treatment of suppliers might invoke real sanctions, our interviews turned up some strong taken-for-granted assumptions about dealings with suppliers. Purchasing managers described the lengths to which they went to keep their suppliers in business: bringing them new products to manufacture, finding them new customers, even orchestrating mergers with other firms. When there were no alternatives to terminating the relationship, a customer might give the supplier notice of a year or two to ease the transition. Customers thus extricated themselves slowly from commitments to suppliers, not just from fear of sanctions but because, they said, this was 'the way things are done' in Japan, and it would not be right (i.e., moral or legitimate) to do otherwise." Economic reasons probably exist for these assembly–supplier relationships, as Ahmadjian and Lincoln (ibid., p. 697) note also that: "for many assemblers and suppliers, close partnerships are still the norm. Cultural and institutional obstacles to severing long-term business ties are important, but these forces of inertia are not the whole issue. There remain real advantages of hybrid organization in flexibility, cost, and speed."
19. The assembly firm's minority ownership position versus its suppliers' means the assembly firm can remain relatively small and allow suppliers to manage themselves independently, thus eliminating the types of agency cost that many large, vertically integrated firms typically suffer.

20. Vertical keiretsu groups discussed here are just one type of keiretsu group in Japan, but their economic characteristics (for example, their efficiency implications) are relatively well understood. Other types of keiretsu groups include bank-based horizontal keiretsu groups, which are less well understood. In most of these keiretsu groups, equity ownership is involved. In some cases, cross-shareholding ("*mochiai*") is practiced, with each member of a keiretsu group owning shares of other member firms. During the 1990s, keiretsu activities (particularly ownership by banks) declined considerably. But there are indications of keiretsu ownership of certain types emerging in relationships in M&As in Japan.
21. Compared to the Japanese keiretsu-based network model, the Silicon Valley network model of innovation and entrepreneurship involves less durable interfirm ties than are typical in Japan and more informal encounters of individuals "doing lunch" and otherwise transacting business in a bounded geographic space (Saxenian, 1994).
22. Japanese equal employment opportunity law was enacted in the late 1980s and has gone through several revisions. Nevertheless, it does not have enforcement power and continues to face difficulty in promoting equal employment practices for women.
23. Most Japanese companies operating in the U.S. and other Western countries generally practice more aggressive equal employment opportunity-based industrial relations with respect to their female workers. This practice, however, has not been transferred back to their home operations in Japan (see, for example, Nakamura, 1993). We also note, however, that a number of lawsuits have been filed against Japanese overseas operations for violating equal employment and human rights laws. These include: a U.S. government suit against Mitsubishi Motor Mfg. of America (the largest sex discrimination case in U.S. history, involving 350 women at the plant in Normal) and a suit against Toyota Motor U.S.A. by a female employee (a US$190 million lawsuit charging that the auto maker's top U.S. executive sexually harassed her and that other executives failed to act on her complaints).
24. Hofstede's (1980, 1983) definitions of these factors are as follows. Power distance: the degree to which less powerful members of organizations and institutions accept that power is not distributed equally. Uncertainty avoidance: the extent to which people feel threatened by ambiguous situations and have created institutions and beliefs for minimizing or avoiding these uncertainties. Individualism: the tendency of people to look after themselves and their immediate family only; in contrast, collectivism is the tendency of people to belong to groups that look after each other in exchange for loyalty. Masculinity: the degree to which the dominant values of a society are "success, money, and things." In contrast, femininity is the degree to which the dominant values of a society are "caring for others and the quality of life."
25. Nevertheless, considerable difference exists between the values for the cultural dimensions that Hofstede (1980) and House et al. (2004) found for Japan. It is possible that this is partly because these authors use different definitions for their dimensions and partly because of Japanese society's changing norms.
26. Alternatively, we may interpret this to mean that the Japanese norm of caring for the elderly has not changed but public expectations regarding the mode

of providing this care may have changed from strictly home care to more publicly funded, or group, care.

27. See Mikanagi (2006) for another view on this conclusion.
28. Jacobs and Potter (2006) explain China's differential policy reactions in dealing with AIDS and SARS in terms of its selective adaptation behavior. Stiles (2006) also notes the importance of local and international norms in the dissemination of international liberal norms in the U.K.
29. For example, the factors that increase state variables such as (s1) below will also benefit all shareholders, including minority shareholders (s5). We define protection of minority shareholders as a separate state variable, (s5) because increased (s1) may benefit large shareholders more than minority shareholders. This is because large shareholders have power over the firm's management and hence can influence it to their advantage, unlike minority shareholders.
30. Highly developed economies, compared to developing economies, tend to have high levels of achievement in these state variables (see, for example, Shleifer and Vishny, 1997; Porta et al., 1999).
31. Since societal norms and business norms are often intermingled and are not generally separable, we discuss them together below.
32. Aoki (1988, p. 154) describes the Japanese firm as a coalition of the two constituent bodies (shareholders and quasi-permanent employees) which share the uncertain returns from the firm's production activities. This model differs from the neoclassical model of the firm in which the shareholders are the owners and exclusive residual claimants. Recent surveys show that Japanese executives think that shareholders are only slightly more important than employees. Executives are still in favor of distributing incremental profits equally among shareholders, employees, internal reserves (profits retained for future use, and cash reserves) and investment (Araki, 2005, p. 51). Jacoby (2005) argues that these views are shared by the general population.
33. Tsurumi and Tsurumi (1991) present empirical evidence that value-added maximization was followed as the corporate norm by Japanese semiconductor firms during the 1970s and 1980s.
34. Note that, unlike stakeholder value or value-added maximization, shareholder value maximization is concerned with firms' residual values net of all expenses including workers' wages.
35. As noted above, new Japanese laws to promote female workers' individual rights and equal employment opportunities over the period from the late 1980s to the early 2000s continue to fail to achieve their intended objectives. One reason for this failure is that there is no enforcement clause and no civil or criminal penalty is imposed on the businesses failing to implement the new laws. But the underlying reason for this is explained using our selective adaptation framework adopted here as follows: even though Japanese businesses see legitimacy in the U.S.-style equal employment opportunity laws and have endorsed the government to adopt them, the businesses (and public) do not necessarily have a strong positive perception about female workers' extensive participation in business activities. They do not see extensive female work participation as complementing or enhancing their normal business transactions either. For these reasons the relevant laws have been adopted but they have not yet been fully enforced in practice.

36. Potter (2003, 2004) proposed using perception, legitimacy and complementarity as instruments in explaining how selective adaptation proceeds in a foreign culture.
37. Note that in our calculation of the above interactions (correlations), the Western norms underlying particular U.S. corporate governance practices that drive each of the state variables are not explicitly enumerated. We use the three instruments instead in these calculations. The use of the instruments in this way allows us to make inferences about Japan's selective adaptation behavior in a practical manner. The use of the instruments in this way would also make it possible to test our hypotheses statistically on selective adaptation when appropriately designed data (such as survey data) on corporate governance became available.
38. See Nakamura (2006) for a brief survey on this.
39. The share of the outstanding shares owned by Japanese banks clearly decreased over the 1990s. Other types of corporate shareholding also declined somewhat, but the majority of vertical keiretsu-related shareholding stayed at roughly the same level.
40. Our conclusion is consistent with Roe (2001) who suggests that shareholder value maximization is empirically less likely to be accepted in countries where product market competition is weak (such as European markets) than in countries where product market competition is strong (such as the U.S.).
41. Most outside directors on Japanese company boards are not really independent directors. Many are sent in by their banks, affiliated companies (for example, a parent firm, a subsidiary firm, a keiretsu firm, and so on).
42. Firms adopting this system have some flexibility in designing how these three committees (appointment, compensation and auditing committees) relate to the board of directors. For example, Sony adopted the U.S.-style system but Canon and Matsushita Electric Industries did not.
43. However, the volume of M&As involving Japanese firms is still small by international comparison. The amounts (in US$ billions) of M&As reported for different countries for the first six months of 2007 were as follows: the U.S. (1,372.7), the U.K. (632.3), Spain (217.6), Italy (208.5), Canada (185.4), France (159.9), Germany (155.1), Australia (110.4), and Japan (81.3).
44. For example, the merger between the Kangyo Bank and the Daiichi Bank, two of Japan's largest banks, which took place with the blessing of the Ministry of Finance, kept two separate personnel management systems under the new merged bank (Daiichi-Kangyo Bank), with all promotions conducted within the respective former systems, for more than ten years. Needless to say, their performance badly lagged behind that of their industry peers during this period.
45. In 2005, there were 3,734 reported transactions of M&As in Japan. Of these, 2,725 (73 percent) were between group (affiliated) firms, while the remaining 1,009 (27 percent) involved non-group firms. Furthermore, the fraction of in-group M&As has been increasing since the early 1990s (Development Bank of Japan, 2007).
46. Prior to the reform, financial statements on stand-alone firms were the only required form of reporting. Firms did not report unrealized gains or losses of the securities they owned until they were sold in the market.

47. An example is the recent scandals in illegal accounting (for example, the creation of non-existent sales between related firms) by Fujitsu's and NEC's related firms (Nikkei, July 3, 2007).
48. A recent example of this involved Mitsubishi Motors Corporation (MMC) selling itself to Daimler-Chrysler, while hiding the company's record on recallable manufacturing defects, and so on. In the end, Daimler-Chrysler sold back all the shares of MMC to MMC and also received compensation for the lack of disclosure of manufacturing defects of the MMC.
49. Shareholding among vertical production keiretsu group firms is often said to be efficiency increasing.
50. The capital tied for stable shareholding purposes is unlikely to generate any meaningful returns.
51. Such stable shareholding prevented hostile takeovers of listed firms in Japan from the early 1950s until recently.
52. These include Oji Paper's attempt to absorb Hokuetsu Paper, Rakuten's attempt to take over Tokyo Broadcasting System and Livedoor's attempt to take over Nippon Broadcasting System.
53. *Yomiuri Shinbun*, Tokyo, May 17, 2007. See also Nikkei, March 12, 2008.
54. Empirical support for this statement, however, is somewhat mixed. See, for example, Bebchuk and Cohen (2005), Gompers et al. (2003), Gordon (2002), Hermalin and Weisbach (2003). However, recent calculations using Japanese data show that firm performance is significantly worse for firms adopting poison pills than firms not adopting them (see, for example, Arikawa and Mitsusada, 2008; Hirose et al., 2007; Nikkei, March 12, 2008).
55. It was reported that the Tokyo District Court decided that: "Ultimately, (Steel Partners) has the view of disposing of its target company assets and must be seen as solely concerned with pursuing its own profit. As such it is appropriate to label (Steel Partners) ... as an abusive buyer" (A. Tudor, Reuters, July 9, 2007). The Japanese Supreme Court also argued that Steel Partner's takeover would not be consistent with Bull-Dog's survival as an ongoing concern. Their argument does not seem to fully support the shareholder value maximization principle.
56. Before appealing to Japan's Supreme Court, Lichtenstein commented: "We feel we have no choice but to appeal to the Supreme Court of Japan as Bull-Dog Sauce's actions breach the principles of shareholder equality. We also categorically dispute the High Court's characterization of Steel Partners as an 'abusive bidder.' Our track record as an investor since 2002 clearly shows that Steel Partners is a long-term shareholder whose interests are aligned with those of the Company." The Court did not agree.
57. This argument, often used by the incumbent management in Japanese firms, can be effective if it has shareholder support. It is, however, not the case that Japanese courts always side with the incumbent management.
58. In the Japanese interpretation, this also seems to be consistent with maintaining the target firm as an ongoing concern.
59. Their expected loss for the first six months of the 2007 fiscal year was over US$10 million. They also expect to register losses for the entire 2007 fiscal year.
60. Whether this has negative economic efficiency implications is another serious question.

61. At its general shareholders' meeting in February, 2007, Tokyo Steel's management proposal to make Tokyo Steel become one of Osaka Steel's subsidiaries was rejected because about 42 percent of shareholders opposed the proposal. The minority shareholders argued that the management's proposal would seriously disadvantage the company shareholders. It was thought that many of the shareholders who voted against the management were individual shareholders owning less than 1 percent of Tokyo Steel shares. We note that this opposition to the management was originally organized by the Singapore-based Strawberry Asset Management which used the internet extensively to achieve this. Without such major efforts by a skillful investment fund, the Tokyo Steel management would have won.
62. These figures are from Recof, http://www.recof.co.jp/column/.
63. In the U.S. it is customary for the company to set up a special committee consisting of neutral directors for dealing with MBO-related negotiations, evaluation, approval, and other decisions. Unbiased opinions from third-party experts are also often called upon. In addition, dissatisfied shareholders may choose to file a class-action suit. None of these actions are possible in Japan, even under the new corporate governance system. The only option open to dissatisfied minority shareholders in MBO situations in Japan is to exercise their rights under the Company Law to ask the company to buy out the shares they own. Even this option may not be very practical because it is the shareholders who are responsible for showing that the TOB price is significantly below the fair price. Proving this can be quite costly.
64. In practical terms, this may occur, for example, when two laws, both of which are intended to promote market competition, are implemented according to selective adaptation in such a way that one law is fully enforced to promote competition while the other is superficially accepted without any real enforcement, thus impeding market competition.
65. As noted earlier, our selective adaptation analysis implies that keiretsu firms tend to choose not to make extensive use of independent directors, which is consistent with empirical findings.
66. Konomi (2002) also points out the potentially serious implications for corporate governance of the inconsistencies in the new institutional and legal settings that Japan adopted in the reform.
67. Japan's revised Anti-Monopoly Law uses a more lax criterion for acceptable mergers in terms of proposed merged company's market share. The domestic market share was used before the reform, where now it's the global market share that will be applied. This will facilitate large mergers.
68. Friendly mergers are often associated with managers' wasteful empire building, resulting in loss of company value. Hostile takeover threats could identify poorly functioning management and improve the value of the firm concerned.
69. Another example is Japanese banks' role in corporate governance. The Japanese reform's intent was to reduce Japanese banks' role in corporate governance to a minimum, thus allowing shareholders to play the main governance role. Japan's Anti-Monopoly Law, limiting a bank's equity ownership in a particular firm to 5 percent, was not changed in the reform, while banks' overall equity ownership is restricted in terms of market value (see, for example, Nakamura, Chapter 7, this volume). The latter restriction was introduced as part of the

reform during the 1990s to greatly reduce the banks' excessive ownership in other firms. However, Japan's reform has not changed the types of roles that Japanese banks can play in corporate governance. As a result, as Japan's stock prices rise, more banks may begin to resume acting as aggressive shareholders. (U.S. banks choose not to play such a role.) It remains to be seen what type of new role Japanese banks play in corporate governance, but they could resume their traditional dual role as the main creditors and shareholders of their client firms, as they did until recently. Japanese banks and corporations may choose such a practice in the present context of selective adaptation.

70. The recent revisions of Japan's Anti-Monopoly Law relaxed the market share requirements and also relaxed the requirements for ownership and control of other corporations by banks and industrial firms. (However, banks are not allowed to own industrial firms in their holding companies.) No rules have been changed or strengthened to regulate Japan's keiretsu relationships.
71. Naturally, this causes a significant loss to the target company and its shareholders.

References

Ahmadjian, C. L., and Lincoln, J. R. (2001) "Keiretsu, Governance, and Learning: Case Studies in Change from the Japanese Automobile Industry," *Organization Science*, 12, 683–701.

Aoki, M. (1988) *Information, Incentives, and Bargaining in the Japanese Economy* (New York: Cambridge University Press).

Araki, T. (2005) "Corporate Governance Reforms, Labor Law Developments, and the Future of Japan's Practice-Dependent Stakeholder Model," *Japan Labor Review*, 2, 26–57.

Arikawa, Y., and Mitsusada, Y. (2008) *The Adoption of Poison Pills and Managerial Entrenchment: Evidence from Japan*. Discussion Paper Series 08-E-006 (Tokyo: RIETI).

Bartlett, C. A., and Ghoshal, S. (1998) *Managing Across Borders: The Transnational Solution* (second edition) (Boston, MA: Harvard Business School Press).

Bebchuk, L. A., and Cohen, A. (2005) "The Costs of Entrenched Boards," *Journal of Financial Economics*, 78, 409–33.

Burt, R. (1992) *Structural Holes: The Social Structure of Competition* (Cambridge, MA: Harvard University Press).

Cailluet, L. (1998) "Selective Adaptation of American Management Models: The Longterm Relationship of Pechiney with the United States," in M. Kipping and O. Bjarnar (eds.), *The Americanization of European Business: The European Response to the US Productivity Drive* (London: Routledge), pp. 190–207.

Chan-Tiberghien, J. (2004a) "Gender as Intersectionality: Multiple Discrimination against Minority Women in Japan," in M. Nakamura (ed.), *Changing Japanese Business, Economy and Society: Globalization of Post-Bubble Japan* (Basingstoke: Palgrave Macmillan), pp. 158–81.

Chan-Tiberghien, J. (2004b) *Gender and Human Rights Politics in Japan: Global Norms and Domestic Networks* (Stanford, CA: Stanford University Press).

Corning, P. A. (1996) "Evolutionary Economics: Metaphor or Unifying Paradigm?" *Journal of Social and Evolutionary Systems*, 18, 421–35.

Development Bank of Japan (2007) *Do M&A Improve Corporate Financial Performance in Japan?* (Tokyo: Development Bank of Japan).
Dixit, A. (1996) *The Making of Economic Policy* (Cambridge, MA: MIT Press).
Dore, R. (1983) "Goodwill and the Spirit of Market Capitalism," *British Journal of Sociology*, 34, 459–82.
Freeman, C. (1991) "Innovation, Changes of Techno-Economic Paradigm and Biological Analogies in Economics," *Revue économique*, 42, 211–31.
Gilson, R. J., and Milhaupt, C. (2004) "Choice as Regulatory Reform: The Case of Japanese Corporate Governance." Columbia Law and Economics Working Paper No. 251.
Gompers, P., Ishii, J., and Metrick, A. (2003) "Corporate Governance and Equity Prices," *Quarterly Journal of Economics*, 118, 107–55.
Gordon, M. (2002) "Takeover Defenses Work. Is That Such a Bad Thing?" *Stanford Law Review*, 55, 819–37.
Fruin, W. M. (1992) *The Japanese Enterprise System – Competitive Strategies and Cooperative Structures* (Oxford: Oxford University Press).
Fruin, W. M. (1997) *Knowledge Works – Managing Intellectual Capital at Toshiba* (Oxford: Oxford University Press).
Fruin, W. M., and Nakamura, M. (1997) "Top-Down Production Management: A Recent Trend in the Japanese Productivity-Enhancement Movement," *Managerial and Decision Economics*, 18, 131–9.
Harris, A., and Nakayama, K. (2007) "Rapid Face-Selective Adaptation of an Early Extrastriate Component in MEG," *Cerebral Cortex*, 17, 63–70.
Hermalin, B., and Weisbach, M. (2003) "Board of Directors as an Endogenously Determined Institution: A Survey of the Economic Literature," *Economic Policy Review*, April, 7–26.
Hirose, S., Fujita, T., and Yanagawa, N. (2007) *Poison Pills and Firm Performance: Japan, 2005 (Baishu donyusaku no gyoseki joho koka: 2005 Nihon)* (in Japanese). Working paper CIRJE-J-182, (Tokyo: University of Tokyo).
Hofstede, G. (1980) *Culture's Consequences*, London: Sage Publications, 1980.
Hofstede, G. (1983) "The Cultural Relativity of Organizational Practices and Theories," *Journal of International Business Studies*, 4 (Special Issue on Cross-Cultural Management), 75–89.
Hofstede, G. (1997) *Cultures and Organizations: Software of the Mind* (New York: McGraw-Hill).
Hoshi, T., and Kashyap, A. (2001) *Corporate Financing and Governance in Japan: The Road to the Future* (Cambridge, MA, and London: MIT Press).
House, R. J., Hanges, P. J., Javidan, M., Dorfman P. W., and Gupta, V. (eds.) (2004) *Culture, Leadership and Organizations: The GLOBE Study of 62 Societies* (Thousand Oaks, CA: Sage Publications).
Jacobs, L., and Potter, P. B. (2006) "Selective Adaptation and Human Rights to Health in China," *Health and Human Rights*, 9, 113–34.
Jacoby, S. M. (2005) "Business and Society in Japan and the United States," *British Journal of Industrial Relations*, 43, 617–34.
Japan Fair Trade Commission (1993) *A Survey of Transactions of Auto Parts (Jidosha Buhin Torihiki ni Kansuru Jittai Chosa)* (in Japanese) (Tokyo: Japan Fair Trade Commission).

Kirby, S. (1998) "Fitness and the Selective Adaptation of Language," in J. R. Hurford, M. Studdert-Kennedy, and C. Knight (eds.), *Approaches to the Evolution of Language: Social and Cognitive Bases* (Cambridge: Cambridge University Press).

Kiyokawa, Y., and Yamane, H. (2004) "Japanese Views on Labor (*nihonjin no rodokan*)" (in Japanese), *Ohara Shakai Mondai Kenkyujo Journal*, 542, 14–33.

Konomi, Y. (2002) *Research Report on Corporate Structural Reforms (Kigyo no kozo kaikaku kenkyukai kenkyu katsudo hokokusho)* (in Japanese) (Keio Business School, Keio University).

Korkie, R., and Nakamura, M. (1997) "Block Holding and Keiretsu in Japan: The Effects of Capital Markets Liberalization Measures on the Stock Market," *Journal of International Money and Finance*, 16, 113–40.

Kremers, J., Stepien, M. W., Scholl, H. P. N., and Saito, C. (2003) "Cone Selective Adaptation Influences L- and M-Cone Driven Signals in Electroretinography and Psychophysics," *Journal of Vision*, 3, 146–60.

Lincoln, J. R. (2006) "Interfirm Networks and the Management of Technology and Innovation in Japan," in D. H. Whittaker and R. E. Cole (eds.), *Perspectives on Technology Management (MOT) in Japan* (Oxford: Oxford University Press), pp. 216–33.

Lincoln, J. R., and Gerlach, M. L. (2004) *Japan's Network Economy: Structure, Persistence, and Change* (New York: Cambridge University Press).

Lincoln, J. R., Hanada, M., and McBride, K. (1986) "Organizational Structures in Japanese and U.S. Manufacturing," *Administrative Science Quarterly*, 31, 338–64.

Mikanagi, Y. (2006) "Review of Chan-Tiberghien, Jennifer, *Gender and Human Rights Politics in Japan: Global Norms and Domestic Networks*, Stanford University Press, Stanford, CA. 2004," *Social Science Japan Journal*, 9, 162–4.

Milhaupt, C. J. (2005) "In the Shadow of Delaware? The Rise of Hostile Takeovers in Japan," *Columbia Law Review*, 105, 2171–216.

Millar, J. A. (1972) "Selective Adaptation," *Policy Sciences*, 3.

Miyashita, A. (2007) "Where do Norms Come From? Foundations of Japan's Postwar Pacifism," *International Relations of the Asia-Pacific*, 7, 99–120.

Morck, R., and Nakamura, M. (1999) "Banks and Corporate Control in Japan," *Journal of Finance*, 54, 319–39.

Morck, R., and Nakamura, M. (2005) "A Frog in a Well Knows Nothing of the Ocean: A History of Corporate Ownership in Japan," in R. Morck (ed.), *A History of Corporate Governance Around the World: Family Business Groups to Professional Managers* (Chicago: NBER and University of Chicago Press), pp. 367–459.

Morck, R., Nakamura, M., and Shivdasani, A. (2000) "Banks, Ownership Structure, and Firm Value in Japan," *Journal of Business*, 73, 539–69.

Nakamura, M. (1993) "Japanese Industrial Relations in an International Business Environment," *North American Journal of Economics and Finance*, 4, 225–51.

Nakamura, M. (2002) "Mixed Ownership of Industrial Firms in Japan: Debt Financing, Banks and Vertical Keiretsu Groups," *Economic Systems*, 26, 231–47.

Nakamura, M. (2006) "Japanese Corporate Governance Practices in the Post-Bubble Era: Implications of Institutional and Legal Reforms in the 1990s and Early 2000s," *International Journal of Disclosure and Governance*, 3, 233–61.

North, D. (1990a) *Institutions, Institutional Change and Economic Performance* (Cambridge: Cambridge University Press).

North, D. (1990b) "A Transaction Cost Theory of Politics," *Journal of Theoretical Politics*, 2, 355–67.

Ogawa, N., and Retherford, R. D. (1993) "Care of the Elderly in Japan: Changing Norms and Expectations," *Journal of Marriage and the Family*, 55, 585–97.

Porta, R. L., Lopez-de-Silanes, F., and Shleifer, A. (1999) "Corporate Ownership Around the World," *Journal of Finance*, 54, 471–517.

Potter, P. B. (2003) "Globalization and Economic Regulation in China: Selective Adaptation of Globalized Norms and Practices," *Washington University Global Studies Law Review*, 2, 119–50.

Potter, P. B. (2004) "Legal Reform in China: Institutions, Culture, and Selective Adaptation," *Law and Social Inquiry*, 28, 465–95.

Potter, P. B. (2007) "Selective Adaptation and Institutional Capacity: Approaches to Understanding Reception of International Law Under Conditions of Globalization," *Sociology of Law*, 66.

Reischauer, E. O. (1988) *The Japanese Today: Change and Opportunity* (Cambridge, MA: Harvard University Press).

Roe, M. J. (2001) "The Shareholder Wealth Maximization Norm and Industrial Organization," *University of Pennsylvania Law Review*, 149, 2063–81.

Sako, M. (1996) "Suppliers' Associations in the Japanese Automobile Industry: Collective Action for Technology Diffusion," *Cambridge Journal of Economics*, 20, 651–71.

Saxenian, A. (1994) *Regional Networks: Industrial Adaptation in Silicon Valley and Route 128* (Cambridge, MA: Harvard University Press).

Shibata, G., Tse, D., Vertinsky, I., and Wehrung, D. (1991) "Do Norms of Decision-Making Styles, Organizational Design and Management Affect Performance of Japanese Firms? An Exploratory Study of Medium and Large Firms," *Managerial and Decision Economics*, 12, 135–46.

Shleifer, A., and Vishny, R. W. (1997) "A Survey of Corporate Governance," *Journal of Finance*, 52, 737–83.

Stiles, K. W. (2006) "The Dissemination of International Liberal Norms: The Case of the ECHR and the UK," *Canadian Journal of Political Science*, 39, 135–58.

Teranishi, J. (2003) "Review of Hoshi and Kashyap's *Corporate Financing and Governance in Japan*," *Journal of Economic Literature*, 41, 566–74.

Tsurumi, Y., and Tsurumi, H. (1991) "Value Added Maximization Behavior of Firms and the Japanese Semiconductor Industry," *Managerial and Decision Economics*, 12, 123–34.

Williamson, O. (1996) *The Mechanisms of Governance* (New York: Oxford University Press).

Yoshikawa, Y. (2003) *Corporate Governance for Improving Firm Value (Kigyo kachi kojo notameno corporate governance)* (in Japanese) (Tokyo: Toyo Keizai).

Zeitlin, J. (2000) "Americanizing British Engineering? Strategic Debate, Selective Adaptation, and Innovative Hybridization in Postwar Reconstruction, 1945–60," in J. Zeitlin and G. Herrigel (eds.), *Americanization and Its Limits* (Oxford: Oxford University Press), pp. 123–52.

Index